THE
WEDGE

Also by Scott Carney

The Red Market

*On the Trail of the World's Organ Brokers, Bone Thieves, Blood Farmers
and Child Traffickers*

The Enlightenment Trap

Obsession, Madness, and Death on Diamond Mountain

What Doesn't Kill Us

*How Freezing Water, Extreme Altitude, and Environmental
Conditioning Will Renew Our Lost Evolutionary Strength*

THE
WEDGE

EVOLUTION, CONSCIOUSNESS, STRESS, AND THE KEY TO HUMAN RESILIENCE

SCOTT CARNEY

Foxtopus Ink

Denver, Colorado

Visit us online at foxtopus.ink

Printed in the United States of America

Book design by Robin Vuchnich

Library of Congress Control Number: 2020900981

ISBN: 978-1-7341943-0-2 (print)
ISBN: 978-1-7341943-1-9 (ebook)

for Emily O'Conner

...and every seeker, everywhere.

WARNING

This book is intended to be a journalistic investigation into the limits and possibilities of the human body. No one should attempt any of these methods or practices without appropriate experience, training, fitness level, doctor approval, and supervision—and even then, readers must be aware that these practices are inherently dangerous and could result in grave harm or death.

CONTENTS

Dave Asprey

It's common to think that your emotions are something that happen to you. When your boss corners you at work, or when you've told your kids to clean up their room for the hundredth time, or when you're stuck in traffic and miss your plane…these things make you feel a certain way.

Or do they?

One of the most profound steps I've taken toward hacking my biology and improving my performance has been to learn how to control my nervous system. Being able to bring myself back to a clear and even space makes all the difference in how I work, my creativity, how I relate to my family, and how much I like my life overall.

Journalist, anthropologist and adventurer Scott Carney wrote this book to show you how to take back the wheel yourself. He has developed techniques to control his emotions, and so much more. He has also been able to master his own biological regulation — things like his heart rate, his internal temperature and stress responses by leveraging a concept he calls the Wedge.

The Wedge is that space between your environment and your reaction to a sensation or stimulus that has been shaped by your life experiences. The first time you experience a sensation, the emotion you attach to it at that time is likely what you'll feel the next time you come across the same sensory input.

When we spoke on an episode of *Bulletproof Radio*, Carney told me that any time you sense something, you're reliving your past. It makes perfect sense. You were born not knowing what sound a teapot makes or what a cat looks like. You were born not knowing whether Mom and Dad are safe people or dangerous people. You were born not knowing whether you like to eat steak or dirty socks.

You spend years of your life exploring the world around you while your brain organizes massive amounts of sensory information that you can retrieve later. You add to your mental files every day of your life. Your interactions with people and objects over the years determine how you experience the world and all of your interactions in it.

Carney shows how you can separate sensory input from your reaction to it. He shows the connect and the disconnect between everything that you're feeling, everything that you're touching, everything that's happening around you — and how your brain processes that information.

Carney illustrated this when we talked. He posed the question, "Does pain happen in your bone or in your brain?" It's reasonable to say, "My knee hurts," and assume your pain is coming from your knee. You can press down on a pain site and it hurts worse, or you can change the way you walk and it feels better.

Truth is, pain comes from your brain. In fact, there are people born without a sense of pain, a condition called congenital insensitivity to pain, or CIP. It's common for someone with CIP to die young because they don't notice the early stages of injury or illness. This condition has to do with the amount of endorphins in your brain, and zero to do with the site of injury.

Sensation in and of itself is meaningless, and it's your brain's job to make meaning out of what you're experiencing. For example, if someone is yelling at you, one of the sensory inputs is "loud." If you're at your favorite concert, the sensation is also "loud." But one input makes you angry or frightened, while the other input makes you dance around all happy. That's where life experience comes in. Somewhere along the line, you attached totally different emotions to each type of "loud."

The best part about the Wedge is, you can use that space between stimulus and response to control how you feel. I've noticed that when I'm doing really intense treatments like Rolfing, or when I'm getting 100 injections of stem cells in one go, or when I have my bone marrow taken out for stem cells without anesthesia, my body initially wants to panic and fight it. I've worked over the years to approach the pain in a different way. I say, "I'm going to welcome this, because this is part of the experience and it doesn't hurt." I'm not going to lie and say that someone hammering a needle into my hip bone doesn't hurt. But talking my brain out of zeroing in on 100% pain and panic makes it far less painful. I'm talking like 5% as much as it would have been.

There's a switch. And you can teach yourself to work your own Wedge to turn down pain, anger or fear, and turn up pleasure and happiness.

Carney is an adventurer, and he weaves incredible storytelling throughout *The Wedge* to show you the development of his own changes over time. He offers practical tips that you can begin to apply right now to sharpen your own Wedge and become the Super Human you were meant to be.

—Dave Asprey, author of *Super Human: The Bulletproof Plan to Age Backward and Maybe Even Live Forever*

FOREWORD

Amelia Boone

It was 4 a.m. on December 18, 2011, in Englishtown, New Jersey. The temperature read 19 degrees Fahrenheit. Close to 1,000 athletes had lined up the day before to compete in a race called the World's Toughest Mudder, where the goal was to run as many laps of a 10-mile obstacle course as possible in 24 hours.

Twenty hours in, after hundreds of obstacles and repeated swims and submersions in icy water, all in sub-freezing temperatures, there were 13 of us left out on the course.

In one obstacle, I had to break through a layer of ice before I could submerge myself under the water. I picked up a sheet and held it up to the last remaining volunteer brave enough to stay out there. "This is fucking ridiculous, isn't it?" I asked, laughing.

"And I've never felt more alive," I added to myself.

So what kept me going on that frigid night when 99% of competitors dropped out? And what enabled me, a corporate attorney with a questionable athletic background, to win multiple world championships in obstacle racing over the next few years, repeatedly enduring conditions horrific enough that I eventually received the nickname "The Queen of Pain"?

It wasn't my gear or some type of superior athletic ability; after all, I was the kid who came in dead last in the 100-meter dash all through her childhood. Based on that, no one would have ever predicted I'd emerge as a world-champion athlete some 20 years later.

I never really had words to describe how it was that I was able to do what I did; I couldn't pinpoint why I was successful. In dozens of interviews over the years, I'd stumble repeatedly when the interviewer asked me how I seemed to be so good at enduring conditions that would lead others to quit. I always assumed it was some type of inherent ability that I was born with, but that explanation never really resonated with me.

But when I met Carney for the first time on a winter night in Denver and he described to me his next book project, which he was calling *The Wedge*, things suddenly clicked. In describing his thesis and all the exploits he undertook to test and research it, he gave a syntax and vocabulary to things that I had felt all along but could never find the words to describe.

Unbeknownst to me at the time of that first World's Toughest Mudder, the key to my success was the Wedge: It was my ability to separate the logical human response ("Stop this miserable nonsense and get out of here") from the stimulus (swimming through frozen ponds in sub-freezing temperatures).

That's not to say that I didn't feel pain, or that there weren't times when I was genuinely miserable. But I was able to create space (a wedge, if you will!) between what was happening *around* me and what was happening *within* me. I took the inputs the environment was giving me, but I altered the outputs. Through that process, I was able to find the joy in misery and, as a result, an ability to keep going where others would give up.

The brilliant thing about the Wedge is that it's not something that's innate in some humans and not others. As you will see in this book, we all use it to some extent at certain times. But the coolest thing is that once you are aware of it, and once you practice using it, the applications are vast and wide-ranging. Sure, you can employ it in long endurance races or climbing shirtless to the top of Mount Kilimanjaro, for example, but it's equally applicable for use while sitting in a traffic jam at 5 p.m. or waiting in line at the DMV.

We live in a world where people are eager to be fed solutions; we all want the secret, but we don't want to work for it. If you are like me, you may have some fatigue around the concept of "hacks." The past decade or so has been full of so-called shortcuts to optimize your life: Eat only meat! Eat only plants! Sleep in five-minute increments! Only take cold showers! The list goes on and on. So you may be asking yourself whether this book is just another book full of them.

Thankfully, it's not. We don't need to be fed more quick and dubious solutions; what we need is a method and a framework to adapt to the ever-changing stimuli and problems in our lives. And this requires practice, hard work, and constant curiosity around how we experience moments in our lives. It's been something that I've honed over years and years of repeated exposure to different stimuli and difficult situations — and, like all things, it's still a work in progress for me. In every race, and every different life scenario, I'm using the Wedge.

Last year, I taped a note up on my bathroom mirror. It read as follows:

"If you expect to be miserable, you will be miserable.

If you think you will be in pain, you will be in pain.

If you tell yourself 'This is fucking amazing and I've never felt more alive,' it's pretty incredible the joy and meaning you can find in any situation."

The mind is powerful. The Wedge is powerful. Learn how to use them wisely, and you will learn to live.

—Amelia Boone, Four-time obstacle racing world champion

SERIOUS BUSINESS

I'm a million miles from anything familiar when I decide to put my life in Tony's hands. He's wearing a red Lycra Adidas soccer shirt, baggy jeans and hiking boots. At full height he comes only to my shoulders, and his belly comfortably precedes him everywhere he goes. He's an ordinary man who wouldn't draw a second glance on any third-world street. But there's something about his eyes and cherubic grin that conveys a sense of contentment.

Luzma translates my vague ideas about connection and consciousness to him.

He nods. Then he raises his hand in the air and makes what little eye contact is possible in the near-total darkness. "You must know that what happens tonight is not theater. This is serious business. Though I look like an ordinary man—and not someone who wears feathers and fake headdresses—I am a shaman. Tonight I will work in the world of spirit," he says, still trying to gauge why I would want to cross the globe to see him for something that wasn't a life-threatening illness.

I've only been off the plane for a few hours. I still smell like international travel. But I'm here with questions that I may never get answers to. I'm terrified of what is going to happen next. Am I even in the right mental state to do this?

For now, I'm going to be open to whatever happens in the ceremony. I will suspend my disbelief and give the experience the full force of my mind. Luzma suggests a mantra for me: "Whatever happens, say to yourself, *'I'm willing.'*"

A few hours later, I'm walking down a deep Amazonian jungle path.

It's a new moon, but the Milky Way lights a bright swath across the sky. The jungle is alive with chirping birds, insects, frogs, creaking trees, vines, monkeys and god only knows what else. It sounds as if every creature in creation is deep in conversation. One animal calls out, and a million buzzes and burps return in answer. I wonder what they are saying. Our headlamps bounce off a muddy path for about fifteen minutes until I spy the hut where the ceremony will take place.

I creak open the door and make out about ten people lying down on cheap foam mats in a circle around the interior of the structure. A single candle in the center of the room provides some flickering light that casts deep shadows up on the roof and along the floor. Deeply stained buckets with gray streaks down their insides sit next to every mat.

Tony arrives about half an hour later.

He's holding a two-liter plastic water bottle that's about half full of a viscous black syrup. He finds a seat on a cube of wood on the west side of the room and fiddles with a bottle of scented water known as *agua de Florida* and a clutch of unfiltered cigarettes.

The room hums with silence and anticipation.

Time passes slowly until Tony lights one of the cigarettes, gets up onto his feet and blows giant puffs of tobacco smoke in the four cardinal directions. The smoke signals the beginning of the ceremony. Luzma whispers to me that the tobacco cleanses the room's energy and invites spirits in. He sits back down, whispers a few words into the open plastic bottle and blows more smoke into its aperture. There's no other fanfare. We've begun. And I have no idea what's going on.

Tony taps his feet gently on the floor in a rhythm that starts as a distant rumble and then grows with the subtle intensity of a heartbeat. He purses his lips and whistles equally as softly. It's a simple tune that I almost remember from childhood, but not one I've ever learned. The whistles turn into a chant that might be Spanish or the indigenous language of Quechua. Then again, maybe they're just sounds that come to him out of the ether with no meaning in particular.

It goes on for a while, and when he's sung enough, he motions to a rail-thin man to his left and indicates that it's time to drink his potion. The man gets up and kneels in front of Tony. He's holding out his hands in a clasped gesture of prayer. Tony grasps the man's bony fingers and they whisper back and forth. Tony is asking some sort of question. Once he's satisfied with the answer, he pours a flimsy plastic cup full of the black liquid and holds it up to the light of the candle. Judging the dose insufficient, he pours a few drops more. The man drinks, scowls at the taste, and makes his way back to the mat.

The process continues for every person in our circle.

I watch as Luzma takes a cup in her hand, looks at the amount, squints her face into a screw and shakes her head no. Tony pours some back into the bottle and offers her what's left. She downs it in a quick movement like she's taking a shot. Within seconds of getting back to her seat, she rinses the taste from her mouth with water from her bottle.

Fifteen minutes later, it's my turn. I make my way over to Tony, and he asks me if I've taken a psychedelic before. I tell him that I ate psilocybin mushrooms a few times in college and how the first time I tried them, I ended up in the hospital. In my psychedelic daze, I told a friend that I thought I was going to die, and he dutifully called an ambulance. They pumped my stomach. Cops got involved. I was wary of hallucinogens after that, but a few years later, I tried them again. On *that* trip, I had a glimpse of something far greater than myself.

I'm oversharing.

Tony nods, probably unsure what to make of my gushing. Then he pours a nearly full cup. He asks me to repeat my name and then whispers words into the brew. When he hands it to me, I look into the syrupy brownness and try not to smell it. I seal the back of my palate so I don't take in any fumes, then down the contents of the cup like a shot. It has the consistency of used motor oil and a taste somewhere between rotting fruit and coffee grounds. The fluid coats the inside of my mouth and slicks down my throat. The taste won't go away no matter how many times I swallow. Once the last in the lineup slurps down the noxious brew, someone blows out the candle in the center of the room.

We plunge into inky blackness.

I'll tell you what hermits realize. If you go off into a far, far forest and get very quiet, you'll come to understand that you're connected with everything.

—Alan Watts

CHAPTER 1

YOU ARE THE UNIVERSE

This isn't going to be easy, but I have something important to tell you. It's the sort of message usually delivered in a scream of unmitigated terror. If you've got a flair for the dramatic, you could change the lightbulbs in your room to a deep hue of blood red. Imagine the whirring urgency of a siren getting ever closer until it demands every last shred of attention that your body and mind can muster. Maybe your skin is beginning to crawl with pinpoints of perspiration and your eyes are dilating in anticipation of what's to come. Has the hair on the back of your neck gone full ridgeback? Can you feel it in your bones? (Incidentally, if you happen not to be human, this applies to you, too. So feel free to wave your flagella, beat your wings, gnash your fangs or swish your fins in anguish.)

Ready? Here goes:

We're all going to die.

Okay. You already knew that. And, yes, maybe I was being a little over the top. There was probably a time in your childhood when the thought hung over your head like a specter and haunted your dreams and waking moments. But by now you've likely pushed the existential dread away enough that you can at least function in the world. Chances are that unless you've had a reason to think about it, you haven't dwelled on mortality in quite a while.

The simple truth is that every living thing has an expiry date. Death is so certain that over the past three billion years or so, the inevitability of cessation hardwires our biology—not only in the way that we reproduce and push our genetic makeup one more lifespan into the future, but in just about every sensation, nerve firing and biological drive that moves us to action.

We spend our time on Earth doing everything we can to wiggle just a little more mileage out of our bodies and maybe pass our unique combination of genetic inputs on to a line of descendants. As far as evolution is concerned, our lives are just grist for the mill, and death is the mechanism that allows for change over generations. But from our own perspective, the evolutionary imperative to procreate and survive is personal. Most of us hold the unspoken position that whatever meat we're made up of is somehow exceptionally well suited to give rise to future generations. And that logic has gotten us pretty far, hasn't it? We all come from a line of evolutionary winners dating back to a time before history when single cells emerged from Earth's primordial slime. That's right: You, dear reader (or bacteria, bird, wolf or fish), are the pinnacle of that several-billion-year process.

But there's a problem. Sometime in the past few hundred years, humanity made a break with its evolutionary roots. When we mastered the technology to control our world, we started paying less attention to our in-built resilience. It might have all started back when *Homo erectus* built the first fires and donned fur clothing. At the time, it was a great leap forward into the world of comfort and convenience. But what cave dweller could have ever imagined electricity? Central air? Or the miracle of Internet-powered food home delivery? The allure of technology even informs the ultimate discomfort: our relationship with mortality. Whereas cave people presumably chalked up illness to mystical forces, modern medicine teaches us that every bodily breakdown can find a fix with a pill or a procedure. Should our state-of-the-art hospitals fail, the specter of comfort is so pervasive that even the funeral business seems hell-bent on making us comfortable in the Hereafter with elegant parlors and cushy silk-lined caskets. Let's face it: Humans love comfort to the point of absurdity. And you don't even have to hark back to prehistory to see it. What would your average Joe in the Great Depression think of you or me suddenly becoming enraged when the WiFi goes out for a few minutes? Imagine him watching us dial up the Internet company on our cell phones to shout obscenities at the poor sap working the call center. Admit it: You've been there. I certainly have. As a species, we love how smart we've become at controlling the world around us. But was this grand movement toward an ideal state of comfort really a good idea?

Here comes the uncomfortable truth: It might not have been. The reason is simple: We may drive cars that steer themselves and get laid to rest in cushy caskets, but we are still the same human beings who slept in the open air on the African plains. Which means that we are built to survive in hostile environments and very uncomfortable conditions. Our nervous systems—our bodies' central command systems, which evolved to endure hardships out the ying-yang—are not like digital thermostats. They're not calibrated for radical comfort. If anything, those mechanisms that let us thrive in harsh and even dangerous environments are even more active now than they were in the past. Instead of out-running or out-fighting fierce predators, we face heavy traffic on the morning commute and read crawling text on the television informing us that our health-care premiums are skyrocketing. It might sound crazy, but our bodies process the unfortunate news of an avocado shortage spiking the price of guacamole at our favorite Mexican cantina with the same underlying biology that our ancestors used to fight off lions, tigers and bears. Our bodies then want to react in a way that protects us from impending doom, even though the threat we perceive is no threat at all.

So, Houston, we have a problem. And it's no small thing.

The result is that as a society, we're crippled with anxiety, autoimmune conditions, fatigue, loneliness, and a generalized sense of unease that no matter how much we insulate ourselves from the natural world, eventually the hard realities of nature are going to win out in the end.

The goal of this book is to reconcile the biology that we inherited from our ancestral past with the world we live in today. I will explore tools that reprogram our nervous systems so that we can live the best lives possible. And to get there, I'm going to have to ask a rather hard question.

What's the point of being alive in the first place?

The way we generally understand evolution, the guiding principle of life on this planet really just boils down to birth, survival, procreation, mutation and death. It's a fundamentally mechanical process that makes the miracle of life pretty darned uninteresting. Evolutionary biologists understand evolution in thousand- and million-year increments. They don't have the resolution to understand individual experience of an ancestral mollusk, platypus or primate. And this has made me wonder whether all those scholars who painstakingly examine endless fossil iterations have gotten it all backward. Perhaps there's something about this moment—right here and right now—that gives purpose to that evolutionary drive, something so obvious that we've just missed it.

Here's what I think: Maybe the point of life is the very experience of being alive—those moments of joy, empathy and love, as well as those of pain, sorrow and loss; things that can never show up in the fossil record. Maybe those feelings are actually what evolution seeks to preserve.

To this day, consciousness and the hidden mechanism that drives it remain poorly understood. But we know this: It didn't start fully formed. It evolved from simpler life forms and the tools they had to sense and react to the environment. Those creatures *wanted* to live. And so that desire to carry on meant that their individual experiences, their totally subjective understanding of the world, was an evolutionary force in its own right. Or, to put it another way, senses and emotions evolved to give purpose to life.

Where most evolutionary biologists see discrete endpoints that add up to the slow process of change over millennia, none of those minute iterations could occur without the unique individual experience of each ancestor along that line. The way we teach evolution makes it seem that the only forces affecting a species are the glacially slow processes of natural selection and gene mutation. To these scientists, evolution is a conversation between the environment and an animal's physique, with nothing in between. This macro-level frame overlooks the individual creatures who had to have a reason to transmit genes from one generation to another.

This book is about the intersection of three things: our bodies—i.e., the physical hardware that we inherit through evolution; our minds—i.e., the subjective experience of our minds; and the world outside, which applies pressure against us, causing us to feel and offering us the chance to adjust to it. In these pages, I will show that we actually have more choice in how we experience the world than we might think—more choice than scientists thought possible.

It's a book about how to be alive.

And that means it's also about death.

All biology clings to life. The threat of death undergirds hormonal releases, muscle contractions and atrial function. It defines sensations through a lens of pleasure or pain, then determines whether or not the actions we take are necessary or needlessly risky. If life were a song, we can be pretty sure it ends in a minor key. But the point of life isn't to land a good job, fund a retirement plan, work 40 hours a week at a desk until you're too old to continue and then die comfortably in your sleep. The point of being alive is to have experiences that make it all worthwhile. Death is the greatest teacher, because it offers us a stake that defines what kind of life we want to have.

This book's title is *The Wedge*. I think of the Wedge as a combination method, practice and worldview that allows human beings to take control of their lives. More about this soon. But first, a story.

...

A few years ago, I wrote a book called *What Doesn't Kill Us*, about my encounters with a Dutch fitness guru and extremophile named Wim Hof. He's known for a number of world records that prove his resilience in the cold—a bare-chested hike three-quarters of the way up Mount Everest, the world's longest ice bath, a barefoot marathon on Arctic ice—as well as his uncanny ability to control his immune system under laboratory conditions. When I learned that he was trying to teach others his method, I thought Hof was a madman and a charlatan who was going to get people killed by urging them to do dangerous things in the ice. Instead, I discovered that I was able to learn to do the same things he could in just a matter of days. And while I learned that Hof was, and probably is, a madman, he's also something of a prophet who is redefining the way humans can take control of their biology. My book is worth reading if you want an understanding of where this all began. However, all you need to know about that book for now is that Hof's practices taught me to find strength by becoming comfortable sitting in ice water, holding my breath like my life depended on it, and ultimately finding a technique to manipulate my immune system.

Indeed, it has helped hundreds of thousands of people redefine their own relationship with their body. Hardly a day goes by without someone sending me a message about how my book changed their life. And among that feedback, there's a common thread: Once people have learned one way to master their reactions in a specific environment (usually the cold), what other conditions can they train themselves to thrive in? This question has driven me to explore the frontiers of my own body and mind. It has pushed me to grow my knowledge philosophically and scientifically, and by expanding the range of my own life experiences. It has led me to develop an approach that I call the Wedge as a way of seeing the world—a way of *being* in the world—that allows a person to cut through the illusions that our fear-of-death-oriented nervous system causes us to have. It helps me survive and even thrive in a world thoroughly tamed by technological bliss.

But there's an important caveat that I need to get out of the way before we go any further. I'm not an endurance athlete, prophet or underwear model, nor am I a tenured professor at one of the world's top universities. For that matter, I'm not at the pinnacle of any particular field. Just like anyone else, I am deeply fallible. The one skill that makes me qualified to tackle such a heady topic is a general willingness to try new things and ask a lot of questions along the way. While I have felt the Wedge and learned many amazing things that have made me a stronger happier person, I am still very much the Wedge's student. There are certain aspects of the Wedge that can't be explained through language; they have to be felt, seen, tasted and relaxed into. I don't have all the answers to life's big questions. Instead, this book records my quest to dig deep into what I've learned and report back. I hope to provide tools for readers to embark on their own journeys and ask their own questions.

To understand how it all started for me, I must take you back to the series of events that shifted my perspective on almost everything. It was a trip that, by many people's reckoning, should have killed me.

After years of training with Hof, I had decided to take on one last challenge that would prove that I'd surpassed what I'd thought were the limits of human endurance. Hof and I, together with an expedition of about 20 other people, planned to hike to the top of Mount Kilimanjaro using just Hof's breathing method. We aimed to do it in under 30 hours, without the normal acclimatization safety stops—which, I was told, would be a record. When I asked members of the United States Army's environmental unit how they thought we would fare, they predicted that 75% of us would have so little oxygen in our blood that we'd have to abandon the effort. A Dutch mountaineering association predicted we would all die. And that was before I told them that I'd be doing most of the trip shirtless.

Suffice it to say, the trip wasn't easy. At 12,000 feet, one woman in the group developed altitude sickness, and medics had to ferry her down the mountainside. At 15,000 feet, things got bad. In a bout of record-focused solipsism during which his own impressive endurance seemed to overshadow the welfare of the group, Hof demanded that we skip lunch before the final ascent. The group descended into mutiny. The professional guides refused to follow because they said it was too dangerous. I was just one of two people to follow him on the final push. I told myself that I had a job to do, a book to write. I followed Hof in protest, angry at the dangers that he was putting me through. Every fatigued step felt more leaden. My eyes dimmed along with the declining levels of available oxygen. I had to breathe harder and faster to make the world brighten up again. And then it happened: I watched Hof slip on a loose rock and almost fall to his knees.

When I saw the indomitable "Iceman" come close to his own limits, I realized two interrelated things. First, that my decision to follow Hof's path wasn't his responsibility; it was mine. And second, that success or failure at the razor's edge of human endurance depended on my relationship with the environment. The techniques I'd learned allowed me a certain margin of error with catastrophe and gave me a little leverage to negotiate survival with the mountain itself.

Instead of the five days it usually took to get to Gilman's Point, I stepped onto the zenith of a bare-chested sprint up Mount Kilimanjaro after just 28 hours. Thirty-mile-an-hour winds screamed over my exposed skin and across the snow-swept ridgeline and echoed off the side of the glacier. The picture of us standing beneath Gilman's Point made headlines around the world. In it, I'm wearing only thin wind pants and a hat. My chest is naked to the elements. I filled my lun~ the cold air. Despite the freeze, I wasn't shivering. In fact,

t warm.

p wasn't supposed to be a reckless death-defying stunt;

ulated attempt to show the world how easily humans

could adapt our physiologies to even the most challenging conditions. We're all stronger than we think.

Our species evolved in ever-changing environments, from parched African deserts to ice-encased high mountain ranges, with only a whisper of technology to aid us along the way. We once thrived on barren Pacific atolls, in scorching badlands and insufferable jungles, and above the Arctic Circle. Those environments forged our biology while our senses guided us safely through the challenges we faced.

So why is it that modern humans aren't quite as robust as the people who came before us? We cringe at the extremes and encase ourselves in cocoons of technological comfort. Climate control, electric lighting, stable food supplies and readily accessible transportation make it impossibly easy for most of us to never leave a narrow band of homeostatic bliss. Most of us don't *want* to feel uncomfortable. We prefer to be numb to the world around us. Indoor lifestyles almost entirely remove seasonal variations in temperature, so that most of us live in a perpetual artificial summer. In doing so, we blunt the environmental signals that stimulate our nervous systems and spark adaptation. In short, we've ignored the power of our bodies in favor of the cleverness of our tools. We've embraced medicines designed to circumvent our mind's built-in healing powers to instead work on our bodies like they're little more than machines. And so many of the powers we inherited through evolution are untouched and underutilized.

I climbed up that mountain in part to show that the biological systems that our ancestors relied on for survival aren't gone; they're just a little dusty. Resilience is our birthright, and the key to regaining that strength is re-engaging with the stresses of the natural world. The feat on Kilimanjaro gave me a certain kind of visceral proof that civilization's dependence on technology and its addiction to comfort undermines our bodies' natural evolutionary resilience. I had a message that was as easy to digest as a selfie. I showed what a pretty ordinary non-athlete could do with cold exposure and breathwork.

But I always knew there were still more frontiers to push, and the protocols that Wim Hof taught me were just the starting point to understanding the deeper principle.

Mastering my reactions to the cold, wind, heat and emotional turbulence forced biological adaptations that play out not only in the narrow band of extreme athletic feats, but also in the world with which we're most familiar.

In today's society, there is a basic assumption that the key to human health rests on the twin pillars of diet and exercise. We tend to believe that if we just eat the right things and then move in the ideal ways, somehow the calculus will yield healthy results. However, there's a third pillar that we almost entirely ignore: all the ways the environment molds our biology. Environmental signals are the levers, dials and buttons that send messages directly to our nervous systems. Our nervous systems, in turn, use that input to direct how our body responds to the challenges around it.

I was drawing on that third pillar when the icy fingers of the upper atmosphere grazed my skin painlessly and the African continent seemed to fall away from my feet. I felt my strength emerging from boulder fields, barren tundra and, eventually, the verdant tropics at the base of the volcano. This bewildering connectedness showed me that survival was a relationship—a negotiation between a person and the environment. And that was when I had the most significant realization of my life.

I wasn't really on the mountain.

In a way, I *was* the mountain.

Every ice crystal on my skin, every gust of wind and stony crag beneath my boots was a vital part of one great living, breathing system. In that moment, there wasn't a distinction between my body and the environment around it. The power to change biology doesn't just stem from grit and determination to overcome whatever obstacles lie ahead, but from the realization that the partition between the environment and what happens inside of us is an illusion. We're not adversaries fighting against the randomness of the world's climate and weather systems; we're connected to those variations through the very senses that define the boundaries of our body and give meaning to life.

The oneness I felt on the mountain made me part of a great living ecosystem that works on scales as large as tectonic shifts, but also at the infinitesimally small level of microorganisms inhabiting my gut and the autonomous cells of my immune system. I live in an ecosystem, and at the same time, I *am* an ecosystem. And everything together is part of a great superorganism of life itself. While I certainly have a perspective of myself on the mountain, my own conscious experience is only a single facet of an infinitely complex system—one that is so vast that I don't think I will ever comprehend it in its totality.

The most profound thing I learned on this journey was also the most difficult to wrap my mind around. If I am the environment, then how can I also be an individual? What is it that senses the world in the first place? As counterintuitive as it seems, at a very deep level, who we are is not who we *think* we are. Instead, our unique perspectives are just one link in a continuous chain of experience between the very smallest molecules in our bodies and the universe itself. Consciousness is mostly just context.

Let me explain. Take that same moment from the perspective of the bacteria in my gut. I need those bacteria to survive; we're symbiotic. They help digest food and provide energy, and they can suppress certain biological mechanisms that would make me sick if they stopped doing their job. They're also with me on top of the mountain, even though they can't conceive of what a journey like that means. The temperature shifts on my skin, lower available oxygen and physical exertion translate into sensations that I feel in my brain. The brain then sends a signal to release chemicals and hormones that alter the environment the bacteria swim in. They sense the changing world around them and respond by secreting chemicals that give me, the shirtless guy who feels himself flagging, more energy. In this way, there's an ongoing feedback loop between the sensations on my skin and the world that my body creates for all the things inside of me. From the bacteria's perspective, Kilimanjaro feels like a bath of adrenaline. I'm that bacteria's lens into the world at large.

Now consider an even larger context. Who would you be without your childhood? Without your friends? Without your habits or education? If you had never moved a muscle? If you had never been sick? Or, to paraphrase the American mystic Alan Watts, "Who would you be without the sun?" Everything that you've ever experienced leaves a mark and makes you you. Without the sun, not only would you not be reading this book, but books themselves wouldn't exist. There would be no society to nurture you and no evolutionary process to form your blood and bones.

This is all to say that what we perceive as an uninterrupted conscious experience is in reality entirely dependent on context. We are the sum of minute interactions inside our bodies—a happenstance of neurology and our relationship with the larger environment all at the same time.

There is no you.

There is no me.

There is only everything all at once.

What we think of as the self is actually a series of relationships and subjective experiences. At times these relationships are nested inside of one another like Russian dolls, with layers of brain, patterns in the nervous system, hormones and physiology wrapped into a single package. At other times we should think of the self as a network of experiences, patterns, understandings and relationships outside of our bodies—layers of that same doll that extend outward into infinity. It's bewildering to contemplate, because we feel like we're individuals: How can we understand the world except through our own eyes? How can we be the universe and be an individual at the same time?

It's the same fundamental paradox that physicists come across when studying light. Depending on how you observe it, light is either a particle or a wave. Somehow it's a discrete object hurtling through space and, at the same time, a ripple of energy extending in all directions. We mostly experience consciousness like a particle with an individual path and direction. However, that experience only comes about when it's part of a greater connected system of relationships.

Luckily, there is a compass through this philosophical morass—two indicators that define who we are and, more importantly, who we *could* be: stress and choice.

It was only when I was on the brink of exhaustion and at the razor's edge of my physical abilities that I truly understood how stress creates a window between the outside world and my inner biology. In that moment, I had a choice about how I could connect the mountain to my mitochondria.

Stress defines who we are mentally and physically. It plays on our consciousness at the same time it initiates biological responses. I discovered on the mountain that the way I feel and react to the sensations around me is a tool to control both my physiology and my relationship to the world at large. In fact, those feelings and reactions define my place in it.

This moment of choice is what I call the Wedge. It's a tool, a practice, and an idea that makes us more real every time we use it.

So what is the Wedge, exactly?

The most comfortable way to think about the Wedge is that it is a choice to separate stimulus from response. Anything that you feel starts out as an impulse from the environment, and then your biology responds to it through nerve firings, hormonal releases and mental patterns. The Wedge is the measure of control that we all have to insert choice into the space between sensation of the outside world and the physiological responses that it triggers.

The Wedge allows you to become healthier, happier and stronger in any situation or environment. It is as useful to embarking on a feat of endurance, a creative endeavor or a business venture as it is to recovering from an injury or illness, mending past trauma or repairing fractured interpersonal relationships. This is because in every situation a human might get themselves into, there's always a tension between the challenge (stress) and the built-in automatic reactions. The Wedge intercedes and introduces a measure of control in things that otherwise feel uncontrollable.

The tricky thing about understanding the Wedge, and what makes it so incredibly difficult to explain, is that you—or rather, your ego—is not always the thing in charge. Remember, there is no self. All the parts of an individual and environment work together to generate an illusion of a self. Ego is just a perspective on the reality that we're part of a superorganism. But illuminating this concept at the scale of the entire universe is too wide a frame to be useful. There's no way to explain the immensity of Mount Kilimanjaro to gut bacteria. So as much as possible, I'm going to discuss the Wedge on a human scale, the way we understand the world from our own perspective. This particular frame is just one Russian doll inside a chain of nested dolls; however, it just happens to be *our* frame. We all have our unique windows into the vastness of the universe. It's a great place to start. But keep in mind that our own perspectives come with limitations.

The Wedge inserts an element of choice into this sensory pathway and alters how we experience the world. I mostly think of it as a proper noun (the Wedge) on a conceptual level—as the choice to intercede between stimulus and response. But it can also be *a wedge*, by which I mean a specific technique, object or intervention that you use to insert that control. So, for example, in the case of cold exposure, an ice bath is a wedge, but the Wedge is the mental trick we use to suppress a shiver response.

Given our biological makeup, there are three ways that we can insert a measure of control to alter our experience of the environment. We can insert a wedge at the point of environmental stress. We can insert a wedge during sensation—i.e., after the stress has occurred and the nervous system is busy transmitting that information to the mind. And we can insert a wedge later, when the mind is making sense of what the nervous system just told it—i.e., mindset. Let's define those.

- **Stress:** Signals from the environment that you experience. Stress is a simple input that comes from the external world and is not inherently positive or negative. Whatever your body can detect from the outside world is a form of stress. For example, stress can come in the form of temperature, pressure, sound and smell (or, more accurately, vibrations and molecules), light and textures. Or it can be a more complex thing, like interactions, threats, ideas and even relationships between you and other people.

- **Sensation:** These are the impulses that your nervous system translates and transmits to your brain that relay information about stress. These signals—touches, smells, images, pressure changes, etc.—are conduits between your mind and the environment, and are the only way you can experience anything physical.

- **Mindset:** This is the way your mind interprets sensations—your mental attitude, expectations, emotions and disposition at the time that you receive sensation from your nervous system. At various places in this book, I'll also call mindset "orientation"; the words are interchangeable. For example, orientations of fortitude, resilience, optimism and joy alter the way you sense stress in a generally positive way. Conversely, orientations of fear, pessimism, hopelessness and panic often make sensations of stress feel worse.

What we know about the world comes through our senses; without them, our minds are like locked boxes, shut off from reality. Stress, sensation and mindset define our experiences, and they are at least partially under our control. Changing our environment alters the sensations that enter our nervous system. Altering our sensory pathways filters the stress before it reaches our mind. Our mindset determines what those sensations actually mean to us (and our bodies), and taken all together, this process determines how our body reacts to the world it inhabits.

Inserting a wedge requires learning the language that your body uses to communicate information about the environment. Its syntax and grammar aren't made of words; they're sensation, emotion, and keen observation of the links between your mind and the external world. And because experience is at least partially based on a biological process, changing an experience will alter physiology. This knowledge is power.

When we relax in the cold, ramp up in the heat, find stillness in chaos and face the things that terrify us, we re-program our nervous systems with a new arsenal of responses. When we're more at ease with the environment, then the processes inside of our bodies are also at ease. The Wedge teaches us to use stimuli that trigger predictable nervous system responses and then yoke those responses to our conscious control.

This works because stress is subjective. The way a person reacts to stress has as much to do with that person's internal mental state as it does with external factors. For someone suffering from post-traumatic stress disorder (PTSD), merely hearing a car backfire in the distance can spark a panic attack. Meanwhile, another person can spend the entire night transfixed and awed by a fireworks display. In both cases, the environmental cues are similar, but the two nervous systems respond in diametrically opposed ways because they disagree with what the sensations mean. In one case, the loud sounds presage catastrophe or even death. In the other, they're part of a ritual that helps people bond with a community through celebration. The key to making the person with PTSD more comfortable with panic-inducing stress is to alter their experience of what it means.

To be clear, inserting a wedge doesn't guarantee the same outcome for everyone. The Wedge offers a way to interface with our nervous systems, whose physiology is largely the same among people, but the actual experience of change is as unique as the practitioner.

The techniques that build and maintain the Wedge don't usually take up a lot of time. They're often short interventions that break up established patterns between automatic stimulus and response. Yes, it can require some maintenance—I do breathwork every day—but the techniques aren't meant to become habits. That would defeat the point.

We don't always have control over every facet of experience. Sometimes we can't select our environment. Other times our minds get stuck and we can't muster a different mindset. And sensory pathways often only respond while we're practicing certain exercises and breathing techniques, or with chemical interventions. However, when we're deliberately trying to influence a particular bodily reaction, we can usually locate at least one place where we can wedge a measure of control into the process and use that new space to train our bodies to function differently.

And make no mistake: We *evolved* to use the Wedge.

In fact, you've been using it your whole life. Any time you make a choice to override your physical reactions to stress, you're using the Wedge. It can be as easy as consciously trying to delay a sneeze or resisting the urge to laugh when someone tickles you. In those instances and a thousand more like them, you focus on your sensations and override what your biology wants to do automatically. In some ways, this is why we have senses in the first place.

If you go back far enough in the evolutionary timeline, life on Earth started with a handful of single-celled creatures about 3.8 billion years ago. Those cells procreated, died and evolved to become trees, mastodons, fungi, butterflies, octopuses, sharks, dinosaurs and, yes, humans. Every living thing has some sort of sensory hardware that detects what's happening around it and mechanisms to adapt.

The sensations that relay information about the outside world correspond to physical changes internally. For more sophisticated creatures—ones with complex nervous systems—it can go the other way as well: Internal shifts in perception can change the way we react to the environment.

Of course, trees, fungi and flowers react to different stimuli than elephants or birds. But react they do. And this means that everything that *your* body does—every type of sensation, physical trait, and autonomic response you have—only exists because evolution put the capability there. Every sense and biological mechanism we have today gave some sort of evolutionary advantage to our ancestors. Sensations are tools, and we are tool users.

The same goes for emotions: We feel love, hate, ennui, angst, depression, fear and everything else because having those capabilities passed on an evolutionary advantage. Emotions create a symbolic link between what's happening in the world and what occurs inside of our bodies. And because evolution is a rather slow process, it would be hubristic to think that the sensory and emotional tools that *Homo sapiens* have access to appeared fully formed when the first member of our species started walking the Earth between 200,000 and 300,000 years ago. Look at the anatomy of any mammal and you'll see familiar structures—bone plans, lungs, hearts, eyes, brains, etc. Those organs were all useful enough to survive the culling process of evolution. And, insofar as cognition relies on anatomical structures in the brain, it makes sense that most other creatures with similar brains have some level of emotional and sensory experience comparable to our own. Consciousness and our sense of self evolved because evolution put it there.

And here's the crux: Because sensation and emotion exist widely in the animal kingdom (and probably to some degree in other kingdoms, too), that means that every creature on Earth has some level of emotional subjectivity. In terms of the Wedge, all creatures have the ability to decide how they respond to stress, and those decisions help determine whether or not they pass on their genes. With just a few exceptions, this is the sort of statement that makes evolutionary biologists cringe. Science wants objective laws that survive in the fossil record. But experience doesn't fossilize, and so many biologists ignore its importance. In doing so, they lose track of a common thread that connects all living things.

Even if paleontologists were able to record every physical data point from an ancient animal, they would still never understand its experience. To steal an example from Brian Mackenzie (an athlete and endurance expert we'll meet later), consider the relationship between a lion and a gazelle. Imagine the moment when the fearsome predator is just about to go in for the kill. At a physical level, both animals have incredibly similar nervous systems; their blood is chock-full of hormonal cocktails that confer super-mammalian levels of energy. Their pupils open up into saucers and their pain thresholds deepen. The only meaningful difference between their two nervous systems is that the lion is the only one that wants to be there. This is the power of subjectivity. Context is everything.

The sensations you feel when you are cold or hot or struggling for oxygen are probably very similar to what a cat or bird might feel when they reach the same threshold of intensity. And yet the actual conditions that might bring other animals to a sensory breaking point are observably very different from where you or I or a person suffering from PTSD might break. In every case, their respective nervous systems are primed to look out for death, but it's their individual experiences that define what anticipating death feels like. Most every other species on the planet inhabits a much broader range of environments than the typical human, who spends most of his or her life in climate control. Animals in the wild experience more stress in their lives, which makes them more robust. It takes more intense stimulation to put them on edge. This is easy enough to observe in the pets we raise in our homes: I've never seen a wolf wearing a puffy jacket or polar fleece, but when I walk down any street in Denver in winter, I see a dozen shivering dogs in coats.

Those thresholds for tolerating stress emerge through the animals' exposure to the environment, and they are the key to using the Wedge.

Sensations tell us a lot about the world, but also a lot about what is going on inside of us. From a purely motivational standpoint, they encourage us to take action—to remove ourselves from some situations and embrace others. If you know how to listen, they also tell a story about the body's hidden programming. For instance, when you start to feel chilly and want to turn up the heat or throw on another coat, what you're really feeling is your metabolism kicking into gear. If you feel cold, you're burning calories—usually fat—to heat up your body, and the cold sensation is telling you to either find some sort of external heat source or make do relying on what you're already storing. This was evolutionarily advantageous in our distant past because our forebears were always on the search for food and calories in order to survive. However, retaining calories is not really a problem in the modern world. Most Americans now suffer from excess stored energy—mostly in fat reserves around the waistline—so perhaps that cold feeling has advantages that we're not primed for. Those warm feelings that you experience most of the time actually signal an evolutionarily mismatched biological program to store fat instead of burn it.

Emotions follow a similar template, except instead of giving us information about our immediate environment, they relate to circumstances in the future. For instance, fear predicts danger or death. The burgeoning love in your chest that you might feel when looking into the eyes of a partner or child corresponds to a sense of continuity that's greater than yourself. It's easy to see how an emotion like love helped groups pass on their genes. Disgust triggers avoidance behavior, while joy reinforces community. Meanwhile, the emotions of frustration and curiosity correspond to the physical process of forming new neural connections in your brain tissue as it stores information about the world.

You can think about the Wedge and the choice it offers as a hack, an interruption of our nervous systems' business-as-usual approach. It affords us choice in how we react to both physical and emotional stress. For example, our bodies react to many negative stresses by withdrawing from the source of the stress. The sensation of discomfort or mild pain tells us that we are potentially in danger: a chill before frostbite, heat before a burn, that run-down feeling before getting sick, fear before panic, or the urge to gasp before passing out. The gap between stimulus and self-protective response is one place where the Wedge comes into play. Remember, we no longer live in a world where our lives are constantly in danger. Most of the stresses are not going to kill us. So inserting the Wedge here, in the split second that transpires between the external cause of pain and feeling the pain, allows us to act out of deeper purpose and make better choices. We get more resilient, both physically and psychologically stronger.

Embracing the Wedge requires practice. Over time, it helps us build endurance and resilience. But that's not all. The Wedge changes us in a far more profound way. It delays the onset of damage to the body, which helps explain how I managed to climb up to the top of Kilimanjaro in minus-thirty-degree winds. The Wedge can reset our bodies and minds to the default settings that we had when we were cavemen and cavewomen. This doesn't mean that the Wedge makes you invincible. As Hof says, "In the struggle of man versus nature, nature will always win." Instead, repeated exposure to difficult environments actually unlocks biological mechanisms that our ancestors trained from infancy. In other words, you will still have all the benefits of a modern human being, but you will also have the resilience and endurance that humans had before we got so damn comfortable.

The Wedge is not exactly a new idea. I didn't conjure it out of thin air. Iterations of this sort of self-mastery date back to the earliest texts written by humans. Yogis in India and qi-gong and kung fu masters in China all draw on a similar set of principles. In ancient Tibet, monks practicing *tummo* melted the snow on Himalayan peaks centuries before Wim Hof was even born. I've drawn influence from philosophers in Europe, Asia and South America. The way I think about the self relates to the sanskrit idea of *atman* and the Christian belief in a soul. Starting in the 1960s, the human-potential movement asked similar questions to the ones I'm asking now. How I write about the Wedge is grounded in several thousand years of tradition, but it benefits from modern scientific understandings.

I would never have conceived of the Wedge without first meeting Hof at his training center in Poland in 2011 while I was on an assignment for *Playboy*. My original intention when I began my research was to try to debunk him as a false guru offering superpowers to a gullible flock. But things didn't go as I had expected. Hof demonstrated nearly complete mastery over his body and let me in on his training secrets. In every instance, he pitted my body's pre-programmed reactions against stressful environments. He wanted me to use my mind to grow the space between stimulus and response. Once, as he treaded water next to me in a pond at the base of an icy waterfall, he taught me to suppress my body's natural inclination to shiver. He insisted that I could will myself to relax in the water. Keeping that urge to clench up and shiver at bay took all of my mental effort, but eventually I let go and fell into a meditative trance. It wasn't long before my body switched from trying to heat itself by shivering to burning fat resources, and I started to feel warm. In this state, I learned that cold is just a sensation, and it was up to me to decide how my body responds.

When I used breathing techniques to learn to stop shivering in an ice bath, I didn't expect that an autoimmune illness that had plagued me since childhood would vanish. Meeting Hof changed everything. And since then, I've met people who use his protocols to treat an array of illnesses, from Parkinson's disease and rheumatoid arthritis to Crohn's disease, lyme disease and lupus. There's the triathlete who claimed it helped him mend a broken humerus, and endurance athletes who modified high-intensity training regimens to push themselves beyond what 20 years of experience said were their physical limits. Their various methods paired mental exercise and exposure with physical stress.

While Hof's method was busy blowing my mind, it was also gaining credibility in scientific circles. In 2014, peer-reviewed research by two heralded Dutch immunologists showed that his method allowed people to consciously suppress their immune responses. A study by Otto Muzik and Vaibhav Diwadkar at Wayne State University in 2018 in the scientific journal *Neuroimage* tested Hof with a barrage of body and brain scans while he was practicing breathing patterns and cold exposure. They concluded that the techniques "might allow practitioners to assert a higher level of control over key components of the autonomic nervous system with implications for lifestyle interventions that might ameliorate multiple clinical syndromes." When I spoke to Muzik on the phone afterward, he told me that he thought Hof had discovered the secret to activating the healing potential of the placebo effect. The Wedge offers an approach to put those findings into practice today.

More than three years after I hiked down from Kilimanjaro, hundreds of thousands of people followed my journey with Wim Hof. Adventurers flocked to Hof's courses. Countless television shows, radio programs, news articles and podcasts retold my story. A whole community of body hackers took up the cause and proclaimed the power of the cold.

Rather than just a method, I've always looked at Wim Hof's teachings as more of a set of principles. The Wedge isn't bound just to ice baths and heavy breathing; it encompasses the entire world of human sensory experience and biological control. We have the tools now to break past a narrow view of human resilience and apply them across all environments. There are other practices out there that draw on the same Wedge-like mental fortitude. Some are thousands of years old, others seemingly invented out of thin air just a few months ago. Whether they admit it or not, many of these methods implicitly draw on each other. And through this mélange of ideas, I want to understand how I can access deeper parts of my physiology by tweaking the conditions around me and the sensations I feel inside. Every one of these techniques is a lens on the Wedge. And that's what brings me back to the keyboard as I embark on a new quest to explore the principles that make my body work. I've been told that I'm something of an astronaut exploring new frontiers.

The comfort provided by technology does too much to frame our experience of the world. It coddles our senses, defines our thoughts and subtly alters our biology. My hope going forward is to untangle the mess we've made and throw off some of the blankets that comfort has given us. If we become less dependent on technology and alter our mindset so that we no longer see the world through a lens of pain and hardship, then we can feel at home anywhere. The Wedge seeps into all aspects of life. The resilience we build by doing this extends to health, happiness and general competence in the face of new experiences and sensations. It's a complement to Western medicine and makes us participants in our own healing.

This book continues a journey that started when I met Wim Hof to fully understand the Wedge for myself and then relay my findings to you. I'm starting out with a few experiences under my belt, but more questions than answers. In the following pages, I'll take wisdom from athletes and scientists, madmen and prophets, shamans and charlatans. All the while, I will learn techniques that offer me mastery over my body and help me develop wedges to open a gap between stimulus and response. Ultimately, I plan to end this journey in a place completely foreign, where risks that I take are only matched by the potential for transformation.

But before I run, I first need to learn to crawl. My very first stop will be to learn about how human physiology forms the building blocks of experience. I'm headed to a neuroscience laboratory at Stanford University to understand my own brain.

Do one thing every day that scares you.

—Eleanor Roosevelt

CHAPTER 2

FEAR AND FOCUS

How many times have you asked yourself "What could go wrong?" before letting your mind spin out a dozen potential catastrophic failures?

I do this all the damn time.

Yes, I've spent the better part of my adult life working on myself—mind, body and spirit. I exercise. I do breathwork. I watch what I eat. When I go on assignment in an exotic, dangerous locale, I do my homework. I plan ahead. I minimize risk out the ying-yang. And still I wake up in the middle of the night wondering what I missed. There must be more I could do.

But there's one irreducible truth to every human endeavor: Risk is risky. We can never iron out all the wrinkles in this life. Nothing is actually easy. Which has led me to this blanket conclusion:

How we resolve the tension between risk and reward defines who we are. And fear is a guidepost for how we use the Wedge. It is as much an involuntary response to a prediction of the future as it is a sensation that immobilizes our biology and stops us from taking action. Mastering fear doesn't mean ignoring danger, but rather finding a reason that makes danger worth it—separating the stimulus from the response. More important, the way that our brain encodes fear gives insight into everything we sense, feel and react to.

About ten years ago, I was reporting a story from a jungle in central India about a war between the government and communist insurgents that had raged on almost since the country's independence. A day earlier, child soldiers with automatic weapons and bows and arrows held me up at a roadblock, but now I was sitting across from an Indian colonel who informed me that he was planning a raid on an enemy encampment. It sounded like something I should be there for, so I asked if I could come along. He said yes, but advised me that there were certain risks I would have to be willing to take.

First, it would be a long hike over grueling terrain.

I was okay with that.

Second, the army wouldn't be responsible for my safety when the shooting started.

That sounded a little dicey, but I figured I could stay far enough away from the bullets. Maybe I'd hide behind a tree.

Third, there would probably be land mines.

My heart dropped into my stomach. I started to sweat. My mind spun out a vision of the future where an errant footstep and explosion ripped off my legs and sent shrapnel through my guts. There would be an airlift, a mournful return home, and years of rehabilitation without prognosis for recovery. I felt queasy. Terrified. I didn't know it before he said it: Bullets and exhaustion were one thing, but land mines were a bridge too far. I'd be happy to read a report about the raid later.

Over the years, I've done a lot of dangerous things. Maybe I've been lucky to escape with my skin intact. But how is it that I can look at one threatening situation with a shrug and then want to hide under my bed when the stakes change just a little bit? Some alchemy must happen at the neurological level that makes abstract ideas into things that I can feel in the pit of my stomach. I want to know what process my brain and nervous system go through to transform a sensation into a thought. Where's the interface between neurology and experience? And how might I use fear as a wedge? I realize I am going to have to call in an expert.

A few years ago, I had a conversation with a neuroscientist at Stanford named Andrew Huberman who had set up a laboratory to study the complex neurology of fear. He was unlocking the mysteries of how our brain encodes sensation and visual stimuli as visceral emotional responses. More specifically, he was looking at how people responded to suddenly being face to face with great white sharks. What could be scarier, right? I called him up again and made plans to meet him at his Palo Alto laboratory. I had a gut feeling he could teach me a lot about about how my brain builds automatic assumptions about the world.

A few weeks later, we're sitting in a trendy restaurant a few blocks from where Steve Jobs lived while building his Apple empire. The menu boasts enough salad bowl varieties to match any fad diet. As we crunch our lettuce and sip iced tea, I am struck that Huberman looks more like a mixed martial arts fighter than a neuroscientist: He's tall, with dark hair and a rigid chin line, and muscles bulging through a Henry Rollins-esque black jacket. Tattoos cover most of his body below his neckline. I begin with the most basic question I can think of: "What is fear?"

Instead of answering directly, he breaks into a story about an experience he had a few weeks earlier while running one of his fear-based experiments. He knows he's got a good yarn to spin, because this time his life was on the line.

He was about 40 miles off the coast of Mexico and 40 feet below the periwinkle surface of the ocean. Above him, a boat packed to the gunwales with state-of-the-art camera and diving gear was his laboratory on the sea. He was here to collect footage of some of the largest predators on the planet in order to reproduce them in a virtual-reality simulator back in his lab. But something was wrong, and it wasn't just the great white sharks circling his cage. Andrew Huberman couldn't breathe.

A long air tube called a hookah line snaked from the boat to the Stanford-based neuroscientist's mouth. Somewhere along the way, it either kinked onto itself, or the pump that forced air through the tube stopped working. Either way, Huberman knew that he didn't have much time; 40 seconds at the most. So he leaned back on his training, cleared his mind, and tried to think his way out of the situation before he ended up gulping down an ocean of water.

The shark cage was a rectangular steel box about five feet at the base and eight feet tall. At opposite corners of the cage, two backup tanks carried about ten minutes of air for emergencies like this. He reached down and put his mouth on the regulator of the first tank. Nothing. He tried the gray metal knob on one canister, but it refused to rotate, as if a pin was locking the mechanism. The other tank offered the same result. With no time to wonder why the backups weren't working, he pushed off the metal floor and carried himself to the top, where he tried to shake the hose free. Still nothing. He drew on the tube again, but all that did was create a little reverse suction, pulling his tongue gently into the aperture. Things were starting to get scary.

Outside the box were at least six great white sharks between 10 and 17 feet long; some weighing as much as 3,000 pounds swam by. While the team knew about the nearby sharks, no one had an exact count on how many hid in the haze just out of range. Huberman locked his eyes on one ancient battle-scarred monster, his brain somehow recording the shark bites that marred its sandpaper skin as it swam toward him. A flick of its tail sent it careening past a diver who was bravely recording the encounters with a special 360-degree camera but had his back to the cage.

Twenty or 30 seconds had passed since Huberman's last breath. The frothy sensation of panic began to well up in his gut, threatening to take him out of the moment and squander any hope of escape. While his life hung in limbo, the wrinkled face of his bulldog, Costello, filled his mind. It was a bit of a non sequitur, a brief interlude in the moment of high drama. But he remembers focusing on his pet and thinking, *I'm going to make it back home to him.*

Between thoughts of Costello and being ripped apart by sharks, he took a moment to assess his options. He had two: He could exit the top of the cage and make a sprint to the surface, or he could try to get the attention of one of the other divers, share their air and buy time. The second option was the best, but no one was looking in his direction. He wrapped his fingers around the hatch above him and tried to calculate his chances of escape. Getting to the surface might not be hard by itself, but the sharks made the errand more complex. Divers who remain calm attract less attention than those who panic. Rapid breathing, fast movements and the hidden signals that we all give off when we're frightened can trigger a predator's hunting response, which can transform an unappetizing neoprene-clad diver from a curiosity into prey. Dashing to the surface right then meant that Huberman would not only be fighting his urge to breathe, but possibly also racing away from a creature that can reach bursts of speed over 35 miles per hour.

Maybe I can go when they're not looking, he thought. It was a risky move. If one of the great whites caught sight of him—a likely occurrence since they have panoramic vision—his last sensation could well be teeth ripping through his wetsuit. On the other hand, there weren't many other options.

Huberman steeled himself for the rapid ascent, picturing the movements his fins and arms would have to make during the sprint. Then, by chance, his friend—who had spent 10 years organizing shark expeditions—followed the path of the battle-scared shark, passing him so that the cage entered his field of view. In a moment of brief communication, Huberman ran his finger across his throat— the signal for being out of air underwater. The dive organizer put his hands up in a shrug, as if to ask, "How is that possible?" Huberman symbolically cut his own throat again. Convinced of the emergency, the other diver swam over, removed his regulator and shared it with Huberman. Another 10 seconds and the situation could have ended in tragedy.

The two men slowly ascended to the surface together, making subtle deliberate movements until their heads broke the surface.

Once he was safe and in the boat, says Huberman, another friend of his on the expedition, a former Navy SEAL, gave him a wry grin.

"So what did you learn?" the friend asked.

I look across the table at him expectantly. "Yeah, what did you learn?"

And then Huberman answers my question.

At one level, he says, fear is a specific type of arousal in the brain stem characterized by the secretion of adrenaline, then discomfort and perhaps a dash of confusion. I can see that he thinks his first attempt at an answer is not quite good enough, so he tries again. "It's the anxiety that you feel when you don't know what behavior can remove a feeling of helplessness in the face of a threat."

He's obviously having trouble pinpointing such an obvious yet ephemeral concept. But he's landing on the same interfaces of the Wedge: There's external stress, a sensation he can feel in his body (anxiety), and an orientation to the threat.

He goes on to recount that it wouldn't have helped him to spend time thinking about all the ways he might die. He was too busy to contemplate alternative endings. Instead, he had to remain calm and problem-solve his way out of the situation. "I still had options," he says. Fear would have meant he was out of control. No choices. So maybe he wasn't exactly afraid in the moment. It was something else.

Huberman decides to paraphrase the great horror writer Stephen King: Fear has a lot to do with time frames. Before the event, a person experiences the dread of anticipation; during the event, there's terror when they're helpless in the moment; and after it's over, a person remembers the experience as horror.

In fact, if you can think back to any Stephen King book (or for that matter, anything in the horror genre), we experience fear more as anticipation than anything else. The build-up to a scary clown lurking in the sewers creates more emotional resonance than the actual moment it grabs you.

As I listen, my mind wanders back to my battlefield experience in India, and I realize that it was an entirely different type of fear than what Huberman went through. In the dread-terror-horror continuum, I felt dread as I anticipated the possibility of stepping on a land mine in India. But for Huberman, the danger was so immediate that actual fear didn't have time to enter the picture. It's only after the event that the story evokes something powerful: a sense of horror when we look back and anticipate what might have gone wrong. In both cases, however, the danger demanded a particular type of mental state to avoid fatal consequences, wedging open a space between stimulus and response. Maybe this is why some people enjoy the anticipation of dread that builds up in a horror movie. They're in a safe space, but they identify with what they see on screen in a way that tickles their innate anxiety. For the record, I'll tell you that I can't even make it through the previews.

The entire reason that Huberman ended up in the waters of Guadalupe, off the coast of Mexico, in the first place was to capture footage of great white sharks with 360-degree cameras. Media engineers in his lab would be able to use the footage to re-create a virtual shark dive. Since most people have a visceral reaction to the ocean's apex predators, Huberman hypothesized that the film could be a standard stimulus to study the biological underpinnings of fear. The virtuality-reality goggles his test subjects wear can track eye movements, dilation and blinking to reveal autonomic responses to whatever he puts in front of them.

And this, in short, is why Huberman's research is so interesting. Fear is an excellent inflection point to demonstrate the physiology of the Wedge. It's powerful, visceral, has a strong influence on our behavior, and yet also preserves our ability to make choices about our actions. We experience fear on both a biological and psychological level. It triggers the fight-or-flight response just as reliably as the cold does, issues a burst of adrenaline, secretes sweat, dilates pupils and ramps up the heart rate. However, with fear, our bodily reactions are based on sights, sounds and our own idiosyncratic assessment of how things are changing around us in a bad way. It starts in the mind, not the body. And this is why I hope that his research into fear can help me dissect every other emotional and environmental interface that contributes to the Wedge.

...

But before we go there, before we can hack our nervous systems, you should know a few things about how it works. The *central nervous system* is everything in the brain and spinal cord, while the *peripheral nervous system* encompasses every nerve bundle that reaches out into the rest of the body. The peripheral nervous system has two divisions: the *somatic*, which lets you direct muscles and sensory systems with conscious control; and the *autonomic*, the parts that regulate background body functions like digestion and heart rate without the need for thought. The autonomic nervous system itself has two main divisions: the *sympathetic*, which governs the fight-or-flight response; and the *parasympathetic*, which controls rest and digestion.[1] When any part of the nervous system kicks into gear, it's considered "aroused."

Fleeing a predator will light up the entire sympathetic system at once. Sleep ignites the parasympathetic nerves. Flipping the switch between parasympathetic and sympathetic defines our "state." Mastering the Wedge puts our thumb on that switch so that we can learn to control the state of our nervous systems, flipping between sympathetic and parasympathetic systems almost at will.

In some ways, you could say that all arousal states are created equal. Consider the example that I mentioned in the previous chapter: If a gazelle and a lion are on the open savanna, and suddenly the lion

---

[1]   There's a glossary in the back of this book to help with the sometimes bewildering number of terms that come up when talking about human physiology.

leaps out of hiding and starts a chase, both animals trigger the same sympathetic nervous pathways. Both animals fire the same hormonal cocktail into their bloodstream to give them a spike of energy. Their pupils open up into saucers and their pain thresholds deepen, and the only difference is that the lion is the only one that wants to be there.

If, for some reason, the gazelle falls down, then the few helpless seconds that it's waiting for the lion to pounce are pure helpless terror. If, for some reason, the gazelle happens to get away—imagine the lion misses its pounce and falls off a cliff—then the memory of the terror that the gazelle felt will live on in its nervous system as horror and will flavor every encounter it has with lions in the future. That memory of fear gets hardwired into the animal's physical anatomy. The experience lives in a neural memory circuits and goes on to in-fluence future experiences. Now imagine that a person could choose what specific experiences become hardwired as a permanent neural circuit and which don't. This is the Wedge.

The three main building blocks of human experience are time, emotion and sensation. The brain must account for all three factors in order to encode information from the outside world.

When the nerves first identify something—whether a visual stimulus like a shark swimming up from the deep-blue depths below, the feel of the ambient temperature and pressure of the water on the skin, or the sound of a respirator suddenly not working—the brain needs to make sense of the situation and come up with a plan of action.

Humans sense the world in two different processes: *perception*, or signals that come in from the outside world; and *conception*, or internal understandings that define the world from the inside. Neurologists call these two types of mental processing "bottom-up," for perception, or "top-down," for conception.

You can think about the nervous system as a collection of branching circuits, where each branch triggers subsequent parts of the network. Raw sensation enters through the nerves in the peripheral nervous system and branches off into two different channels: internal and external. Internal channels provide information about the state of the body—hunger, pain, overheating, etc.—and external channels deliver information about the state of the environment around the body.

Both processes only take a fraction of a second as nerve pathways fire and make sense of the environment, but a lot happens in that infinitesimally short period. Sensory information and cognitive processing take slightly different amounts of time to process, and as the brain organizes different streams of information, it creates a filter between experience and raw reality. This organizing process means that humans are always living in the past. And because of our peculiar anatomy, sometimes it's a more distant past than you might expect.

Stimuli from the internal channel trigger two responses, starting in the lower areas of the brain stem. The first signals immediate physiological processes—digestion, heart rate, blood flow—without asking higher areas of the brain for any input. The reactions happen automatically; there's nothing you can do to directly influence them. The second response occurs at an instinctual level. It is a sensation, like hunger, pain or cold, that prompts you to take action. These sensations can be strong, weak, or anything else that could fit on the volume knob of an amplifier; they don't yet have a quality that the body can understand beyond a primal level. They're effectively meaningless. But things get interesting once these signals travel to the next-higher brain area. Because while you can't affect how they feel, you can control whether or not you want to respond to them.

The *limbic system* interfaces raw sensation with higher cognition. Some limbic structures you may have heard of, including the amygdala, the hippocampus, and maybe even the insular cortex; these regions serve as relay and processing centers where sensory information becomes experience. I like to think of the limbic system as a sort of library whose main role is to pair emotional values with sensations and then store those pairings for future reference.

When the limbic librarian receives a sensation, it checks its records to see if the nerves have sent along something similar before. If there's no record, the librarian passes the sensation along to the *paralimbic cortex*—the center for emotions—to figure out how to categorize the new information. The paralimbic cortex pairs the new sensation with the brain's current emotional state and creates what Muzik and Diwadkar call a "symbol." Symbols are the books in the limbic library. Once it's been created, a symbol is filed away in the brain stem by the limbic librarian. The next time the librarian encounters the same sensation, it won't need to consult the paralimbic cortex again; it just pulls the old record (the symbol) off the shelf and passes it to the brain's higher-functioning centers. And whether it's relevant to the current situation or not, that old emotional value gets passed along, too. In effect, this means that every time you feel something you have felt before, you're actually reliving part of your emotional past. This is the neural vocabulary that locks all animals together in emotion, time and sensation.

Neural symbols are the building blocks for all higher cognition. They are the bits and bytes at the center of all of our brain's software, because without them, the sensations we bring in from the outside world wouldn't actually *mean* anything; it would all just be data. The unique architecture of the brain means that everything we sense from the world carries an old emotional value along with it. Everything we experience is inherently a blend of objective data from our senses and the total subjectivity of our emotional state. And while this might not seem like the most efficient system, once we understand the architecture, then we have the opportunity to intentionally create our own new neural symbols to hack our biological software from the ground up. This is the physiological underpinning for how we experience the Wedge.

Because this is such an important concept, I'm going to explain it again by going back to the sharks. Initially, photons enter the eye, forming the sharp edges of a toothy sea creature. If you've never seen one before, the fish might be meaningless; you might associate it with warm, fuzzy feelings of weightlessness and underwater exploration. However, if you happened to have seen the film *Jaws*, then your brain could cross-reference the memory against the terror you felt imagining a giant shark chasing you on a family swim. In this case, the paralimbic system can identify the potential threat, cross-reference it with an earlier emotional state, and notify the sympathetic nervous system to kick into action. This process allows an animal to swim away from the threat, to play dead, or perhaps to stage a last-ditch fight to the death without spending a lot of time reasoning out the best course of action. The symbols are an emotional shorthand that allows for quicker action in the present moment—and as far as we can tell, it's pretty much the same process for any mammal.

Our brains use symbols as the basic cognitive vocabulary that allows for long-term planning. On their own, symbols don't hold a ton of information, but when you put enough of them together, they start to form complex thought. What we think of as "thinking" happens mostly in the cortical gray matter—in particular, those parts of the frontal lobe involved in planning and execution, such as the prefrontal cortex and areas within it that allow us to share a complicated language.

Without these structures, humans probably would not have evolved to become the apex predator on this planet. These higher brain areas allow the body to develop strategies around symbols that surpass the immediate ability for other animals to respond to the world around them. Instead of simply inscribing emotional reactions to a single stimulus, the cerebral cortex can pair symbols together in novel ways that build complexity, similar to the way that computers make billions of ones and zeroes turn into full-fledged programs.

The brain does this in part by using the grammar and syntax of neural symbols to account for the passage of time. It recalls symbols and recombines them so that they can anticipate what emotional state you might feel in the future. No matter how it reorganizes this data, all of these symbols start as sensations that first came up from the lower levels of the brain and peripheral nervous system. Without that data, the brain doesn't have anything to process.

For instance, let's imagine a young child reaching a hand up to the glowing coils of a hot stove. At first the pleasing orange glow and vague heat might draw on positive associations of warmth and spark a curiosity to learn more. However, contact with the coil triggers an immediate reflex to withdraw, followed by lots of tears. This entire experience creates a new symbol that the limbic librarian will file away for later: Glowing red tubes of light pair with the emotional pain of the injury. Now, a few months later, let's say that same child sees a neon light with a glow similar to that of the electric coil. The limbic librarian might pull the symbol of the earlier experience off the shelf, note the emotion and surprise, and signal danger even where there is none. This only changes when the child creates a new association to neon lights. Over time, there are enough symbols in the library that the child can form a generalized understanding of the world informed by the combination of sensory and emotional information.

In this way, every shark image, business plan, mathematical formula, memory of a long-lost lover and decision to mull over whether to buy a luxury car or econobox sedan started as a sensation that bonded with an emotional value and then was processed in the higher brain areas. In other words, the brain never comes up with anything new on its own. Instead, it can only recycle old symbols that it already has stored and combine them in different ways.

This is why the Wedge is so powerful. If you can alter or bond new sensations to emotions, then you can insert a level of control directly into the fundamental grammar of your brain as you create new symbols. Instead of passively waiting for emotional states to bond with particular sensations, you can choose *which* emotions you want to hardwire into your nervous system. By giving yourself intense sensations at the same time you have a mindset of joy or determination or whatever else, you give the limbic librarian more symbols to draw from in future situations.

Here's an example of how that might work. Let's say you feel an aversion to public speaking. If you focus on your nervousness as your next speaking event draws close, you're likely to go into a panic. However, if you instead focus on a fun or rewarding aspect of the experience as it draws near, then you can attempt to attach a different emotional value to it. If the event goes well, then the next time you have to speak in public will be even easier. You'll have created a different neural symbol for public speaking.

Emotions and sensations are the building blocks of everything you experience. They're so primal that it might not even be possible to have a thought without them. This is why extremely abstract ideas with little direct emotional or sensational resonance often fail to make an impression. If you want to make a convincing argument for just about anything, the best tactic usually relies on triggering visceral and emotional details rather than employing logic and abstract reasoning. In other words, I'm much more likely to capture your attention if I start a chapter of my book with an anecdote about a minefield in India or someone swimming with sharks than with a drab academic summary of neurological vocabulary.

Luckily, humans are pretty sophisticated, and our cerebral cortices allow layers and layers of neural symbols to come together to form bewilderingly complex thoughts. This despite the fact that no matter how logical we feel, emotions and sensations underpin the way that a person decides whether swimming with sharks is a good idea, ponders the cost of airfare, and ultimately decides to instead visit sharks in a comparatively safe virtual-reality simulator many miles from the coastline. I can thank my cerebral cortex for the ability to want a meeting with Huberman's lab in the first place.

Still, actually planning that meeting required my brain to both recognize and organize symbols, and also an ability to keep track of time. And this is where things get tricky. Neuroscientists and lifelong meditators have long known that our minds slip from past to present to pondering the future, often without any obvious connection between reference points.

In moments of perfect focus or meditation, we might be able to experience the present. We simply put the limbic librarian to sleep and experience raw sensation. But those moments are few and far between. Usually our minds are all over the place—what Buddhists call the "monkey mind," meaning that we are so easily distracted that our minds don't have significant continuity from one moment to the next.

Monkey minds aren't great for the modern world. Think about the million instances every day in which you should be fully engaged but aren't. Perhaps it's driving a car, where you are literally in control of several tons of metal speeding down a road along with hundreds of other high-velocity vehicles. The stakes are huge, and so, too, are the consequences if something goes wrong. Still, one ding on your cell phone and your attention drifts from the threat. Or maybe your brain wanders in emotional contexts. Perhaps you're in the middle of having sex with your partner and your mind slips inexplicably to the work that you still have to complete tomorrow. Or maybe you're taking a look over your finances—doing battle with the existential problems of the future—but can't wait to get home to dinner. Visual information, physical sensations, memory and emotions all pull on our attention so that the human mind almost can't help but wander, moving from one point in time to another with no apparent direction.

But as scattered as we are, we *can* actually focus; sometimes it comes naturally. While it might be impossible for me to pay attention to anything specific when I'm sitting at a cafe trying to write—I usually end up watching people for the duration of a cup of endless drip coffee—if I sit on my couch at home, I can devour a book in a single sitting. Focus requires the ability to shut out other stimuli and fix our attention to one place in time.

Focus lets us intentionally form and file symbols. With it, we temporarily hire the librarian to pull specific symbols from the paralimbic library and then escort them into the higher brain areas.

Focus is a kind of wedge at the root of everything we do. It's as easy as breathing. It allows us to take control of how we want to experience the world. However, we can't focus all the time. Instead, we use focus to help give the limbic librarian new instructions for how to continue when we're not paying attention.

While most of us maintain an illusion of continuity in our daily lives—a sort of story that we tell about ourselves that proceeds from our earlier memories until our last days on Earth—consciousness doesn't experience all those moments at once. Most of the time we're on autopilot.[2] We make ourselves real by the amount of attention we're able to summon.

---

[2]   So far in this chapter, I've written a lot about how our jumble of neural connections creates a unified and indivisible self. Unfortunately, that's just a story that our brain likes to tell us. A series of experiments starting in the 1950s demonstrated that there is more than one you in your brain. The brain has two hemispheres connected by a thick bundle of nerves called the corpus callosum that transmits information back and forth. Each hemisphere has a full set of cognitive hardware for forming thoughts and generally controls all the sensory hardware for one side of the body. Each side gets an eye and an ear, but only the left hemisphere can control the language center.

Occasionally, people are born without a corpus callosum. Some have brain injuries that sever the connector. And a few epileptics have surgery that disconnects the two lobes of the brain. With the connecting nerves cut, researchers realized that it was possible to devise experiments that would allow them to communicate with just one lobe of the brain at a time. A typical test looked like this: The researcher would cover the eye associated with the left hemisphere and then show the person a picture of a bell. The patient would report that they couldn't see anything. However, when the researcher asked that person to draw what they saw, the patient had no problem drawing an image of the bell on a piece of paper. This was because the uncovered eye attached to the opposite hemisphere still controlled the hand and could communicate independently. When the doctors removed the eye covering and asked the patient why they drew a bell, things only got stranger. Rather than be baffled by their own drawing, the patient instead invented an elaborate story about how they saw a bell on the way to the test center and must have simply doodled it on the paper.

So when confronted by a discrepancy that undermines the story we tell ourselves about a unified consciousness, the human brain would rather offer leaps of absurdity and even outright lies to convince us that we have only one consciousness in our heads.

Roger Sperry, who won a Nobel prize for his work on split brains, wrote, "Both the left and the right hemisphere may be conscious simultaneously in different, even in mutually conflicting, mental experiences that run along in parallel."

Perhaps this is why it's so difficult to shift our own perspective of self into larger or smaller contexts when thinking about the Wedge. Not only are we an ecosystem to the bacteria in our bodies, but also, apparently, an ecosystem of independent consciousnesses that all somehow co-exist in our physiology.

Still, I'm thankful for the story. I don't know how I'd ever get anything done if my various competing consciousnesses started to disagree with one another. And that's more than just a flippant sentiment. With consciousness as messy as the spaghetti plate of neurology in our heads, the only solid thing to hold on to is what we're thinking and experiencing right now in the present.

This idea of focus is related to the way that we talk about mindfulness, which is popular today in self-help and spiritual literature. Huberman says that on one level, mindfulness is great, because focusing on the present moment and sensations cultivates a solid anchor for focus to flourish—but mindfulness alone isn't enough. "If a person just experiences the present moment, then they won't be able to plan for anything in the future or remember the past. Yes, in intensive meditation states, people can feel bliss and timelessness, but if you go too far in that direction, you don't have any drive. You aren't an actor in the world anymore," he says.[3] If you want to be a complete person, you need to know how to be in the moment, and how to connect those moments to other places, ideas and memories. And this is why we need the Wedge: because it forces us to focus on the connections between the environment, sensory system and conscious experience. When we consciously form new neural symbols, we aren't just acting in the present moment; our choices and emotions right now also inform how we feel in the future.

...

With all of these thoughts buzzing around my mind in the cafe just a few blocks from Stanford, I have to wonder how it all connected to Huberman's experiment with the sharks. How does the virtual shark footage unlock the mysteries of the brain?

To show me, we walk together toward his laboratory, past rooms full of impossibly expensive microscopes designed to help technicians dissect mouse brains, and small centrifuges that spin who-knows-what at incredibly high speeds. Huberman gestures to a half-dozen pictures of Costello the bulldog, as well as beautiful hand-drawn sketches of the optic nerve that hang on his wall. Then he leads me

---

[3] See my earlier book *The Enlightenment Trap* for the sometimes-fatal consequences of extreme mindfulness.

down an industrial hallway. The otherwise drab office door opens up to what at first looks a little like a recording studio.

The control room features a standard computer monitor and an undergraduate lab tech by the name of Troy Allen Norcross, who looks out of a bay window into an adjoining room fitted with gray padded walls. The tech looks on through a glass panel into the VR chamber. Each corner of the room features a motion-capture camera that records every movement that happens inside. A set of VR goggles dangles from a cable on the ceiling, and a small foam bat hangs on the back right wall. Norcross gives me a wand that I'll use to interact with things in the new environment and acts as a proxy for my hands.

"It's not a mental institution. We had to pad the walls because people kept walking into them," he offers when I give the insulation a raised eyebrow. Huberman instructs me to sit in a rolling chair in the middle of the room and don the goggles. He then clamps two headphone speakers over my ears.

When the visor powers up, I find myself sitting in a digital reproduction of the room I was just in. The walls don't quite have the reflective quality of the real world, but when I move my head left and right, the display compensates for the changes so that the virtual space feels real. Or at least about as real as a video game could ever possibly feel. I'm not wearing any sensors on my hands, feet or body; the computer can't populate them into the visual field. So I'm really just a floating head hanging in a digital world. I also can't feel anything that I see in terms of touch, smell, pressure or whatever else. But as long as I try to ignore those details, the setup *almost* feels, well, real.

Once I'm settled, Norcross fires up the first script of the day. At first the machine needs to calibrate itself to my own individual eye movements. A red dot bounces around the edges of the goggles, and I follow its path with my eyes. Sensors will record the way that my pupils dilate over the course of the experience. Those changes indicate how my autonomic nervous system responds to whatever scenarios they throw at me—giving away telltale signs of how my visual processing center detects threats. If, for instance, my pupil dilates when it perceives a barking dog in the virtual distance, it could be a physiological sign of a latent phobia and a signal that my sympathetic nervous system is firing too early—whereas a control group might not react at all.

The program starts, and I'm transported onto a boat deck somewhere off the coast of Mexico. I can see the gray outlines of sharks swimming after chum in the water below. The headphones relay the gentle rhythmic tapping from some sort of cable on an iron pole. There's a cut in the scene as I go beneath the water in scuba gear. The respirator translates a passable Darth Vader impression through the headphones. As I swing my head left and right, I have a panoptic view of the school of virtual sharks from one of Huberman's expeditions.

In this scenario, I'm supposedly part of a dive team with a group of fellow researchers. It feels a little like being in a movie where the film continues around in 360 degrees. At first the sharks lurk in the distance, where the gray-blue predators appear indifferent to the underwater film crew, but I look back to my left and catch a glimpse of a majestic toothy fish swimming toward me. Just as in a real undersea dive, the danger could come from anywhere. Unlike in the real world, however, I don't have any control over where the script goes, only where I look. There's also a safe word: If I feel panicked, I can tell the guy in the booth to stop the experience. Or I can just take off the goggles. So it requires a bit of imagination to gin up any real responses.

Over the next hour or so, Norcross puts me through three or four other simulations. There's one for arachnophobes, where I play a tic-tac-toe type game on a wall with a virtual mallet while the simulation unleashes a tarantula-sized spider in my peripheral vision. I take a few swipes at the creature but never am able to squish it. In another, I play with a dog who pretends to attack me, but it's wagging its tail the whole time—a clear indication that it's enjoying itself and not about to take a chunk out of my leg. In a program for claustrophobics, I get stuck in an elevator with five or six graduate-student actors as they run through a script talking about how bunched up they feel.

In another scenario, I stand on a ledge a dozen or so floors above a virtual cityscape. The program urges me to step forward along a precipice, and I have to resist a sense of vertigo. When I cross a bridge between two buildings, the ground beneath me crumbles, and all of a sudden I'm plummeting downward. It actually feels like I'm falling. Or maybe a better way to put it is that it feels like I'm falling in a dream. There's no rush of air or confusion as I accelerate down, but my heart starts beating faster and I'm a little dizzy. When I hit the ground, my knees buckle ever so slightly as they brace for the impact. For that second or two, simulated motion overrides all of the associations and sensations that were telling me I was safe. It must have accessed a symbol in my mind that was already there about the meaning of falling. It was an ever-so-brief window into what it feels like to lose control, and a taste of what some people with generalized anxiety try to avoid. And this is the closest I've felt to an actual sensation of fear in Huberman's lab.

I'd come to his lab with the intention of getting a crash course in neuroscience to understand how the brain moves between stimulus and response. I'm using the tool that he designed to test and shed light on those questions. However, part of me wishes that the scenarios conjured stronger feelings. I'd hoped that he'd have a high-impact device that would make me tremble with anxiety so I would find tools to overcome fear in any scenario. Unfortunately, that's not really the point.

Huberman had a very specific audience in mind for the simulator, and I'm not it. The program is really meant for people diagnosed with generalized anxiety disorder, whose brains have already encoded symbols that automatically trigger their fight-or-flight responses. For the virtual program to make them anxious, a patient has to be so primed for anxiety that merely the suggestion of a threat is enough to make them nervous.

To be clear, I am not immune to fear. But 20 years of taking on dangerous assignments, and nearly a decade of breathwork and cold exposure have, apparently, made me immune to virtual sharks. Instead, Huberman offers, I would make a really useful member of a group to establish low-anxiety baseline controls against his subjects.

For Huberman's target patients, the VR simulations are direct conduits to their nervous systems. Their attention is so heightened to potential threats that their bodies don't notice the lack of water pressure on their skin, the silly goggles or the padded room. Their eyes take in the visual information and their body screams "SHARK!" before their minds can catch up.

And if you think about it, these hundreds of patients in Huberman's lab are heroes. Their bodies are primed for catastrophe, just as I would be if I were offered a chance to walk through a minefield. However, their nervous systems are so sensitive to fear that Huberman doesn't need to use dangerous scenarios to measure their anxiety. And this is helpful for everyone. Because while fear is subjective, just as with the gazelle and the lion, the biological responses are the same for everyone.

Huberman's lab is still refining the process. Looking for physiological measures of anxiety isn't an absolute science...yet. There isn't a single physical measurement that Huberman can point to that could stand in for a diagnosis from a psychologist. Instead, he homes in on changes in breathing and heart rate, pupil size and, in patients with electrodes in their brains, the way that their amygdala fires in response to the virtual environment. There's so much data to access that he needs powerful computers and machine learning to suss out the patterns. And although he hasn't published the results yet, he sees a signal in all that noise.

A more accurate method for visualizing which structures are involved inside the brain could have involved an MRI machine to track how different areas light up in real time. But since those machines require being perfectly still, it isn't a practical option. Alternately,

Huberman could have implanted sensors directly into my brain, but as he pointed out before the demonstration, "I would have had to involve the guys at neurosurgery, which, administratively speaking, would have been a pain. Also, we would have had to remove a section of your skull."

So the next best thing is the virtual-reality tracker. In the simulator, potential threats appear at different distances to trigger predictable responses in the control subjects. By measuring thousands of people's eye movements, Huberman has developed baselines for what a normal reaction is in the program and which markers point to pathological responses.

Again, these scenarios aren't made to arouse people like me. In the Huberman Lab, they're purely here to research the physiology and anxiety responses, but similar labs are starting to use VR to help people with phobias and anxiety. In cognitive behavioral therapy (CBT), therapists gently expose their patients to the things that make them anxious in order to relieve their symptoms over time. In a typical series of CBT sessions, the therapist gradually introduces the fear-inducing stimulus and then increases its intensity to build up tolerance. This could mean showing a snake-o-phobe a picture of a snake from across the room one day, a video of a snake on another, and then, much later, letting the patient hold a real snake.

Eventually—and if everything goes according to plan—the phobia goes away because the patient has been able to wire new neural symbols that override the terror that they initially encoded. The virtual room offers another step in that training process, as well as a controlled stimulus that the researchers can test and generalize across a population.

Anxiety disorders occur when autonomic systems bypass the mind and hijack the stress response. The emotions that created neural symbols in the first instance were so powerful, and tied together so tightly, that they hardwired stress into the patients' systems. Exposure therapy in CBT is a way to access the Wedge. Patients control their anxiety in the face of something that stirs up their emotions, so that they can gradually desensitize their reactions. It's often a slow process, and the key is that a person needs to feel something emotional in the presence of the stimulus.

However, people who don't have anxiety disorders need stronger stimulation to trigger a useful sensory response to use the Wedge on.

But what if the stimulus were different? Whereas people with anxiety disorders are fighting their neurobiology just so they can function in the ordinary world, people without disorders might be able to learn to hijack their sympathetic responses by repeated exposure to what feels like a life-threatening situation. It should be possible to train away a panic response. If I were going to try this, I'd have to find something that scares me and provokes a sense of anxiety, then bond it with a positive emotion. The limbic librarian would take care of the rest.

A couple of weeks ago, Huberman inadvertently had a chance to test his own response to danger in a sea of great white sharks.

"It was a grim situation. In the best-case emergency scenario, you form a plan and work through a protocol to survive," he says. This feels like the understatement of the century to me, but he's a scientist, after all. "We all imagine that in a high-stress situation we'll be deliberate. But reflexes are faster than higher cognition. When I reached down to an air canister and tried to breathe and instead swallowed a mouthful of water, I almost gagged. That would have been the end. But a strange thing happened. I couldn't help it—I started thinking of my dog, Costello, and I knew that there was a time in the future that I would see him. It gave me a reference to think about. Now, who knows if that's what saved my life—there was absolutely a lot of luck—but it's one of my clearest memories of my escape: my dog's face," he says.

Huberman thinks that it's possible that the image of his dog was his brain's way of telling him that his life was worth living—and that his struggle for survival in this moment would have a reward in the end. The goal of the Wedge is to separate stimulus from response. There's no more important time to do that than when your life is actually on the line. The memory of his dog might have helped keep him calm long enough for a solution to emerge. If that were the case, then maybe Costello was a symbol that allowed Huberman to focus his mind during the emergency. Perhaps the thought of his dog was what he needed to overcome brewing panic and gave him the crucial few seconds he needed. What is certain is that Huberman didn't spend those moments underwater dwelling on failure. He didn't freeze in terror and then suck down an ocean of water. Whatever happened in Huberman's mind to keep him in the present moment is worth considering. That ability to respond to the danger around him let him not only survive the immediate threat, but, on a larger level, keep contributing to the superorganism of life itself. In this way, Huberman's individual agency was also part of a larger whole.

And while it will take some time for me to really let that lesson sink in, for now I'm going to have to continue my quest to understand the Wedge in a new context. I need to find a stimulus with higher stakes that evokes a real sense of danger. It doesn't have to be a minefield, a shark attack or a gunfight in India. But it can't be something that I can just brush aside, either. I need something just dangerous enough to demand my attention and focus my mind and body together.

...

When I leave the Huberman Lab, there's already a message on my phone from a friend of mine in the Bay Area, saying that he knows I don't have much time, but there's someone that I just have to meet. Over the previous few hours, I'd learned something about how the brain and nervous system encode sensations and emotions together. I now know that neural symbols are the underlying building blocks for everything that I think and experience. But I don't have a new practice to put that knowledge into action. I want a technique that's easy to learn but also triggers enough of a response that it keeps me attentive. The message from my friend baits the hook with a line designed to grab my attention: "He uses kettlebells to put people into instantaneous flow states."

My eyes linger on the word "kettlebell," and I sigh. A kettlebell: The sphere of iron eight inches in diameter with a horseshoe-shaped handle on top is a staple of gyms everywhere. I've always associated them with Russians with too-huge necks who forgo social encounters to pump iron. I can't remember the last time I've been to a gym. I don't much like weights. But I have a rule when I'm on reporting trips that either ends up getting me into trouble or landing me in unexpectedly enlightening situations: Unless something is likely to get me killed, I try to say yes to all opportunities that present themselves. Maybe this person will have some ideas about what I couldn't find in Huberman's lab. At least the word "flow" sounds promising.

I must not fear. Fear is the mind-killer. Fear is the little-death that brings total obliteration. I will face my fear. I will permit it to pass over me and through me. And when it has gone past I will turn the inner eye to see its path. Where the fear has gone there will be nothing. Only I will remain.

—Frank Herbert, *Dune*

CHAPTER 3

FROM FEAR TO FLOW

It's two hours after leaving Huberman's office, and I'm crouching low and squared off against a predictably gorilla-esque man. We're on a hill in San Francisco where gangs used to settle scores with bats, knives and whatever other weapons they could get ahold of. My bare feet grip sand that once was speckled with blood clots. I'm holding 25 pounds of cold iron in my hands. He wants me to throw it at him. The kettlebell would make a lethal, if cumbersome, weapon. And right now, in this moment, the thought of what happens next makes me nervous. Will I kill him? Will he kill me? My hands sweat on the handle and my heart thumps rapidly in my chest. This isn't something that I've ever done before.

Obviously, we're not really fighting. But I can't help but dread what could go wrong. The two of us lock eyes. I swing the kettlebell low and backward between my legs. There's a pause, and then it reverses direction. As the bell swings forward, I feel it build momentum. I see him stretch his hands out in front of him. I swing the bell back a third time. As it arrives at the apex, I release my grip. The bell flies out of my hands. I watch as it flips perfectly backward over itself in the air. It traces an arc across the empty space. And then the bell lands in his grasp. It follows the pivot of his shoulder along a delicate sine wave though his legs. He guides it through his legs, and the force of my throw exhausts itself. His forearms press against his thighs. Then, with only the slightest twitch of force, he swings the bell forward and releases it. It flies through the air in a perfect arc toward me. *Jesus!* I think. I pucker, ready for a potential impact on my leg. But my hands grab the handle. I catch the weight and let it fall between my legs. And then return it to him again.

A slight misstep could mean a weight missing its mark and crashing down onto a knee, shin or foot—at best leaving a nasty bruise, at worst crushing delicate bones. But somehow, that's not what is happening. Despite the threat—or rather *because of it*—we're focused. The potential for someone getting hurt is the wedge that forces us into coordination.

"Normally, the only time that men face off against each other is when they are adversaries," the gorilla, also known as Michael Castrogiovanni, tells me later. Thank goodness for small favors, because if he were my adversary, I'd be dead. The man is built like a truck. He waits for the next pass with his legs rooted into the ground like tree trunks, arms like ham hocks in front of him and his butt projecting backward. The position makes him look more simian than human. "If we throw kettlebells like we're trying to win, then we both lose," he says, finishing his thought.

...

We continue in this way, playing catch with an iron ball. Soon, my anxiety falls away. I relax. The great battle that this felt like a minute earlier feels like a dance now.

After five minutes, what I thought would be a dangerous practice is feeling fun—light, even. The thrill of watching the bell fly though the air delivers a mini version of the feeling of a roller coaster just starting its descent after a climb.

A few throws in, and I know this is something special. It's answering a question that Huberman's lab left lingering in my mind:

What sorts of practices trigger a loud enough emotional volume to train the Wedge? Getting hit with a kettlebell doesn't meet the same danger threshold of, say, surviving a war zone, jumping out of a plane or rushing into a burning building. I'll survive if it lands on my foot. But the threat is more real than a virtual shark swimming behind a set of high-tech goggles. The nervousness I felt when I first contemplated throwing the metal at Castrogiovanni was *visceral.*

I realize that this shift from fear to fun is exactly what the Wedge is about. In a mere five minutes, I've dismantled and then rebuilt a neural symbol from the ground up.

Throw. Catch. Return. That's all that matters. And the kettlebell lands beautifully. His pass becomes the logical precursor to my catch and vice versa. I feel as if we are intimately connected to each other—body and mind—by the arc of the weight. We're dancing. This is what my friend meant by flow.

...

No matter how large or small, all threats trigger the same biological reactions along the sympathetic pathway. As far as your body is concerned, a shark, a killer clown and a kettlebell all act on the same system. The only difference is the volume of the signal. What sets this practice apart from Huberman's lab is that it carries enough consequence to keep my nervous system in a heightened state of awareness. The threat wedges me into a place of laser-like mental focus.

The risk of injury guarantees that I'm emotionally engaged. At first my mind runs through the worst-case scenarios. I don't want to get hurt, and I don't want to hurt anyone else. Yet because we're engaged in a set of physical movements, the emotion of fear bonds to the sensations of our dance. I'm working on the neural grammar of my brain.

...

Though kettlebells originated in Russia 350 years ago, in the past few decades they've taken off in America in a big way. A typical kettlebell swing works in semi-circular motions between the legs and over the head, incorporating multiple muscle groups at once. But kettlebell passing—literally flinging the iron balls to another person to catch—is the sort of fitness innovation that, on the face of it, doesn't make a whole lot of sense.

But Castrogiovanni saw its potential.

Castrogiovanni has pretty much always self-identified as a "meathead." At 14, he begged his parents for a gym membership, and he's been honing his simian profile ever since. But just being strong was never enough.

At first throwing bells was just a lark. When he was 27, Castrogiovanni filmed a short video series on fundamental kettlebell exercises with a strength coach in Southern California. He and his partner started riffing off each other's movements, then wondered what would happen if they started throwing a kettlebell around. The motions of the bell through the air—deftly caught by a partner and then returned—ignited something in Castrogiovanni's soul that has never gone out.

He understood that throwing bells isn't just about flow or physique. It's about making connections with other people; it's a spiritual practice. Indeed, it takes someone special to see an exercise like throwing kettlebells as something more than a muscle-building routine.

Castrogiovanni isn't a monk, but he's spent at least four years of his life at the New Camaldoli Hermitage in Big Sur. When he first arrived at the monastery in his early 20s, he was eager to find a purpose in life, and liked the idea of being in service to God. Taking work in the maintenance department appealed to him because he found physical labor rewarding.

He infuses a sense of devotion into every pass, because throwing weights was never about the weight. The goal is to cultivate inner growth as much as develop muscle. And so while Castrogiovanni's kettlebell system started in the gyms of Southern California, the Hermitage is its spiritual home.

Over the next few years, Castrogiovanni filled his work days chopping wood, clearing brush and moving dirt. In his free time, he honed a system of throwing kettlebells on the monastery's grounds that ran counter to the systematized protocols of repetitive deadlifts, swings, cleans, snatches, jerks and presses that are the mainstay of the popular Russian Kettlebell System.

After three years, he felt that he'd come up with something special that didn't exist anywhere else. Kettlebells were almost universally an individual exercise, but Castrogiovanni had made it a group effort. He probably wasn't the first person to throw a bell, but he's likely the most passionate about it. The movements weren't hard to pick up, and just about anywhere he went, he could take a bell out of his trunk and, if he was lucky, find a person to throw with. No one was as skilled as he was, but he liked that every person came to the technique with their own inborn style. The more he watched people throw, the more he discovered that he was learning about not only their physical skills, but the way they communicated their thoughts and intentions through movement. He could tell if someone was anxious by how they gripped the iron handles. When he introduced couples to partner passing, he could see the issues in their relationships play out in the arc of their passes. It becomes kettlebell therapy. After all, throwing a lump of iron between two people requires an absolute amount of trust. People who can't overcome their issues don't tend to pass kettlebells very well. They shy away from the incoming missile or jerk the bell out of its natural arc—expending more energy than they need to along the way.

The magic happens when people stick with it, says Castro-giovanni. "As two people overcome their physical resistances to the kettlebell, they're also overcoming their emotional hangups." By passing the bell, partners face fear together and then break past those barriers and wedge in new emotional symbols as they gain competency. They build trust without words as the movements join their bodies and minds.

And all of this makes me want to know more. In the limited time I have with him on this hill in California, all Castrogiovanni can offer are the basic moves. But after just a few hours, I'm already feeling the transition from fear to flow. This was the Wedge in action—an emotional and physical crucible that I hadn't come across since learning to breathe with Wim Hof. Over the next few months, I purchase a kettlebell of my own and rope Laura, my wife, into throwing weights with me when I'm back in Denver. Pretty soon a neighbor down the street joins me in a few sessions. Even so, there's a problem: I understand the value of the practice, but at best, I'm a novice without any business instructing anyone in the fine art of slinging iron. I need to see the gorilla in person again, so I book a flight back to California.

...

What does kettlebell tossing teach us about the Wedge?

Throwing kettlebells is a stress that my senses detect through my visual and somatic pathways and that my mind has already predicted is a potentially dangerous exercise. Initially, it triggers an innate orientation of fear. As the bell moves through space, my visual system naturally modulates my sympathetic response. With each successful throw, the fear disappears and my brain can focus on other aspects of the practice. Over time, this transforms the sensation of fear into joy. My brain is *in* this. I'm focused on what's happening in front of me, and my mind is completely in the moment. Castrogiovanni is, too. We're both here together. We keep our focus on the bell and then enter into that shared mental state called "flow" that my friend had texted me about. I've moved from fear to fun. From fear to flow.

In the past decade, scientists, psychologists, athletes and mental health gurus have looked to flow states as one of the keys to optimal human performance. In flow states, actions don't originate from well-formed thoughts in the cerebral cortex; they bypass the higher brain and just sort of happen.

University of Chicago psychologist Mihály Csíkszentmihályi describes flow as a psychological state where the ego falls away and people are able to complete every action with their whole being. It's a state of peak performance and creativity. While athletes might talk about flow as "being in the zone"—think of Michael Jordan on his best game or Bruce Lee simply knowing the ideal contortion of his limbs to tackle the next threat—flow doesn't only need to be an individual experience. It can also be something that's shared, the sort of mental state that multiple people sync into simultaneously. For instance, right now Castrogiovanni and I are focusing our attention on the kettlebell. We're not exactly thinking about what movements the other person is making; the kettlebell movements direct how our bodies move together. To take part in the dance, all either of us needs to consider is the object between us.

There is something about flow that speaks to the idea of a shared sense of consciousness. And it makes me remember what it felt like to be on the top of Mount Kilimanjaro doing something impossible. The individuals of Castrogiovanni and Carney dissolve into the shared movement we participate in together. Flow offers a peek into what it means to be part of a superorganism.

Most of us experience collective flow states every day. Take, for instance, what happens on a typical American highway. When you're behind the wheel of your car, you limit your attention to just a few things: what's directly in front of you as well as the relative movement of cars in your vicinity. It's so easy that a lot of us feel comfortable checking our phones (bad idea), daydreaming or talking to friends, despite the very real consequence that a mistake could kill you. At any given moment, thousands of cars move together (almost) seamlessly in an incredibly complex system of moving parts. Yet most turns of the wheel and presses on the gas pedal barely register in our conscious brains. On the roadways, we subsume our own egos and contribute to a larger superstructure of the city's traffic patterns without even realizing its bewildering immensity. Every driver's attention centers on the things in their immediate vicinity. In this way, all drivers together form a sort of huge attention network.

There's no way that you could orchestrate a highway by giving instructions to every individual driver from a central command center—instead, those drivers have to make decisions for themselves according to the information in front of them. Together those decisions give an overall character to the entire system.

There's a relationship between attention and risk. If you can remember back to when you learned to drive—those initial moments on the highway before jamming your foot onto the gas pedal and lurching forward—you probably felt at least a hint of fear imagining what might happen if you made a mistake while surrounded by tens of thousands of pounds of steel all moving at sixty-plus miles an hour. I know I did. Over time, the stakes slipped to the back of my mind once I realized I had mastery of the process. Competence meant that I didn't have to focus my attention on every detail, and that I learned to trust the patterns of drivers on the highway. The flip from fear over to competence is the moment when the Wedge starts to pay off. The worries haven't gone away, but my nervous system has accounted for them so I can focus on other things. Now I trust that when I enter into the flow of the highway, I'll be more or less safe. And this is exactly what happens with kettlebells.

While our attention is locked on the movement of the bell, we instinctively know what the other person is going to do, which forces our minds into a group flow state. Once I learn to trust this connection, the fear and emotion that I felt at first will give way to competency. That's the sensation of the Wedge working. And it could never have happened if I wasn't first afraid of getting hurt. Castrogiovanni has opened my eyes to a technique that I think will allow anyone to break into a flow state.

...

Fast-forward to winter, when the sea undulates with cold, unstoppable swells until the water crashes against California's rocky coast. Every movement pushes the Pacific just a little bit farther inland as it slowly erodes the continent. I'm piloting a small rental car down the Pacific Coast Highway. Over the course of the journey, the halting traffic of the Bay Area gives way to an intermittent caravan of gravel-laden trucks. A few miles later I pass a prison crew dressed in orange jumpsuits and a flashing sign warning of a controlled burn in Big Sur.

Even though he lives most of the year on the road, I've come all this way because Castrogiovanni still spends several weeks a year as a groundskeeper at the Hermitage and has done his part to subtly transform the grounds into a sacred space for human performance.

Castrogiovanni is waiting for me when I get there, beaming like an old friend. He's dressed in a thick black sweatshirt that smells like chainsaw fuel and sawdust. He's been chopping wood all day, he apologizes. His facial hair is thick, black and scraggly, but his eyes are kind and brown—kinder and more sincere than any I can remember. Even though we barely know each other, he greets me with a close, tight hug. For Castrogiovanni, connection is king.

"Before we talk about our plan for the next couple days, I want to know your intentions. What do you want to get out of this experience?," he asks.

Like him, I say, I'm after connection. I hope to find another facet of the Wedge through throwing kettlebells. I don't want to simply understand the principles intellectually; I want to feel them for myself. I want it to hit me in the gut. To make me scared, so that I can transcend my own fear.

He nods.

Training starts tomorrow.

...

At noon the next day, we climb up to a bluff above the cloisters called Fox Point. It's a perfect spot, with one side shaded by oak trees and the other an ocean overlook. We arrive at a place that Castrogiovanni cleaned the brush out of years earlier with the idea in his head to make it a contemplative, peaceful destination for training. I ask him what it was about kettlebells that made him dedicate his life to throwing them.

"I saw an opportunity to be creative, to have fun, and to connect at a fundamental level with another person," he tells me. Kettlebells became his spiritual practice, one he pursued with monk-like devotion, but with no ordination. This answer doesn't surprise me. Just about everywhere I've gone looking to deepen my knowledge about the Wedge, people have spoken about similar connections between spiritual ideals and physical practices. While the Wedge is not always something that I can describe perfectly in every context, whenever I've been successful in pushing up against my physical limits, I also feel a deep connection to something greater than myself. That experience gives me insight into the nature of a collective consciousness and a superorganism. As a Christian, Castrogiovanni feels a divine inspiration. As far as I'm concerned, it's two sides of the same coin. At the end of the day, I'm not sure that there's much of a difference.

The first time I met him, I knew so little about weightlifting that he had to show me the basics of a deadlift. He told me to keep my back straight as I crouched down and to stick my butt out behind me. He showed me how my head was supposed to continue straight off my spine so that I'd be looking down ever so slightly. I learned how to grasp the handle and then turn my hands inward to engage my lats. "Lift with your glutes and remember to keep your back straight," he said.

Form has never been my strong suit, but I pushed off the ground and brought the iron up to waist level.

Most popular fitness routines confound me. In America we work out to get fit, to get six-pack abs and impressive biceps, or just to "look better naked." A glance at the cover of any fitness magazine offers top health tips and quick ways to lose that belly fat, as if the aesthetics are all that matter. I think that we've got it all backward. I don't want to work out on behalf of my abdominal muscles. I want my abdominal muscles to work for me. They should help me do things in the world. When we put aesthetics before function, it makes them joyless and cements anxiety into every physical movement.

This is a problem, because when our brains encode sensory information, every emotion and sensory stimulus affects the neural grammar of our minds. If we work out because we think we look fat, that emotional assessment infects the very core of the workout. It transforms exercise into a neural symbol of anxiety.

Alternately, if we work out with a purpose—for the sheer joy of the experience—that positive association hardwires joy into our nervous systems. If I look forward to a workout and am excited for what I'm about to do, then the entire experience draws on positive programming.

We are all reflections of the environments that we inhabit and create. If we sit at an office desk all day, we make a body perfectly attenuated to sitting. Line cooks in fast-paced restaurants get bodies fit for kitchens. Cyclists, gym rats, soldiers, swimmers, fencers and couch potatoes all create physiques that match their actions. No activity in the world outside of bodybuilding competitions requires a six-pack. Impressive forearms don't allow anyone to experience joy more fully. Meanwhile, climbing a mountain, going on a hike or running an obstacle course can be incredibly fulfilling to a certain type of person, while another might find it underwhelming.

A few months before I met Castrogiovanni, I realized that I don't actually like running. It's not only that I'm not very good at it—a goofy duck-walking gait along with my tendency to walk on my toes makes it a physically painful and rather slow affair—but more than that, I just don't enjoy it. However, there are things that give me joy. In the past five months, I've logged almost a thousand miles on a bicycle. With cycling, my funny stride doesn't matter as much. The rhythmic mashing on the pedals makes cycling a sort of meditation where the bike feels like an extension of my body, and I look forward to the eventual fatigue I feel at the end of a particularly difficult ride. I don't know *why* I enjoy it; I just do. So I stick with it.

Of course, this is my personal baggage. What works or doesn't work for me will be completely different for another person. My wife genuinely loves the gym. She sees something in it that I don't. And that's okay. That's human.

However, Castrogiovanni wants me to find joy in something new: lifting and then throwing a kettlebell. Just as we did in San Francisco, we start this session by going over basic form: a swing between the legs where the bell hinges just behind my butt. The weight hangs loosely from the joints at my shoulders while my forearms press at the inside of my groin. The power of the forward stroke comes from both the conservation of momentum of the natural swing from the bell and then a gentle hip thrust forward to help it along. It's not supposed to be much effort, but I struggle a little bit making the arc exactly right. There isn't supposed to be any strain on my back or shoulders. It takes about twenty swings until he nods.

He shows me a few moves where I can flip the bell to myself, a little like juggling. There's a two-handed throw where the bell flips forward and comes back into my hands. And one where it flips backward at the risk of rapping my knuckles with iron if my timing is just a little off. We go through one-handed variations, and a long swing where I pull my leg behind and follow the rotation to its top-most point with my body in a half-twist. These movements are all pieces of a freestyle vocabulary we're going to put together when we start passing. This is the grammar I want to bring home.

And then he says something that I don't expect.

"When you throw it, throw it with love." More than exercising muscles, kettlebell throwing means exercising emotions.

I'm hooked.

I'm also still a little terrified. When I hold the bell in my hand and think about what might happen next, I feel a pit in my stomach. I still feel a similar pit before I jump into an ice bath. Even though I've practiced the Wim Hof Method for years and done crazy feats in the cold, ice water still provokes a twinge of fear for me. Yes, I've done it before, I think to myself, but what if *this time* it doesn't work? It's only after I take the plunge that the anticipation turns to relief and joy. The kettlebell provokes the same thoughts. Even after a few months, throwing a piece of metal at another person is intimidating. It's one thing to take a risk where the consequence is hurting myself. It's quite another matter when a mistake means hurting someone else. I'd much rather drop a weight on my own foot than live with the knowledge that I'd broken his. And in this mutual feeling of shared consequences, we both must give every throw our best and most concentrated effort. And that's what he means by love: We give the practice our best because it elevates us together.

Before every passing session, Castrogiovanni insists on a basic protocol that confirms the gravity of the situation to both partners. We run through it again.

It starts with me looking him in the eyes and asking if he's ready. We're focused on each other. He replies, "Yes," and then I count to three as I start swinging the bell.

"One." I say as the bell reaches the top of its swing still in my hands. He's smiling.

"Two."

The bell reaches the same position, and we move our eyes from each other and deliberately down to the weight, transferring our attention to the bell as a proxy between us.

"Three."

The bell flies from my hand, looping end over end, reaching its apogee in the middle of the space between us and then traveling in a downward arc. Since it's spinning, the handle moves in the opposite direction of the swing and lands smoothly into the cup of his downward-facing hands. From there it follows effortlessly down between his legs to the nadir and then along an upward arc formed from the fulcrum of his shoulder until it loses its energy at a new apogee behind his butt. Next he pushes slightly off from his wrists and thighs and returns the kettlebell along the same path until it arrives perfectly into my hands.

Ideally, the path of the flying kettlebell would be as smooth as a complete sine wave as it moves back and forth between two points. Just like with the Chinese martial art qi-gong, the best kettlebell passing relies strongly on conserving momentum and energy. It isn't supposed to be a lot of work.

"Keep your hands in position and I'll get it to you perfectly every time," he says.

And with that, we're in flow again. It goes back and forth about twenty times before he starts to mix up his passes—crossing it over from one hand to the other, around the back, rotating the bell sideways and frontways until we are playing in a dance of improvised kettlebell swings and throws. In a matter of minutes, we are in the same mental place that a capoeirista finds in the acrobatic moves of the Brazilian martial art capoeira.

This is not to say that I ever expect to be a kettlebell master—it's clear that it's the type of skill that can develop endlessly over years of practice—but I have a glimpse of what happens on the other side. Flow deepens with skill, but even though I'm a novice, I grin from ear to ear at the sheer joy of dancing and throwing iron. The fear recedes. I'm in the moment and loving it.

And this is where Castrogiovanni's dreams come in. At the moment, he calls his system Kettlebell Partner Passing, and it is pretty much unknown outside a few niche enclaves in California and New

Mexico. I ask him what he would do if, hypothetically, his training program caught on and it started making money. He smiles and confides in me that he'd like a bed of his own, and maybe a small house that could anchor him so that he didn't always have to be on the road. After that, his ambitions tend toward charity. "One day I'd like to build an animal shelter, and then give back to this monastery. They've been so generous with me that I feel it's important to give back," he says.

What Castrogiovanni has discovered is more than an exercise; it's the perfect everyday execution of what Huberman is building in his laboratory. It's a physical movement that poses just enough danger that it keeps me present. It's an example of the Wedge in action: the sensation of overcoming stress gently pulls a person from an orientation of fear into confidence, connection and flow. The individual motions are all easy enough to master that just about anyone can take it on. Once the initial fear falls away, partners learn a whole new form of wordless communication and awareness. And as strange as it might sound, that mutual sensation of flow is the force that connects the two partners into a frame of reference that is bigger than just two people on a grass field: It's the connection that all living beings share in the superorganism of life on the planet. This relatively simple kettlebell exercise offers one lens on how we all experience being individuals and part of the universe simultaneously.

After two days at the Hermitage, I head back on the road up to San Francisco, and from there back to Denver. I already have plans to show my neighbor a few new throws so that we can start a dance together. Maybe one day I'll even start up a little group.

Of course, it's also one practice of thousands that might offer similar results. My quest for digging deeper into the Wedge is still just beginning. I've considered deepening my knowledge with martial arts masters, yogis or accomplished meditators who have their own techniques to separate stimulus from response. I'm sure I would learn a lot. But I've decided that my next stop will be with something that

I've studied for years. It's the first place that just about every esoteric tradition explores even though it takes a lifetime to master. I'm going to return to the breath.

Breath is the bridge which connects life to consciousness, which unites your body to your thoughts. Whenever your mind becomes scattered, use your breath as the means to take hold of your mind again.

—Thich Nhat Hanh

CHAPTER 4

BREATHE IN

A brisk frost coats the windows of a yoga studio not far from my house in Denver. Outside, people walk by with scarves bundled up to their chins, hunched over to keep the cold at bay while cars zoom up and down the busy street. Inside, the space's womb-like interior is warm and quiet. Two dozen humans lie down on yoga mats with their faces pointed toward the roof. Most of us have our eyes closed.

Unlike in a typical class, the teacher isn't leading us through sequences of sanskritized stretching. Instead, we're breathing in unison. That's all. Long, deep inhales followed by equally long exhales. This is the sound of humans doing what is absolutely necessary to be alive. Inside our bodies, our lungs perform a bit of chemistry. We take oxygen into our bloodstreams and then exhale the acidic byproduct of respiration: carbon dioxide.

I'm relaxed and stretched out on my mat. I inhale, then exhale, urged onward by the rhythm of the music. We start out slowly at first, but as the session proceeds, the instructor urges us to pick up the pace. We breathe until our fingers begin to tingle and our legs come alive. I'm dizzy, but still putting effort into every inhale and exhale. We work on our breath together, reaching new peaks of exertion, then slow down into relaxation.

As I lie there, I am amazed at how odd the bodily function of breathing really is. Nearly all respiration runs on autopilot, without any need to consider how important it is. It just takes the slightest effort to consciously hijack control and determine for ourselves how deeply we breathe, how often, and even stop it altogether for long stretches until our bodies have no choice but to wrest back control when we pass out. This makes breathwork the perfect wedge between our autonomic and somatic systems. And yet the control switch between consciousness and unconsciousness is so perfectly smooth that we don't always notice what a feat it is.

I'm enjoying the gentle way that the teacher leads the group into connecting to their own bodies by alternating between deep, focused breathing and long breath holds. There's something amazing about breathwork in a group that is impossible to duplicate at home. I feel myself going deeper into my own mind with every pattern.

Elizabeth Lee, our guide, takes us through the basic Wim Hof Method. We start to breathe faster as the music from her portable speaker matches our pace. When we're lightheaded, she tells us to exhale and hold long enough so that the automatic urge to breathe starts to become uncomfortable. Many of the people in the room have never tried Wim Hof breathwork before, and Lee is watching everyone closely to be sure they stay with her script. She doesn't want to push anyone too far.

Lee, who goes by Elee, is a slight, elfin lady in orange psychedelic-patterned yoga pants; she calls out to the room with the voice of a person who has made breathwork a central part of her life. She's a Wim Hof Method instructor with a breezy style of teaching. The real reason I'm here is that she asked me to give a talk at the beginning of the class about my own journey with Hof and the power of breathwork. But I have stayed to experience the energy of the group breathing together. I'm glad I did. I'm learning a few new things, diving deep into my experience and reconnecting with my own Wim Hof journey, which began almost a decade ago. My experimentation with the Hof Method was the gateway into my curiosity about hacking the human nervous system. My own journey has developed over the years.

In the beginning, I'd almost always feel slightly lightheaded, have tingling in my hands and feet and see an array of colors flash behind my eyes—and then I'd experience intense euphoria between tension and release. Over time, as my practice matured, those feelings fell into the background. I've conditioned my body, and because of that, the luster of newness has dulled.

But it's different in the group experience. Now I feel connected back to those first sensations of the method. I am going deeper. My breath holds are getting longer. A shifting pattern sparks behind my lids, and I realize that my body is primed to do a maneuver that Hof once taught me that will send my consciousness to a place I seldom try to visit. I start to stray off Elee's script into what Hof calls "DMT breathing," and I'm so deep that I'm not thinking about how it might look from the outside. If I were a fly on the wall, I would have seen that Elee was getting concerned about me. It's understandable. It must have looked freaky, as if I were actually taking the drug DMT, this breathing method's namesake.

...

The breathing pattern gets its name because it produces a particular type of hallucination that resembles the experience that people report when they smoke the chemical DMT (N,N-Dimethyltryptamine). Aficionados of psychedelics, often called *psychonauts*, consider DMT to be one of the most powerful and profound chemicals on Earth—characterized by brief but intense visions of spirits, aliens and even traveling to other worlds. What makes DMT so fascinating is that many people report seeing the same exact hallucinations and meeting the same otherworldly entities in their visions. Some claim that the visions are a peek into what happens during death. The chemical basis for so-called near-death experiences occurs when the pineal gland releases DMT into the brain and you take your last gasps.[4] While difficult to prove, this is why DMT sometimes goes by another name: the spirit molecule. Whether or not the breathing pattern does release DMT has never been the subject of medical study; nonetheless, many people initiated into the practice report life-changing experiences from the protocol. Regardless of the mechanism, I'm getting to the point in the breathing where I can trigger my own near-death experience.

Giving into my impulses, I shift away from Elee's instructions.

At first I concentrate on that familiar lightheadedness and tingling in my fingers. Then there's a swatch of colors behind my eyelids, and I know that I'm getting somewhere. My chest heaves up off the mat thirty more times. And then, just like that, the room disappears. Now I'm traveling down a tunnel of concentric halos. Splashes of color arc across the walls, interspersing deep pitch-blackness with smatterings of violet, red and yellow. I take another lungful of air and hold it at the top of the inhale. Following a protocol that I've been tweaking for years, I clench the muscles in my feet, legs, stomach and chest, one after another, like I'm pushing blood and air up to the top of my head. This process, called a "push," intensifies the experience. Suddenly everything goes white, like I'm staring into the flashbulb of a camera. After a few seconds, the glow fades into a familiar bearded face. Then I'm rushing forward again, down an infinite plane of shifting colors toward...well...I don't know exactly what. Maybe I'm reaching the end of something. Or the beginning. I'm not even thinking about how long it's been since I've taken a breath.

---

[4]   This often-repeated statement is controversial among neurobiologists. While it's well known that the pineal gland produces melatonin and DMT, identifying exactly what chemicals release at the moment of death proves predictably difficult to study. A similar controversy surrounds whether or not the pineal gland ever releases enough endogenous DMT to even spark a hallucination. Chemical similarities between DMT and melatonin (the hormone that regulates circadian rhythms) have caused some scientists to speculate that maybe DMT also occurs naturally in the lungs, and not the pineal gland at all. This is because DMT is just one carbon dioxide molecule away from melatonin—which is exactly what is released during an exhale.

Parallel to whatever might or might not be happening with DMT in my brain chemistry, the body responds in predictable ways to long breath holds like the one I'm doing now. When starved of oxygen, the brain starts turning out the lights—shutting off higher cognitive functions in order to concentrate energy on the life-sustaining systems in the lower brain stem. There's a certain magic to this moment, because as long as I don't push it too long, I can remain conscious of that process and turn it into a lens into my lizard mind. It doesn't feel like I'm being turned into a lesser version of myself. I feel expansive.

...

My experience in Elee's class makes sense. The breathing method has starved my brain for oxygen. But I don't experience this as impairment. Instead I feel expansive, as if I'm moving into a higher state of consciousness. It's paradoxical, but I feel *more* connected to the world when my higher brain functions take a back seat. With the thinking brain turned off, I've stopped seeing all the ways that I'm separate from the world around me. Instead, I'm experiencing the way that I'm part of the universe.

The philosopher and CERN [European Organization for Nuclear Research] scientist Bernardo Kastrup recently wrote in the *Journal of Cognition and Neuroethics* that mystical and spiritual experiences often correlate with neurological impairment in the brain. Drawing on research from cases of hypoxia—oxygen starvation, where parts of the brain turn off—as well as instances of chemical impairment through drugs and even brain injuries, he shows how diminished brain function correlates with feelings of expanded consciousness and spiritual insight. Kastrup writes, "A potential explanation for this is that brain function impairment could disproportionately affect inhibitory neural processes, thereby generating or bringing into awareness other neural processes associated with self-transcending experiences."

I've used the Wedge to get here—first priming my body with an exercise that pushes me toward a physical limit, then breaking beyond the barriers of my body's programming by adding just a tiny bit more stress. And I believe that states like this that put breathwork in the center of spiritual practices across the world. Indian yogis wrote about this 5,000 years ago. Indeed, there have been thousands of different related protocols—from the earliest form of breath control, called *pranayama* in the yogic tradition, to the Tibetan tradition of tummo, which builds up heat in the body, to the hallucination-inducing holotropic breathing from the 1960s and the easy-to-learn box breathing that predictably lowers the heart rate. Like them, I'm approaching one of life's thresholds simply by manipulating a tool with which all of us are born with. After all, breathing means life; not breathing means death.[5] In other words, as I manipulate my breath, I'm pushing a wedge in the space between life and death.

Outside of whatever psychedelic space I've vaulted into, in the real world—the one where I'm lying on the floor with a bunch of other heavy breathers—Elizabeth Lee is worried about me. I'm on the floor at the top of a several-minute-long breath hold and my skin is turning bright purple. She's worried that I might pop.

She puts her hand on my chest and shakes me gently. "Are you okay?" she asks. When I don't react to her voice, she suggests that maybe I should just take a breath.

But back in the tunnel, whatever is happening in the yoga studio doesn't seem so important. I know that a woman is next to me, and I can feel her concern. Unwilling to open my eyes and not exactly thinking clearly, I conjure an image in my mind of the person who I

---

5   The Vinaya—one of the earliest Pali texts that are sacred to Buddhism—contains the story of Migalandika from the Buddha's earliest years, when he decided to teach his followers the surest path to enlightenment. The first method he revealed revolved around contemplating our own inevitable mortality in open graveyards in front of rotting corpses. Unfortunately, his followers did not take to the lesson the way he anticipated, and they began to commit suicide. Sensing he had made a terrible error, the Buddha came up with a new pedagogy that focused instead on watching the rising and falling of the breath. For more about this conflict in the earliest years of Buddhism, see my book *The Enlightenment Trap*.

think is talking to me. I imagine that she's a woman with dark flowing hair and a wide beaming smile. (Later, I'll look back on that image and realize that it's not Lee I'm seeing.) I don't want to come back just yet. I feel like I'm getting somewhere I've never been before. I'm not connected to my body

She shakes me again, this time hard on my sternum. I reluctantly abandon my travels in the kaleidoscope. I open my eyes and take a breath. The flush leaves my face and I feel comfortable and relaxed. More than that, I feel filled with love and gratitude for the world around me.

For her part, Lee looks stressed. Her eyebrows furrow upward in the middle. After the workshop, she says that I hadn't taken a breath in at least five minutes and was turning purple. Whatever blissful plane I was headed toward, she was the one responsible for a room full of people on their own individual journeys and wasn't interested in having any casualties.

Make no mistake: It was irresponsible of me to indulge this way in her class. And while definitely alarming to look at, I've used these breathing patterns dozens of times before and don't think I'm any worse the wear for it. In my experience, I don't believe it's actually possible to completely shut off the autonomic nervous system. The ability to override breathing patterns only works while I'm conscious. Eventually, when I hit the limit of oxygen starvation, I'll pass out. The lowest area of my brain stem will simply take over, and breathing will continue on autopilot as usual. It's not unlike hitting the reset button on a computer. This is why it's a *near*-death experience and not just straight up death. I've seen this happen to other people. Then again, human biology is complex, and I don't know for sure how much danger I was really in while Lee looked on in horror. I do wonder what I'd find at the end of the tunnel. Maybe nothing. Maybe I just passed out. Either way, as I gaze upward at the ceiling of the studio, I'm filled with gratitude for the experience.

Whatever the case, breathwork like this shows how active protocols create physical changes that directly alter my experience of consciousness. However, this type of exercise is only one of thousands. There's too much ground to cover in just one book, or maybe even a library of books. Suffice it to say, breath is the most basic wedge—one that that we're all born with. In Elee's yoga studio, I turned off parts of my brain, which I believe made me look deep inside my internal physiology. The diminished higher brain functions provided a peek at the interior layers of the Russian dolls that make up my consciousness at the same time that I connected to something greater than myself. It could be that the cognitive complexity of the human brain evolved in order to force a sense of absolute individuality—even isolation—onto the way we experience the world. This may have made it easier to pass on our genes, but that always-on filter can also prevent an inherent sense of connection to our environment. I wonder whether our ability to circumvent that filter is a bug, or a feature of being human in the first place. Whatever the truth, breath is also a wedge between the body and the environment—the outer layers of the Russian dolls. Instead of using it to delve inward and shut down, maybe I can also use it to reach outward. To do that, I'm going to have to head back to California.

Breathing is a rhythmic activity. Normally a person at rest makes approximately 16 to 17 respiratory incursions a minute. The rate is higher in infants and in states of excitation. It is lower in sleep and in depressed persons. The depth of the respiratory wave is another factor which varies with emotional states. Breathing becomes shallow when we are frightened or anxious. It deepens with relaxation, pleasure and sleep. But above all, it is the quality of the respiratory movements that determines whether breathing is pleasurable or not.

—Alexander Lowen, *The Voice of the Body*

CHAPTER 5

BREATHE OUT

A few months after Elee's breath workshop, I journey to San Mateo, California, to the home of Brian Mackenzie, one of the world's foremost experts on human endurance. I arrive at his architecturally unique bungalow. Inside I find a gym, his personal library, and more than a few strange experimental body-hacking devices—one of which looks a little like a miniature Tesla coil. There's an assortment of high-end athletic gear in his garage-turned-weight room: stationary bikes, pull-up bars, road bikes and a dozen or so kettlebells (some molded into monkey faces and skulls), as well as a flag featuring the five interconnected Olympic rings. This unassuming skunkworks is actually a pilgrimage site. Each year, dozens of athletes and journalists seeking answers to the next fitness revolution come here to sit at the feet of the guru.

Mackenzie has authored several best-selling books on human endurance, and, depending on whom you talk to, is either a pariah of the fitness world or its savior. His most notable claim to fame is his insistence that short spurts of high-intensity workouts and breath regulation are a far better way to train for endurance events than the standard approach that requires building up increasingly long distances over weeks, months and years. He espouses a quality-over-quantity approach that examines the concept of endurance holistically. Though not its inventor, Mackenzie was ahead of the curve promoting HIIT. Many now take his word as gospel.

I take a seat on a long orange sofa and ask about the chest freezer brimming with icy water in his backyard. He tells me that the contraption has been the DIY solution for people who want to have access to an ice bath but live in areas where cold water is scarce. Every morning, Mackenzie takes a five-minute soak in his freezer and then warms up in his sauna. Later, when we jump into the heat together, we wear bell-shaped Russian banya hats made out of boiled wool to keep our heads cooler than our bodies. Mackenzie is the sort of guy who goes full-bore to chase any idea that might give him an edge in training the next crop of professional athletes. But he's also constantly scrutinizing the results to track where he goes wrong.

One reason I'm here, of course, is to discuss how Mackenzie's research taps into hidden reserves of human strength. I suspect that his breath routines and endurance protocols speak to what I've experienced with the Wedge. The other reason I'm here is that the last time I met him in person, Mackenzie had been using Wim Hof's breathing method to give his athletes a boost on the field. I wrote about his training program in my earlier book about Hof. But recently he's begun to turn away from Hof's protocols. I want to know why.

...

But first, some Hof basics: One of the most stunning hacks offered by Hof's method is that the same tweak that lets a person hold their breath for an exceedingly long time also makes them capable of brief spurts of incredible endurance. (You can find the exact protocol at the end of this book, along with other techniques from these chapters.)

A typical Wim Hof session revolves around three or four rounds of rapid controlled breaths followed by empty-lung breath holds—a variation of what I'd been doing in Lee's class. The super-ventilation alters the ratio between carbon dioxide and oxygen, which tricks the body's sensory system and pushes off the urge to gasp. It's a physical wedge that creates space between stimulus and response. With each repetition, the breath holds lengthen until, for me, after the third round I hold for about three minutes. On the fourth round, you do something different. Instead of just holding your breath on the mat, you get up and start doing push-ups (or any other similar exercise) while holding your breath on an exhale. Most people discover that push-ups are much easier after hyperventilating. When I first tried the method, I doubled my push-ups after just one breathing session—going from 20 to 40 in a matter of minutes. After a few months, I worked my way up to occasionally hitting a breathless 80.

In the Wim Hof Method, the athletic boost comes from a well-understood pulmonary and circulatory hack. For reasons lost to evolution, our bodies can't detect oxygen levels in the bloodstream, and instead only monitor the acidic byproduct of respiration—CO_2. When carbon dioxide concentrations hit a certain level, the brain broadcasts a panic signal urging you to stop physical activity, trigger a gasping reflex, or shut down entirely. Wim Hof's hyperventilation techniques artificially lower CO_2 levels and trick the body into producing more physical output when it would ordinarily shut down. This is partially why I was able to hold my breath for so long in Elee's class. It pushes you past your limits, a turbo boost—or as Mackenzie puts it, "It blows off the roof." Another way to look at Hof's method is to say that it works primarily on the sympathetic nervous system because the rapid breathing mimics the unconscious physiological effects of fight and flight. Over time, Hof's protocols allow a person to take control of these unconscious stress processes and put them under conscious control. It seems like an athlete's dream.

I'd seen the performance boost in my own training programs. I even have data. Before and after testing at a sports lab in Boulder, I showed staggering levels of improved endurance on something called a VO_2 max test. But I've never been an elite athlete, and Mackenzie was seeing something different with the people he worked with.

I turn on my recorder and repeat the question. "So why the shift?" I ask Mackenzie.

"With Wim's method, when you blow off CO_2, it's like taking the ceiling off your workout; the limits just sort of go away. But the catch is that it only works while you keep up with the breathing. I wanted my athletes' physiologies to adapt long-term, but what we found is that while hyperventilation might give a person a personal record, it doesn't allow them to reach new athletic peaks when they're not doing the breathing," he says.

When Mackenzie first heard about this strange performance boost, he reasoned that combining Hof's hyperventilation and breath retention with HIIT programs would create long-term athletic gains in the coterie of athletes that he trained. When we first met a few years ago, I was struck by how much more power I had on a stationary bike as he took me through his protocols. But after publication and several more years of examining biomarkers, resistance training and competition results, Mackenzie started to back away from the program. Something was wrong, he says now. People were performing better in his gym, but the changes weren't translating to success on the field.

Mackenzie realized that while controlling sympathetic activity is an important tool in a person's kit, it's only half the equation. He doesn't just want to blow the roof off of physiology; he wants to raise the floor. If you think of the body as a car, the sympathetic responses kick in as it reaches the RPM red line. People don't usually live on the edge of their capabilities; instead, most of our lives take place in a balanced place between fight and flight and rest and digest.

At a neurological level, sympathetic and parasympathetic impulses travel through the body on the two opposing branches of the vagus nerve, the twisted central conduit for most of our unconscious neural responses. Resting, it turns out, doesn't mean simply lowering the volume of the nervous system; rather, it entails activating a different branch of the vagus nerve. While both sides of the vagus stay on in continual operation most of the time, one branch takes precedence over the other depending on the situation at hand. By controlling the floor and ceiling for athletic performance, Mackenzie is, in effect, training his athletes to consciously choose which branch of the vagus stays active. They're training the way that their body reacts to stress, and over time, they wedge control over their vagus nerve.

Mackenzie wants to find a way to maintain a high level of physical activity in his athletes without relying on the sympathetic boost of adrenaline. In other words, he wants to maintain high parasympathetic "tone" during high-intensity workouts. And that means he needs to invert the paradigm and become the yin to Hof's yang.

Of the thousands of breathing methods that exist, they all break down between those that ramp you up and those that bring you down. As a general rule, if you take more air in than you let out, you up-regulate your body, giving yourself an energy boost and heightened alertness. If you let out more air than you take in, you down-regulate, meaning you will relax and fall asleep easier. At a physiological level, down-regulation correlates with higher CO_2 levels in the blood and pulmonary system, and up-regulation means lower CO_2.

Mackenzie speculates that he didn't see long-term changes in the athletes he trained with hyperventilation because they never adapted their bodies to operate with high CO_2 levels. They only learned how to boost their adrenaline.

But what would happen if a person conditioned their body to tolerate high CO_2 levels in their blood during high-intensity workouts and then used super-ventilation during competitions? Such a training program would both raise the tolerance floor and allow them to blow off the roof when they need an extra boost. Mackenzie's protocols call for building up high loads of CO_2 in the bloodstream and then conditioning the body to get used to the discomfort.

Before I flew out to see him, Mackenzie asked me to figure out my own CO_2 tolerance. The instructions he sent were surprisingly simple. With a stopwatch in my hand, I took three full relaxed breaths, and then, on the fourth, a full inhale. Then I started the watch and began exhaling as slowly as possible. I was supposed to stop the timer when my exhale ended. This is more difficult than you might expect, and harder than a simple breath hold. When air leaves the lungs, CO_2 builds up in the blood, as do feelings of claustrophobia and panic. Since the exhale lowers the overall volume of air in the lungs, the CO_2's signature is stronger than usual.

The second part of the test is a 28-point questionnaire that Mackenzie developed in conjunction with the Huberman Lab at Stanford to measure emotional reactivity. The self-assessment posits different ways that a person might react in stressful situations and asks subjects to rate their likely responses on a scale of one to four. At first the two components don't seem interrelated. After all, how does measuring how long I can exhale determine how angry I get when someone cuts me off in traffic?

After testing more than 400 people in his protocols, Mackenzie says that physiological reactivity correlates strongly with emotional reactivity. Indeed, therapists who ascribe to cognitive behavioral therapy will sometimes use gas masks that deploy CO_2 in order to trigger panic attacks in a controlled setting as part of the therapeutic process. In CBT, the purpose of the training is to teach the patient that panic attacks aren't as bad as they expect; in fact, it's the anticipation that causes the most emotional pain. Mackenzie posits that there's an added benefit to his training program: If you improve your CO_2 tolerance, you won't just be a better athlete, but you are likely to be more emotionally stable, too, which translates to making better decisions on and off the athletic field.

Another way to look at this would be to go back to neural symbols that encode emotion and sensation together. If low CO_2 tolerance leads to pervasive feelings of anxiety, it would mean that if you can't breathe correctly, every new symbol you generate has the physical sensations of anxiety baked into it.

Most people who come to Mackenzie can maintain their exhale for 20 to 40 seconds. When I try it, I make it to 72 seconds, which puts me in the advanced category. Most likely this is because of the amount of breathwork I've already done. I'm unusual, he says.

"Athletic prowess doesn't predict good breathing," he notes. "I meet pro footballers all the time who can't exhale more than 20 seconds. We're training the pulmonary system to work more efficiently. You can't out-fitness breathing."

The questionnaire backed up his prediction. With high CO_2 tolerance, I was also generally calm in stressful situations. This might explain how I've spent much of my career in stressful environments— the middle of war zones in India, the tops of African mountains, amid organ traffickers and Mafia bosses—without any post-traumatic symptoms that I'm aware of. Could it be that I'm naturally a good breather?

Certainly, much of the world isn't very good at it. Mackenzie says that most people who don't do breathwork are chronic over-breathers.

"Peek around your office some time and take a look at how people breathe," he suggests. Most of us never learned to breathe right in the first place and, as is the case with our penchant for temperature comfort, put in the least amount of effort possible. "Most people breathe like this," he says, and then starts taking shallow breaths through his mouth. It goes on for a few seconds, and he notes that it comes out to about 20 to 25 breaths every minute. Mindful breathers should be at around ten. Mackenzie says he averages about eight.

"Breathing is the brain's remote control," he says, letting the rest of the sentiment hang in the air. It's the quintessential tool of the Wedge. Master breathing, and you can control your physiology.

Then he asks me if I've ever heard of George Catlin. Indeed I had; lately, Catlin has had a bit of a resurgence among a certain breed of biohackers who look to evolution for answers to human health. Born in 1796, Catlin was a renowned explorer, painter and ethnographer who spent much of his life traveling among indigenous tribes of North and South America. He traveled with William Clark (of Lewis and Clark) on explorations of the Missouri River and had the opportunity to meet tribes and communities who had never encountered white men before. Toward the end of his career, Catlin began to wonder why it was that nearly all of the tribes he encountered had incredibly low instances of chronic diseases. He claimed to have met "more than two millions of wild peoples" during his journeys and concluded that the secret to their health lay in two primary causes, which he described in one exasperatingly long run-on sentence.

"There is no animal in nature, excepting Man, that sleeps with the mouth open; and with mankind I believe the habit, which is not natural, is generally confined to civilized communities, where he is nurtured and raised amidst enervating luxuries and unnatural warmth where the habit is easily contracted, but carried and practiced with great danger to life in different latitudes and different climates; and in sudden changes of temperature, even in his own house."

To Catlin, the breathing habits of the Western world were inherently unhealthy. His book *Shut Your Mouth and Save Your Life* claimed that the secret to longevity rested in breathing through the nose as well as a healthy dose of temperature variation. Catlin encouraged people to train themselves to sleep with their mouths closed, arguing that the nose is a natural filter of pathogens.

While much of Catlin's logic remained mired in the scientific understandings of the 19th century, Mackenzie and others like Patrick McKeown, author of *The Oxygen Advantage,* have reincarnated the philosophy for the modern world. The nose is nature's most effective air decontaminator, and it also conditions our bodies to handle stress. Mouth breathing—of which I have an almost-40-year-long habit—is for emergency situations where the power boost that comes from a rapid gas exchange is more important than the nose's filtering properties.

To put it another way, breathing through the nose creates parasympathetic tone, while mouth breathing activates the sympathetic nervous system. Mackenzie starts to tell me about how the nose naturally humidifies and conditions incoming air to a steady 96 degrees before it hits the lungs, and how the sinuses will release nitrogen-oxide—a vasodilator—during nasal breathing. As I dutifully take notes on the miracle of nasal breathing, he gets more animated and pulls up a list of citations that correlate respiration rates with different diseases.

Where healthy people move six to seven liters of air through their lungs in a given minute, diseases seem to increase respiration rates. He starts reading down a list of medical citations. "Diabetes 15 breaths per minute, asthma fourteen, heart disease 12, cystic fibrosis 18, liver cirrhosis 18..." He trails off and just forwards me the studies over email. I imagine a hospital full of enfeebled mouth breathers, drowning in air. While the studies check out, it's important to note that just because disease pathology correlates with higher respiration rates, it doesn't mean that higher respiration causes the illnesses. What we can infer, however, is that sick people breathe more, which likely means that people who are sick don't breathe as efficiently as those who are well. It's not too far of a stretch to think that good breathing hygiene might also help keep someone healthy. By expressing choice in how you breathe, you have the power to wedge in control over your overall well-being. With training, the conscious programming eventually forms a habit that turns nasal breathing to autonomic control, and you've hacked your health.

Beyond the disease correlations, for Mackenzie, nasal breathing is also one of the easiest ways to build up CO_2 tolerance. While mouth breathers exchange air easily, they also habitually blow off more CO_2 than they should. Over time the passive hyperventilation becomes the norm, and it's harder to go back to a nasal baseline. This is why many people find it difficult to start nasal breathing once they reach adulthood.

I ask him to show me his program, and he suggests we try a little experiment on a stationary bike. He straps me into a heart monitor and ask me to warm up on something called a Concept 2 stationary bike.

The goal of the new training program is to keep a parasympathetic tone during a heavy workload—but first, as always, we need a baseline reading. The ultimate goal will be to train the resting metabolism for high performance. Mackenzie's hypothesis is that breathing through the nose during training periods will allow for higher performance when you switch over to sympathetic workouts at higher intensities.

He shakes his head when he sees how my feet make contact with the pedals. I have walked with my feet tilted outwards like a duck for my entire life, which translates into being a pretty terrible runner. This is why I've always preferred bikes. "Straighten out your feet and each stroke will give you more power," he says. When I ask how someone is supposed to correct a lifetime of bad habits, he shrugs and says, "It's just a mental thing. Your brain gives the new instructions, and eventually your body will follow." Here, the repeated activity is a wedge that trains the nervous system to transform the gait over time into something that I don't have to spend any mental energy on: using conscious effort to lock in changes so that they become unconscious. So I tweak my legs back into the alignment he asks for. True to form, pushing the pedals has more power. The wattage on the bike jumps upward. He flashes an "I told you so" smile. I was losing torque with my ordinary gait. In a way, correcting breathing patterns will rely on the same sort of willpower. My ordinary gait is a habit, but it's a habit that I can (theoretically) correct with a little conscious intervention. The same goes for breathing.

I warm up on the bike until my heart rate peaks at 170 beats per minute (BPM), and then he tells me that he wants to see how long it takes me to recover. I'm supposed to try to bring it down to below 100. At first I sit on the bike and breathe slowly, but my heart barely budges. I migrate to the rubber mat on the floor. It takes a full seven minutes before I get to 100. Mackenzie says that ideally, a person should be able to recover to a resting BPM of 100 in under two minutes.

We take a rest and come back to the bike about an hour later. This time, he says, he's going to put me through a staged intensity test, where I'll just use my nose to breathe. We start at a meandering pace of 120 watts per minute, and every minute, I'm supposed to increase my physical output by 10 watts. The test will end the second that I start to switch from nasal breathing to mouth breathing. That switch is the inflection point at which parasympathetic tone ends and the sympathetic system takes over. He figures I'll make it 10 stages.

After eight minutes, the slow movement of my nasal breathing gets deeper and faster, and I focus on a single point just above the wattage monitor—trying to sink deeper into my sensations and widening my peripheral vision, which Huberman told me activates parasympathetic responses.

"You're doing much better than I expected," Mackenzie comments as I push the pedals. I wonder if that's an invitation to stop, but I don't feel near done yet. Two stages later, I'm still going strong. Then my nose starts to run. A long, clear dribble threatens to escape. I wipe at it, not wanting to open my lips and give in before I'm done. Two more stages and the pattern of air out of my nose is more ragged. My heart rate is closing in on 170. He tells me to dismount and recover again.

I'm down to 100 BPM in six minutes. It's a modest improvement, but something that he's sure I can train.

"One of the differences between a good athlete and a great one is how quickly they recover," says Mackenzie. "And our hypothesis is that we can train recovery." It's a game-changing notion. If you can tweak how the body deals with stress after exertion, then even resting becomes an active part of an athletic training program.

Mackenzie's own workouts are an order of magnitude more intense than what he's having me do on this stationary bike, and he's been a lifelong athlete and endurance runner who is no stranger to suffering. But after switching to nasal breathing, he says, his recoveries are so much easier. "I just don't feel sore anymore."

Mouth breathing during intense workouts allows a person to blow off CO_2 too quickly. This helps buffer the intensity of the pain of exertion and artificially lowers blood acidity. Nasal breathing does the opposite: Acid levels rise sharply during the workout compared to hyperventilation. It's a little counterintuitive. Part of me thinks that more acid in the workout means more acid in recovery, and thus more soreness afterward. But that isn't what happens. According to Mackenzie, soreness occurs because the body has to restock the lost CO_2 that it blew off during the workout so that during recovery, acid levels actually go higher. It's sort of like a hangover after the euphoria of being drunk: Every chemical high gets balanced out with a chemical low over time. The high-intensity exertion pushes the body into a sympathetic state, and since you can't blow it off quickly, CO_2 builds up in the system. The body has to develop a tolerance to the acid, and during recovery, you don't have to compensate and restock levels as much.

Tomorrow, after I'm rested, he plans to test me again—this time with just mouth breathing. The idea is that I'll be able to complete more stages and maintain a higher heart rate. And a higher heart rate is the marker for what a recovery will feel like.

...

That evening, I'm sitting at the long wooden dinner table in his living room. We nosh on plantains and enchiladas that his wife picked up from somewhere across the Bay. I've learned a lot, but I'm still curious about how an elite training program can benefit the average Joe. After all, not everyone needs to be a super-athlete. How does his breathwork translate into an everyday wedge to make us more resilient?

I ask him why ordinary people would want to go through all these new breathing protocols if their lives are going along fine as is. He nods. "I'm not doing this just to make someone's gym workouts that much more hard-core. It's about being a person with a body. I want to find that razor edge in all things, where you aren't so agitated that you make mistakes, but aren't so relaxed that you don't notice the environment around you. At the end of the day, the Wedge is about balance. And once you discover that mental state where you're connected but objective at the same time, you have an edge in all aspects of life," he says.

The next day, it doesn't go exactly the way of his earlier hypothesis. I go through another 12 rounds of exercise with only breathing through my mouth. Perhaps it's because I already have a high CO_2 tolerance from practicing extended breath holds for the past few years, but the results surprise him. In both tests, my heartbeat spikes to high levels almost immediately—proving once again that I'm no super-athlete. Well-tuned athletes' heart rates move upward smoothly, without sudden spikes. Strangely, my heart rate was higher when only breathing through the nose by three beats per minute. This is the opposite of his usual predictions, but perhaps, he says, it's because I'm already so good with CO_2. Whatever the case, he urges me to keep nose breathing when I do longer bike rides back home in Colorado. It will be a slower process, but he predicts that I'll raise the floor. Time will prove him right.

And that notion of floors and ceilings leads me to another question about human baselines for stress in general. Breathing is a powerful wedge to alter internal states, but there are floors and ceilings to every type of stress level. It stands to reason that a chaotic environment triggers chaotic bodily reactions while subdued ones lead to relaxation. After all, we *are* the environment that we inhabit. So when we alter the outside world, it's really a wedge into our internal state. And the changes don't only affect the present. Our brain lives in perpetual past, so as we create more neural symbols, those past environments continue to affect how we feel and respond in the future. The choices about our environment that we make in the moment both defines who we are as individuals and how we connect to the universe at large.

So far, I've learned important ways that my relationship with the environment alters my internal state. In Huberman's lab, I learned that human consciousness is a recursive process: Every sensation I feel bonds with my emotional state to create a library of neural symbols that my lizard brain uses to make sense of the world at large. I've found how I can use this underlying mechanism to transform fear into joy and see the world from the perspective of flow. Next I delved deep into a breathing pattern that shut down my higher mental functions and, inexplicably, felt connected to something greater than myself. With Mackenzie, I've learned how my automatic breathing patterns can trigger anxiety or contentedness and that I might be able to train anxiety away through breathwork alone. All this new information has helped me gain a deeper understanding of how the Wedge operates at the synaptic and physiological levels. Decisions about mindset alter our symbolic neurology, while breathwork changes the sensory pathways that the body uses to make decisions about the outside world.

Now I want to think about all of this from the perspective of the sequential lineup of Russian dolls. If all I am is the sum of internal and external influences, then what happens to my sense of self when I remove my body from as many external inputs as possible? How does the superorganism affect the body when it's cut off from the outside world? This time, I don't have to go back to California to answer a big question.

Instead, I'm headed to Oklahoma to isolate my brain.

As hunter-gatherers, we foraged for food. Now we forage in our minds.

—Amit Sood, *On mind wandering, attention, brain networks and meditation.*

...

He referred to his being a grown man bobbing around in the dark in a tank of water in a hole under the hospital. "Besides," he added, "this isn't producing any data for the doctor, anyway!" He commented and questioned whether he really was hearing "some noises." Abruptly, he pulled off the mask and left the tank.

—Jay T. Shurley, M.D. *Profound Experimental Sensory Isolation*

CHAPTER 6

A TANK FULL OF NOTHING

A young doctor in slacks and a sweater sticks a heart monitor to my chest and then tapes down the mechanism with clear medical tape to ensure that water won't leak in. She gives me a small PVC pipe box with what looks like the rubber ball of a turkey baster caulked onto the other side. I'll need it later. We're standing in a laboratory bathroom. As she's leaving, she tells me that whenever I'm ready I can strip off the terrycloth bathrobe and make my way to the tank in the adjoining chamber to begin the test. She'll be nearby, monitoring everything that happens.

I do as she says. The tank room is encased in a series of jury-rigged frosted-glass shower panels like you would see in a cheap hotel room, and the water glows with a dim blue light. I stand over a circular pool that is about eight feet across. The air is sticky with humidity and smells faintly of brine. I feel relaxed and a little excited to climb into the tepid water. It feels slippery against my skin. I notice immediately that I float instead of sink. The briny smell in the room is from the hundreds of pounds of Epsom salts that saturate the pool so thoroughly that a human body can bob on the surface. The lights go out. It's pitch black and beyond quiet. There's no difference between having my eyes open or closed. Soon the gentle movement of water against my skin fades into the background. Once again, I'm an astronaut on a journey into the unknown. My head rests gently on the surface of the water. It almost feels like I'm floating in a tank of nothing at all. This is the point. Without external stimuli, there's no choice but to go inward. And so I do.

The first things I notice are the sounds of my body. They are impossible to ignore. I hear breakfast gurgling through my digestive track. I hear my joints. The smallest movement of my body sends creaking sounds through the water. I hear my heart. It thrums at a slow and steady clip. It's so quiet...and so noisy at the same time. Despite the deafening silent-noise, I find it easy to relax. It doesn't take long until I'm somewhere between deep slumber and an alert meditation.

And then I hear a recorded male voice issue calm instructions over the intercom. The voice reminds me that my goal for the next hour is to try to tune into the sensations of my own body and try to detect the rhythm of my own heartbeat. The turkey baster-PVC contraption connects wirelessly to a computer in the next room. The voice explains that in ten minutes it will ask me to squeeze the baster in time with my heartbeat.

I lie there, awake to my breathing and cueing into the cacophony of my body. I wait for the voice to tell me to sense my heartbeat. Has it been almost ten minutes? Time feels different. I suspect it will be easy to hear my heart. On an ordinary day, I like to think that I have at least some ability to sense my own heartbeat, even at rest. There's always a faint rhythm in the background of my mind, and the slightest feeling of pressure going up and down in my circulatory system. If I focus, I can detect that subtle rising and falling of my blood pressure. It should be simple in the tank, where the drumming is almost impossible to miss.

After some time, the man's voice chirps up again. He instructs me to start squeezing the ball in sync with my heart. Later they'll compare my squeezing to the data in the heart monitor. I give the ball a few squeezes, but I'm not at all confident it matches what I'm hearing in my body. I'm trying to sense every beat and then squeeze. But it's so quiet that the creaking in my finger joints seems impossibly loud. Triggering those tiny muscles at the same time that I'm attempting to relax into my body is harder than I thought. I'm not very good at this. I'm off rhythm. The voice tells me to relax and get ready for another minute-long test run, so I try to focus harder, this time anticipating the beats as they're about to come rather than trying to first feel my heart and then squeeze accordingly. This time I think I'm a little closer, but things still don't feel right.

...

In the past few months, I've tried to wedge my perspective into frames of reference that are both greater and smaller than myself. I've seen how a subtle shift in perspective can translate fear into joy. And how breathing underpins my consciousness.

Now I'm floating in a pool of water, attempting to completely extricate myself from every possible environmental signal to find out what happens in my brain when my body stops sensing the outside world. So far my explorations with the Wedge have looked at the space between stimulus and response—but what happens if the only stimulus I feel comes from inside?

This is exactly the sort of question that Justin Feinstein has built his career on. The lanky doctor with a shock of red curly hair met me in the lobby of the Laureate Institute for Brain Research in Tulsa, Oklahoma earlier that morning. He's a clinical psychologist and neuroscientist sporting an earnest Californian smile. He's the only researcher in the country with an entire lab dedicated to studying the clinical benefits of flotation, or what he calls Reduced Environmental Stimulation Therapy (REST). Other people might call what he studies by an older term: sensory deprivation.

His research suggests that turning down the volume of all external stimulation allows people to get in touch with their own bodies and take control of sensations that drive anxiety. This has everything to do with neural symbols.

To quickly review an earlier chapter, neural symbols form when the limbic system bonds new sensations to a person's current emotional state. The next time that person feels a similar sensation, the brain identifies what the sensation means by accessing the previous emotional value. In effect, your body is always reliving its past.

Feinstein takes this idea and pushes it a step further, noting that our bodies don't ever truly experience any given sensation in isolation.

Right now, as my fingers crunch this paragraph in my computer, I can hear the traffic from a nearby main road and the bell from a church. There's also a dry warmth to the summer as it filters in through my open window. There are smells, qualities of light and even odd thoughts running through my head. I'm not just feeling one isolated sensation, but dozens, maybe hundreds, all at once. Every one of those sensations carries some sort of emotional stake that my brain encoded long ago. While my attention only registers a few at a time, my nerves constantly transmit information from the outside world to my brain, leaving me to re-experience old emotions at the whims of whatever sensations drift into my nerves.

And that's just the external world. I'm even less aware of sensations welling up from my body itself—the dull ache in my leg from sitting too long, the pumping of blood through my arteries and veins, aches, pains, digestion and thoughts. All of these sensations also have the potential to form neural symbols and thus retain an emotional value. We've seen these values before in how people who are over-sensitive to CO_2 reinforce constant feelings of anxiety. This internal awareness is what neuroscientists call *interoception*. It's a critical sense to hone the Wedge because it allows people to identify subtle sensations inside their body that they don't often notice consciously.

Feinstein's research indicates that even brief periods of turning down external stimuli can force people to turn their attention inward—heightening their interoceptive abilities—and break the feedback cycle that reinforces anxiety. And that's why he thinks flotation can be so powerful: It's a wedge to help people turn their attention inward.

For example: Imagine a new soldier walking down a road in Afghanistan. He can smell the scent of car exhaust and of flowers just beginning to bloom. He can feel the sensation of wind on his arms and the idle chat of his fellow soldiers fighting off boredom. And then, in an instant, the world turns upside down in a fiery conflagration of chaos, injury and death. It's a roadside bomb. He's thrown to the ground. He can hear the thrumming of his heart and his own deep, panicked breathing. His body goes on high alert, and so his limbic system registers *everything* around him and starts to encode it all into his nervous system for reference later. Beyond whatever physical injuries he might sustain, in the moments leading up to the explosion, his brain was making associations between sensations and relatively low stress levels. Now all of those innocuous environmental sensations—even ones that went below conscious observation—are part of new neurological associations that tie back to the trauma of the explosion. In the most extreme cases, any sensation at all adds to a constant anxiety feedback loop. This is the fundamental process that makes post-traumatic stress disorder so difficult to tackle. Float tanks can interrupt that loop and give people space to form new associations with their bodily processes that don't tie back to the original trauma.

You can think of anxiety disorders as the inability to find the body's baseline state of normal, aka *homeostasis*. Disturbing sensations in the environment create negative feedback loops that redefine the baseline and make it impossible to return to. This new baseline is what psychologists call *allostasis*. In the case of anxiety, environmental signals constantly trigger sympathetic nervous-system responses that keep a person in fight or flight instead of in balance.

The human body is a homeostatic system. It's always trying to return to a baseline state where it has positive associations. Even the most primitive areas of our brain want to be healthy, happy and strong.

So the idea is that if you throw a wedge into the feedback cycle, it's possible to interrupt the constant reinforcement, and then the natural tendencies of the body will take over and bring the body back toward homeostasis. Floating perturbs the status quo for patients by giving them an entirely novel environment that is so quiet, it upsets their heightened sense of normal and they return to their original baseline.

This isn't just idle New Age speculation; there's data to back it up. A month before I arrive, Feinstein released the first peer-reviewed paper on how flotation affects patients with PTSD, panic, agoraphobia, social anxiety, generalized anxiety and major depression. He located 50 severely anxious patients and put them in his state-of-the-art open flotation pool for an hour. The results weren't only intriguing, they were groundbreaking. Every patient reported that their anxiety went down measurably after just a one-hour session. "The results were really surprising, because you'd think that at least some of them would have felt panic or anxiety or something off-putting after an hour alone with themselves. But we had 100% improvement," says Feinstein. He remembers that the patients' faces were drawn and unhappy when they came into the office, but that when they left the tanks, it was as if they had been transformed.

At the end of the paper, he includes post-float statements from all of the anxious floaters. One stood out to me:

"In there, just being so much more body-aware is just very different for me. The only time I usually notice my heart as much is when I have very high anxiety…matter of fact, I've been to the hospital a few times in the past thinking I was having a heart attack when it was really anxiety. During the float I would notice my body some, I could feel my body. But I felt so relaxed, it was almost like, at times, my body was one with the water."

— Subject 30

Of course, a therapeutic program would use multiple sessions in a tank, but these are the sorts of results that have made Feinstein a hero to float aficionados around the country. It was the first scientific validation that floating is not only a cool way to understand the mind, but it can actively repair it. What's more, it was serious relief without any need of drugs or extensive in-person therapy.

...

In short, this is how I end up with my fist wrapped around a turkey baster in one of Feinstein's float tanks. I'm trying to both report and feel my body at the same time. Things aren't going particularly well. Flexing the muscles in my fingers feels loud. It's distracting. In a way, studying the exact moment that I'm conscious of my pulse invokes a similar problem that physicists call the *observer effect*. It states that merely observing or measuring a phenomenon changes it. Although a turkey baster in a float tank is a universe away from a high-energy supercollider, interoception is still a pretty hard thing to record. I'm having trouble being completely relaxed while simultaneously maintaining enough alertness to report my sensations accurately.

And yet I might have some good company. Before I got in the tank, I had a chance to speak to another doctor at the institute, Sahib Khalsa, who told me that early in his career, he once tested Tibetan monks who claimed to be able to slow their hearts on command. It was something that the medical literature said wasn't possible, but having grown up in India among the esoteric spiritual and meditative traditions of Sikhism, Khalsa was willing to give the claim a chance. He recalled that when he hooked up the monks to monitors, his enthusiasm came crashing down even before all the results were in. Not only did the monks fail to lower their heart rate through meditation, but most of them couldn't even press a button in sync with an ECG. As far as his test was concerned, they couldn't even *sense* their cardiac system, let alone control it.

Now I'm starting to wonder if the monks were swept up in the same confusion that I'm having. After the disembodied voice runs me through three or four squeeze tests, I'm finally allowed to give myself over to the darkness and the subtle relief of the water. Without the pressure of observation, my mind simply floats away. And this is when it starts to feel amazing. Without any responsibilities, I really start looking inside. I'm somewhere between wakefulness and dreaming. At one point I see an image of a llama—not the Dalai kind, the South American camelid kind—dressed up in glasses and a suit teaching a classroom full of kids. Later, I see my father's face in the gold wire-rimmed glasses that he used to wear in the 1990s. My heart thumps loud and clear. I sort of wish I had the baster again. When the lights go on in an hour or so, I want nothing more than to keep at it a little longer. I get out refreshed and relaxed—and maybe a little miffed about my performance on the test.

Feinstein goes over the results with me. I expect to hear that I failed, but I'm pleasantly surprised to learn that I only botched the first few trials. After I'd relaxed into it, by the third test I'd correctly squeezed the baster in sync with 85% of my heartbeats. Feinstein comments that I'd become a "true interoceptor."

I grin.

We have a long conversation about my journey so far, and he's impressed with how I've been able to train my body in cold water. He's even more impressed with the breathwork—particularly the way that I can hold my breath for up to three minutes at a time. That's when he smiles and leans back in a rolling chair. "You know what? I'd like to run a test on you. Are you game?"

Of course I'm game.

...

A few years ago, Feinstein got interested in people with Urbach-Wi-ethe disease, who grow lesions on their amygdalae and, as a result, lack the ability to feel fear. It's an unusual condition but far from unknown. Many well-known daredevils and stunt performers—like Alex Honnold, who recently climbed the sheer rock surface of El Capitan without any ropes—show lesions on their amygdalae. Feinstein wanted to figure out if this sort of brain damage only protected from fear outside the body. Might someone who could jump a motorcycle over ten flaming cars be equally immune to internal anxiety?

Nearly all creatures share an innate aversion to high levels of carbon dioxide. Even fruit flies flee when they get near a CO_2 source. In humans, a high dose of CO_2 provokes a desperate need to breathe and triggers an immediate and primal fear of death. However, in small doses of a breath or two, CO_2 is relatively harmless. Our bodies are just super-sensitive.

Feinstein found a group of these fear-immune folks and hooked them up to a bag of air that was 35% CO_2. Ordinarily, humans exhale about 5% CO_2, so this is a huge dose. No one really expected that the amygdalae-damaged patients would react to the gas.

An excerpt from his paper on the experiment describes what he saw:

Immediately following the inhalation, SM began breathing at a rapid pace and gasping for air. Approximately 8 seconds following the inhalation, her right hand started waving frantically near the air mask. At 14 seconds post-inhalation, SM exclaimed, "Help me!" while her right hand gestured toward the mask. The experimenter immediately removed the mask from SM's face. As this was happening, her body became rigid, her toes curled, and her fingers on both hands were flexed toward the ceiling. As soon as the mask was removed, SM grabbed the experimenter's hand and in a relieved tone said, "Thank you." The skin on her face was flushed, her nostrils flared, her eyes were opened wide, and her upper eyelids were raised.

Thirty seconds later, the patient returned to normal and reported that after she took a dose from the bag, she was sure she was going to suffocate. For someone biologically immune to fear, this was a surprising discovery and made him believe that chemoreceptors that monitor blood circulation around the heart and brain stem triggered a response that completely bypassed the ordinary fear center.

This was something of an *aha* moment for Feinstein, who guessed that perhaps we've gotten anxiety wrong all along. He started to see the same thing that Brian Mackenzie had: Instead of anxiety stemming from events in a person's life, perhaps it can also start as misfiring chemoreceptors signaling false alarms to slight changes in CO_2 levels.

Feinstein tells me about his experiment and says that he'd like to run the same one on me. Both the Wim Hof Method and Mackenzie's breathing protocols build up CO_2 tolerance over time. I'd been doing nose-breathing workouts for a few months by this time and had almost seven years practicing the Wim Hof Method. I think it's a great idea, and we walk back to his lab, where he shows me a tiny room with a white plastic bag taped to the wall containing about 30 liters of a 35% mixture of CO_2.

I sit down at a small table in front of a computer and a breathing apparatus that can switch between the bag and ambient air. He fiddles with some Velcro straps and fastens a breathing mask around my face. Then he boots up a program on his computer that can measure all of the gases going in and out of my lungs. It's the same setup—indeed, it's the same room—that he used for testing patients with damaged amygdalae. He starts off by explaining that the test entails what he calls three vital-capacity breaths. This means that I will exhale fully and then draw in as large a breath as possible of the CO_2 mixture before I exhale. "You don't need to hold when you're at the top; just let it go," he says, then reminds me that this test is absolutely safe and there's no chance that I'll get brain damage or die, even if I might feel like that's the case.

There's a dial on the computer in front of me that I can turn to self-report my level of anxiety, starting from a green zero for nothing at all to a red I-think-I'm-dying ten. Whenever I'm ready, I can press a button to take my first breath. I cover the button with my finger and worry that I'll make a fool of myself ripping off the mask, fiddling with the door handle and fleeing the office building in total panic. I sincerely hope that I can maintain at least a level of decorum.

I center myself and let all the air out of my lungs. Then I press the button. The gas tastes faintly acidic, with an electric mouthfeel reminiscent of taking a bite out of a citrus fruit. I fill my lungs and hold it briefly at the top and let it out. For a second I don't feel much at all. Then my vision clouds over a little bit. The world turns slightly red, and my field of vision constricts slightly into a tunnel. It's a similar feeling to what I have during a long breath hold after a few rounds of Wim Hof super-ventilation. It's a feeling I'm familiar with. Indeed, it's a place that I kind of enjoy visiting. I smile under the mask.

Feinstein's jaw drops as he stares at me in disbelief. "Whoa, I don't think I've ever seen a person react so little to this test," he says.

A minute later I press the button again, for a similar, if slightly diminished, effect.

I press it again and try to hold my breath at the top with lungs full to the brim with the acidic mixture. The test is supposed to take 30 minutes, because most subjects need a long time to recover between inhales. Yet I'm just over four minutes in and I've completed the protocol. I ask him if I can press it a few more times to see what happens. I feel the biggest effect from the CO_2 after I've exhaled and taken a breath. Perhaps the training I've done with the Hof method has reframed the meaning of the CO_2 alarm bells going off in my head. The Wedge hasn't just created a short-term habituation to discomfort; I've actually adapted my biology to react to CO_2 in a different way.

After I've gone through six or seven breaths, Feinstein brings up the data from the test on his computer and shows me a series of angular graphs that measure my lung capacity, blood oxygen, CO_2 levels and heart rate. A healthy CO_2 level during ordinary respiration is about 5%. After an exhale, that percentage drops and then builds up during the ordinary spaces between breaths. After a dose of CO_2, most people take a minute to come back to normal, hanging out at the 10% mark and slowly recovering.

"What's amazing here is that you just snap back to 5% in just a breath or two," he notes, showing that not only does my brain process anxiety in a different way, but my body clears the gas more efficiently, too. He's also never seen a person press the button again after the test is over. "You've reprogrammed this part of your body. I would love to see more research on this, because if it's true that we can adapt the way we process carbon dioxide, it stands to reason that we can also lower anxiety for anyone who can train their reaction to CO_2." Indeed, a few months later, Feinstein will write to tell me that he's gotten a new research grant from the National Institutes of Health to study just that. His working hypothesis is that if he repeatedly exposes anxious patients to high doses of CO_2 in a safe setting, they will show lower overall anxiety once they become habituated to the gas. He'll tell me that the results are promising so far.

These two tests together—the float tank and the CO_2 blast—tell me a lot about how the various Russian doll perspectives fit together in the context of anxiety. On the one hand, cycles of external stimuli keep reinforcing neural symbols that bring up past traumas. On the other hand, those same traumas also link to internal sensations that link back to the same traumatic event. Reinforcement happens through both top-down and bottom-up processes. However, both feedback loops can cave to conscious intervention. It's possible to use the Wedge to interrupt them and return to normal.

With these thoughts in mind, I'm excited to head back to Denver to extend floating into my own wedge tool kit. Luckily, flotation isn't only in the realm of professional researchers.

...

While flotation centers haven't exactly taken off across the country, it's safe to say that America is at least flotation-curious. At about $50 per 90-minute session, they cost just slightly less than a trip to a psychologist. According to Float Tank Solutions, which conducts a yearly survey of float centers across the country, in 2011 there were fifty flotation centers in America. By 2018 there were 300. It's been reported that the Navy SEALs and other Special Forces military branches use flotation tanks to help soldiers cope with battlefield stress. I find one a few miles from my house called Samana Float Center.

The business is tucked into the back of a brick building behind two breweries, a billiards hall and a few fashionable clothing boutiques. Inside, paintings of geometric shapes, jaguars and cosmological themes decorate the waiting room walls. I meet Paul Clift in a back room.

Clift spent 20 years in commercial real estate before deciding he needed a change, and he first came to floating through the world of psychedelics. He tells me that he met a shaman in Texas who introduced him to the ritual use of ayahuasca, a potent hallucinogen from Peru that has been used in religious ceremonies for at least 2,000 years. The experience of drinking the brew, and his subsequent exploration of his psyche while in trance states made him question the connections between his body and his mind.

Clift's background reminds me of the strange early history of flotation research back in the 1950s, '60s and '70s. That history makes most people today think flotation is kind of strange, and possibly even dangerous.

The very first float tanks were part of NASA-funded research for space flight and for understanding human consciousness. However, things got strange pretty quickly. John Lilly, one of the original pioneers, and Jay Shurley were connected to CIA-funded research linked to the MKUltra experiments and Cold War interrogation techniques that involved dosing unwitting subjects with high doses of LSD.

Lilly decided to bring his new sensory deprivation device into Timothy Leary's psychedelic revolution. He hoped that by combining flotation immersion with powerful hallucinogens, he would be able to peer into the darkest corners of his mind. Lilly continued to publish books, and his work captured America's imagination and culminated in the 1980 movie *Altered States*. In that film, a rogue scientist tests LSD, ketamine and mescaline in an isolation tank, and it ends in the scientist's devolution into a cloud of pure consciousness. As bizarre as that sounds, the movie was a hit.

Under Lilly's direction, things got real weird real fast. Within a decade, he'd set up a new laboratory in the Virgin Islands, where he believed he would be able to learn to decipher the language of dolphins while he was on LSD. The unorthodox method wasn't successful in turning the aquarian mammals' clicks and whistles into English, but Lilly's experiments continued to receive millions of dollars in funding. Eventually—you can't make this up—a scandal erupted around his lab when it came out that one of the researchers in his unit had developed a sexual relationship with a dolphin. By the time he died of congestive heart failure in his 80s, Lilly was likely addicted to ketamine and, by some accounts, almost unrecognizable to his friends and colleagues.

In short, while other researchers did use flotation tanks to ask important psychological questions, most people today associate the tanks with their colorful past. It's good that a new generation of researchers like Feinstein are bringing them back to the mainstream.

Paul Clift got into floating because of Lilly. Like Lilly, he felt similarities between what happened in the tank and what happened when his mind was chemically enhanced. Floating was legal, however, and after a few experiences, he knew he wanted to bring floating to the masses.

When I told him about my project, Clift offered me ten floats at his center so that I could start to understand how the experience changes with steady practice. "When we take time to slow down, we find that we can do more later," he tells me before setting me up in one of his tanks.

I strip off my clothes and don neon-orange earplugs to keep the saltwater from filling my ear canals. Getting into the tub feels a little like climbing into a fancy bath. At Samana I have the option to keep the lights on and listen to soft New Age music, but I opt for complete blackness and silence for my 90-minute float. It only takes a few minutes in the water before I am calm enough to hear the thump of my heart, the sound of my own breath and the occasional creak of my joints as they acclimate to a world without pressure or tension. It's nice to not be part of an experiment. My mind wanders at first, and then, maybe 45 minutes in, my thoughts simply stop forming. I have a brief window where I'm just, well, floating. Time passes almost without my own internal clock tracking its progress, and my body seems to just disappear. I'm awake and aware, but it's like I've been forced into a deep meditation. Perhaps it's a little like what early psychiatrists guessed would happen to an isolated brain: I simply stop responding to the world. When it's over, I'm so inspired that I gush about it to my wife and ask her to come with me next time.

A week later, we make an appointment at Samana for separate tanks. On the car ride over, we get into a small, relatively unimportant marital argument. We bicker all the way to the door of the center and then plunge into darkness within the first five minutes we're there. There is no resolution, so we float in our mutual saltwater baths, and the disagreement rots inside of us. The dark walls of the tank seem to seethe with resentment and exasperation. The tank becomes an echo chamber that amplifies every negative thought. Part of me is aware that it isn't healthy to dwell on what is objectively a small disagreement, but the absence of anything else that might interrupt that nightmare stream of consciousness borders on obsession. When we get out 90 minutes later, we're both in foul moods.

In the car on the way back home, the argument starts up again, until one of us asks, "Do you think this is because of the float?" We both agree that we've blown things out of proportion, but even after identifying the source of our consternation, we both stay angry and irritable for the next three or four days. It's like we're having an emotional hangover.

This is an important lesson. None of my explorations with the Wedge happen in a vacuum. No technique or device can truly take two people out of their own contexts. Laura and I brought the outside world into the float experience and unwittingly created a negative feedback loop—a negative wedge. There are always some potential risks. But I still see rewards in the float tank. So the next time I go to float, a few weeks later, I'm mindful to not jump in right after a domestic argument.

It should go without saying that lessons from Feinstein's lab don't have to require a trip to a float center. You don't need state-of-the-art facilities to find other, maybe less dramatic, ways to turn down the signals from the outside world and look inward. Even simply lying down in a quiet, dark room can be enough to allow you to pay attention to your breath and heartbeat. Hundreds of meditation practices over the past 3,000 years cultivate the mental focus of looking inward. All of them build interoceptive awareness in one way or another and expand our ability to modulate and respond to stress. For the most part, all of these traditions agree that such moments of interior quiet are also ways that we as individuals direct our awareness outward into things that are greater than ourselves—whether that is a divine connection, a sense of universal awareness, or the mystical state of oneness that yogis call *samadhi*.

And there are still other sensations to turn down that affect us every waking moment. Just about every mystical tradition in the world also teaches the value of asceticism. During Lent, Catholics cut out certain foods from their diets as a symbol of piety. The same impulse drives the fast during Eid in Islam. Jews fast on Yom Kippur, and many Buddhists restrict the sorts of foods they eat during prolonged meditations. All of these practices share the idea that diminishing food intake will make people more sensitive to the world around them. While those traditions use diet as a conduit to the divine, our relationship with food is also a wedge that defines our relationship to the world.

Scott Carney and Wim Hof at Gilman's Point on Mount Kilimanjaro.

A woman covered by foliage lies down inside a Latvian *pirts*.

Shaman Tony peeks out from behind a leaf at the Trocha Amazonica in Peru.

Tony cuts a path through the Amazon with a machete at the Trocha Amazonica.

Michael Castrogiovanni throws a kettlebell high above his head.

Luz Maria Ampuero blows smoke into a kettle of ayahuasca.

The view from inside the Huberman Lab's virtual reality simulator.

What swimming with virtual sharks looks like from the outside.

Scott Carney prepares to catch a kettlebell.

Elizabeth Lee (Elee) and Wim Hof at a training session in Colorado.

Brian Mackenzie controls his reaction to ice water at his training center outside San Francisco.

The first attempts to create sensory deprivation at Jay Shurley's lab in Oklahoma often resulted in patients having panic attacks.

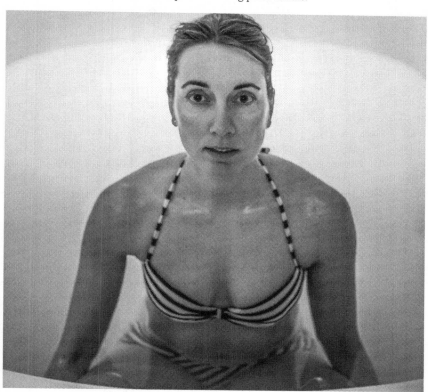

Laura Krantz gets ready to lie down in a modern flotation tank.

Scott Carney with the remnants of Tony's fire in the Peruvian Amazon.

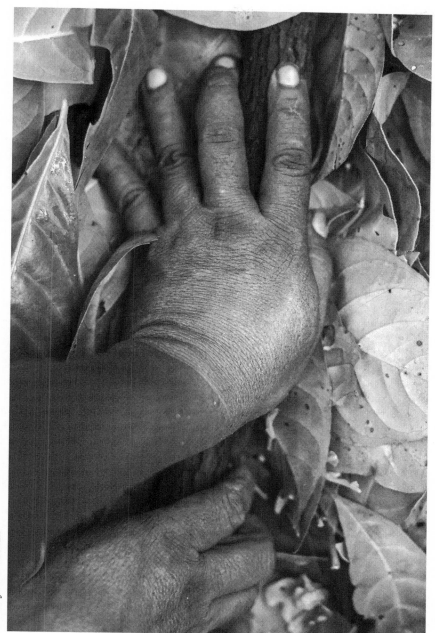

Chakruna leaves brewed into a pot of ayahuasca vines.

A man walks down the street.
He says, "Why am I soft in the middle now?
Why am I soft in the middle?
The rest of my life is so hard."

—Paul Simon, "You Can Call Me Al"

CHAPTER 7

A DELIGHTFUL LACK
OF TASTE

The grocery store located a mile from my house sometimes seems like an amusement park. I push a cart past shelves bursting with colorful boxes of breakfast cereals that promise both happiness and improved athletic performance. The dozens of yogurt variations boast recipes from distant lands. I can't decide if the packaging wants to inspire me to travel more or stuff my face. A bag of chips clearly wants to throw a party in my mouth, while a jar of coconut oil promises that it will make me smarter. Even vegetables get in on the game. One brand of broccoli suggests that simply eating it will help save the world. And let's not even talk about what's going on in the candy aisle.

Everywhere I look, shimmering packages of food are trying to tell me something vital about who I am and what I could be. The messages appeal to deep-seated emotions that I've carried my whole life. I feel hungry for whatever it is they're selling. But at the same time that I desire all these amazing, world-saving foods, I feel a little manipulated. What sort of party is that bag of chips really going to throw? I know the broccoli won't do a damn thing to curb climate change or stop mankind's indifference to the rest of the species.

I avert my eyes from the onslaught and walk to the back of the store, where I grab two large bags of red and brown potatoes, drop them into my cart and head to the register. The clerk, a young woman in a green apron, sees the pile of root vegetables and raises an eyebrow.

"Whatcha makin'?" she asks.

"Just potatoes," I say.

She probably imagines that I'm making a delectable starchy side dish. Nope. I really am making *just* potatoes.

For the next few days, I'm going to try to disentangle the emotional associations I have with food from actual hunger by eating just one rather bland thing. The humble potato is my wedge to isolate hunger from everything else I bring to the table.

...

Just a dozen generations ago, our ancestors only had access to food that grew a few miles from home. A thousand generations before that, our forebears ate mostly roots and vegetables they gathered from their immediate area and supplemented that with occasional meat when they could hunt it. No matter where they lived, geography and seasonality limited their food supply. If any of us traveled back in time for a cave banquet, not only would we find it incredibly bland, but we would also have almost no idea how much effort it took to assemble the meal.

Our sense of taste evolved to tell us important things about our environment and how the things we consume affect our body. More than just a pathway to pleasure, our palate gives us information about the nutrients that we need to survive. Sweetness means energy. Bitterness urges caution. The experience of sharing food, what anthropologists call *commensality*, helps maintain social relationships and community.

In the current interconnected world, the original purpose of our sense of taste is all but obsolete. The multi-billion-dollar food and beverage industry hijacked the ancestral sensory responses and injected brand awareness into social behavior. These changes happen at the societal level from the top down, and the neural associations get wired into our bodies. Together these forces are a persistent society-level wedge into the way we relate to food. If society operates as a superorganism, then the food supply has become something of a leash that removes us from our immediate environment and lets our biology draw sustenance from the entire globe at once. There are many positive aspects to this sort of globalization, but can we even know who we are without it? Omnipresent marketing lives in our mindsets, and easy access to calories permeates everything around us. We have so much available to us that the nuances of taste have been lost on us—often in favor of simple intensity. Many of us would rather have the highly engineered flavor burst of a Dorito than the simplicity of a root vegetable.

Even so, we can still try to understand how flavors shape our understanding of the world by borrowing a page from Feinstein's float research and attempting to turn down the signal. Because it is so pervasive and easy to access, flavor is almost an environment unto itself. As I walk down the grocery store aisles, my mouth waters with Pavlovian discipline. Even when I'm not tasting it, my mind remembers. If I cut back on the variety of flavors available to me, then perhaps my disposition toward the world will change. Indeed, I expect that by removing flavors from my diet, I'll become much more sensitive to other sensations that I tend to drown out with high-flavor food.

In other words, I want to know how my sense of taste affects my own life. How does the anticipation of what I can put into my mouth frame the way I perceive the world around me? And can I interrupt the feedback cycles of flavor and emotion so that I can feel something about the true nature of the food I eat?

It's a worthwhile goal. In the developed world, we no longer suffer from diseases of deprivation; now we suffer from diseases of excess. It's not very likely that you're going to starve in America. And yet the aristocratic diseases of too much sugar—diabetes and gout—have seen exponential rises in the last couple of decades.

At first I contemplated doing an all-out fast for a few days to help reset some of my taste associations. Nearly every spiritual tradition has a long-established fasting practice associated with cleansing the body and ritual purity. Jesus fasted in the desert for 40 days. Mohammed and Buddha fasted, too. In previous books, I'd written about a group of people known as breatharians who decide to forgo food altogether in the belief that they can survive on the energy of the universe—prana—in lieu of calories.

That second group made me reconsider my approach. The Wedge is a tool that separates stimulus from response; in the case of an all-out fast, that could mean learning how to dissociate the stimulus of hunger from the response of eating something. There is absolutely no doubt in my mind that such a thing is possible. But it's not hard to see how that's also a stepping stone to an eating disorder. Denying myself food for an extended period of time to overcome the biologically important hunger signal—or through popular intermittent fasting protocols—would no doubt change my relationship with food. But it's not the way that I *want* to apply the Wedge. This is because hunger isn't really the problem I'm struggling with; rather, it's the association I have between a world of abundance and my impulses to eat emotionally. What I was looking for was something that satiates hunger without stimulating too many food associations.

And then I found the Potato Hack.

I don't know exactly where I first heard about the Potato Hack, but it has done the rounds on podcasts and social media for at least a few years. It would probably be accurate to call it a fad. It received some acclaim when the formerly-rather-obese-and-now-sort-of-gaunt magician Penn Jillette subsisted on only potatoes in a crash diet that allowed him to lose 100 pounds. The idea is fairly straightforward: You eat just potatoes for a short stint of three to five days and then lose a bunch of weight. This doesn't mean French fries and baked potatoes stuffed with bacon and sour cream. At most, you can add a pinch of salt or a sprig of dill for garnish. Just potatoes means just potatoes. Nothing but potatoes. So help you God.

It's a bland counterbalance to the oversaturated palate that we have a hard time escaping. It also has a sort of absurd aspect that I find deeply appealing. Who, after all, doesn't like potatoes? They're starchy, cheap, sort of bland and go with everything. I would be hard-pressed to find anyone in America who hasn't had some variety of potato in the last week. The potato diet is a sort of reverse gorge. And there is some rather interesting science that makes potatoes look a little like superfood for fasting.

In 1995, food researcher Suzanna Holt at the University of Sydney wanted to find out which foods make you feel the most full—a quality that she called *satiety*. She defined satiety as the feeling of fullness that you have when you eat a specific number of calories of any one type of food. Doughnuts and Mars Bars sit fairly low on the satiety scale, with satiety factors of approximately 75, meaning they gave you a lot of calories in return for barely taking away hunger pangs, while steak and beans sat closer to the top of the list, with factors of about 180. However, in the study Holt put together, one food stood out head and shoulders above the rest, at 325. The average human needs to eat about 2,000 calories a day to maintain a stable weight. Potatoes are so satiating that you only need to eat 800 to 1,000 calories' worth of them in order to feel the same level of fullness that you would with an ordinary diet. In other words, there's a magic tipping point at which you can eat enough potatoes to not feel hungry anymore but still build up a serious caloric deficit. It's scarcity without the cost. Thus, a hack.

...

Since a lot of people use the hack to lose weight instead of a method to supercharge their senses, it's useful to know how the digestive system processes a potato-only diet. Potatoes are packed with vitamins, minerals and protein, which will keep your critical systems functioning, but starch makes up the vast majority of their mass. Starch sounds like a lot of empty calories, but it's not just any starch. It's what nutritionists call "resistant starch," because it resists the gut's efforts to break it down. Starch is more resistant when it hasn't been cooked, which means that you can find the perfect amount in potatoes that have been heated and then left to cool down or are mostly raw in the middle. Potatoes more or less pass through your system without adding any real caloric load to your body's metabolism. Since your gut can't chew its way through potatoes, your body needs to find energy elsewhere in the body and starts to burn white fat instead.

There's reason to believe that the potato hack might also be good for general gut health. After passing through the stomach, food passes through the small and large intestines and then the colon; each stage has its own bacterial profile. In Western diets, we often have too much bacteria in the small intestine and not enough in the lower areas of the gut. The small intestine can't break down resistant starch in potatoes, but the large areas can. Gut bacteria ferment and digest the potato starch in the lower regions of the gut and then send it on its way. So flushing just potatoes through the system can help rebalance the gut microbiome. Rebalancing confers all sorts of health benefits and bodily regulation upon the superorganism that is you.

...

I return from the grocery store and pile ten pounds of gold and red potatoes on the kitchen counter. I arrange them in a pyramid inside of a large serving bowl. As with many of the wedges I've explored, Laura is coming along for the ride once again. She looks at me with all the excitement that a person who is about to eat nothing but potatoes can muster. Which is to say, not very much excitement at all.

The next morning we weigh ourselves on our bathroom scale. I'd be lying if I said I wasn't curious about how eating only potatoes might alter my waistline. But it has to be said that measuring our weight is in many ways an arbitrary metric, and the number on the scale cannot ever tell the whole picture of what is happening inside our bodies. A person's weight tends to fluctuate a great deal on any diet; we tend to shed water weight first, and eating soft foods reduces the overall mass of undigested material in the intestines. So whatever readings we get over the next few days are simply an aggregate reading and don't really indicate whether or not we're losing fat or if we're getting any healthier. That said, it's a metric that most people can relate to and can measure at home. There's something to be said for simplicity.

The first order of business is to put a pot of water on the stove, throw in seven or eight potatoes, and set it to boil. Laura wrinkles her nose at this idea of "cooking." Much more so than me, she aches for variety, and when in command of the kitchen, she can make just about any type of cuisine. I marvel at her ability to look at what I think of as uninspiring cupboards and refrigerator shelves and return a half-hour later with a gourmet meal. I am a creature of habit. I once went an entire year eating nothing but egg sandwiches for breakfast. It's that sort of habituated monotony that makes this an easier diet for me than for her. According to the rules, we are at least allowed coffee and tea, which makes breakfast a little more appealing than what we'll make the rest of the day.

If, before we started the hack, there was a certain romanticism to eating only potatoes, the first bite through the skin of a red instantly disabuses me of the notion that this is anything like surviving on French fries. Potatoes do have taste, just not much of it. I supplement each bite with a pinch of salt for enough flavor to keep on chewing, but it's clear that our palates won't get much nuance in the days to come. In the morning we boil potatoes; for lunch we mash them up in a bowl and add sprigs of dill. In the evening we grate spuds and press them into oil-less hash browns.

It doesn't take long for the cravings to set in. You're not supposed to engage in vigorous exercise while on the hack, but I do manage to fit in a few rounds with a kettlebell with no obvious negative effects. Afterward, though, I notice that my mind flits regularly to my pantry, where I've got a stash of assorted nuts and snacks. I think that a banana would be pretty nifty.

At one point, some unconscious ghost takes control of my feet and absentmindedly walks me over to the refrigerator to pull out a yogurt. It's only when I'm peeling back the lid that I realize that my brain brought me here on autopilot. It's not that I feel hungry; the potatoes more than satisfy the ache, or perhaps pain, in the stomach that it gets when it's empty. Instead, there's a sort of full-body craving for nutrients that hijacks my movements. It's as if my cells registered a complaint with my brain to feed them strawberries or steak. Later in the night, I want chocolate and maybe a glass of whiskey on the rocks.

The automatic movement toward my cupboard probably isn't the result of a deep connection to an ancestral relationship with nutrients. More likely, the pull stems from subconscious patterns where I have learned to use food to alleviate boredom or satisfy some vague emotional need stored in a barely discernible neural symbol. After all, I learned in the float tank that my brain is constantly taking cues from the environment and chewing on neural programs that never enter conscious thought.

And yet at some point, those urges must hide a deep-seated evolutionary purpose.

There's a story about pregnancy that just about every mother I've met recounts in one way or another. Sometime in the middle months of carrying a child, an expectant mother has an uncontrollable urge to raid the refrigerator for strange things. I've heard of women sending their husbands out of the house on an emergency food run for pickles. There are tales of women going into the garden to eat handfuls of dirt. Others gorge themselves on brownie mix, raspberries or Cheez

Whiz. One reading of these odd cravings is that the pregnant woman suddenly senses a lack of a certain nutrient, and her unconscious mind triggers a desire for a specific flavor that it associates with a specific taste. I've met other people who eat like this almost exclusively. Once when I visited Wim Hof in Poland, he came back from the grocery store with a bag full of pickled clams and mayonnaise. And although the Dutch occasionally dabble in culinary oddities, this was assuredly not among them. Perhaps he was just listening to what his body told him it needed.

I'd only felt sensations like these when I was reaching the limits of my endurance on the last leg of Kilimanjaro. We stopped on a slope of jagged and loose rocks, and I fished out the only food that any of us were carrying from my backpack: a single granola bar. I broke it into three pieces and shared it with the people I was climbing with. And the sugars and carbohydrates in that mouthful spoke to something deep inside my body. I could feel its energy in a way that I could appreciate how many more steps upward each chew lent my reserves. I knew this information the moment it hit my tongue; it was a type of knowledge I never knew I was capable of.

I felt the tangible relationship between energy and taste when I was pushing the limit of my capabilities. Of course I've been hungry before, but never so starved for food that my life depended on it. It's been rare for me to have to wait more than a few hours for a meal if I wanted it.

Most of us take flavor for granted. Like any sensation, our experience of flavor first enters through the affective nervous system as a measure of volume and intensity before we encode an emotional response to its profile somewhere in the paralimbic system. These associations live on inside of us as neural symbols. Throughout my near-40 years on this planet, I've developed associations and flavor habits that subtly regulate my mood and anticipate the sorts of energy that I would most like to deploy in a given day. The instant that a food touches the palate, our brains associate the flavor with the incoming nutrients—we experience this as taste—but the meat of our body likely experiences it as data and fuel. We need different nutrients and vitamins to keep our bodies running, and I'm a little surprised that after only a few hours of just potatoes, I'm starting to feel those nutrients again individually. I don't actually need to touch on a life-or-death physical threshold. Cultivating the interoceptive link between flavor and nutrients is as easy as decreasing my food's flavor profile.

...

The modern-day messiah of the potato hack is an Air Force retiree in Alaska named Tim Steele, author of the aptly named cult-classic biohacker manual *The Potato Hack*. In it, he outlines his own history with crash diets and constant weight-management routines that never quite seemed to work. Then one day he stumbled across the April 1849 edition of *The Water Cure Journal*, which described a "Potato Diet" of prisoners in England and Ireland. Wardens supplied the inmates only the cheapest food available—potatoes—and much to the surprise of the vindictive guards, after two or three months the inmates no longer had their characteristic bouts of indigestion. "Lean men grew fat, and fat men lean." The article called for severe restriction of all other foods—"no salt, or butter or condiments of any kind"—and promised that in a few days, all digestive troubles would miraculously vanish. (Interestingly, when I looked up that issue, the journal also had articles on cold-water therapy, which just goes to show you that history moves in cycles.) Taking heed of the old-timey advice, Steele followed the prescriptions for a two-week potato-only fast and went from 190 to 179 lbs. After a few shorter potato-only stints, he hit 170. At 5'11", he was trim and in the best shape he'd been since his early 20s.

Thus a potato proselytiser was born.

Of course, every diet plan out there has testimonials like this. The American weight-loss industry is just as prolific as the one that encourages us to feast: They go by names like the Paleo Diet, the 4-Hour Body, the Alkaline Diet, the Baby Food Diet, the Israeli Army Diet, the South Beach Diet, Fit for Life, SlimFast, Weight Watchers, Sugar Busters, the Morning Banana Diet and so on. To some degree, these fads are successful because in at least some—perhaps many—cases, they work for people. Following a strict protocol, almost regardless of the specifics of said protocol, adds an element of mindfulness to eating, which can absolutely garner results.

...

What separates the Potato Hack from other methods is that it's not really a diet so much as it is a hack. There's no reason for anyone to build their life around potatoes. In fact, if you do, it will probably result in an eating disorder. But as a short-term intervention, the potato hack doesn't require as total a lifestyle change as, say, veganism, where fully adopting the ethos seems to infect every part of your life and politics. Every meal you go out to doesn't have just to revolve around an odd number of restrictions. Indeed, you're unlikely to go out at all while you're actually on the hack. Its rules are simple: If all you're eating is potatoes, you're doing it right. The hack is a limited venture, not something that's supposed to continue for months on end. It's a three-to-five-day reset. You could call it an intervention in ordinary patterns—something to shake up established routines but not replace them altogether. It's a wedge. Though I shudder to use the word for its tech-bubble connotations, it's *disruptive*. In terms of what I learned in Feinstein's lab, it's something you can use to interrupt self-reinforcing feedback loops to return to your baseline.

This is the real lesson that I've begun to take away. Yes, we denizens of the modern world have a pretty dysfunctional relationship with food, but that doesn't mean that the only way to correct course requires an entire change of lifestyle. Too many diet programs offer results by completely remaking a person from the bottom up by counting calories, or cutting out sugar-fats-carbs-shellfish or whatever else. Any way they couch it, the key traits for success are discipline and grit. But maybe it's just as important to find ways to break up established patterns as it is to remake all of your habits.

Most of the interventions in this book that have helped me understand the Wedge don't take a lot of time. They're short and simple and offer a brief glimpse into a different way to organize the pattern of interactions and reactions that proceed on autopilot. After the intervention, the body has an opportunity to reset to a homeostatic baseline.

...

After a day of just potatoes, I am more sensitive to what my body is telling me it wants. It is similar to what it would be like to sit in a soundless room and be able to hear my own heartbeat. The following morning, I weigh myself in and find that I am down two and a half pounds. That morning, we bake potatoes in the oven and garnish them with truffle salt and smoked paprika. The second day is entirely easier. The cravings change from a search for quick, fast and fatty calories to a mind focused on fruits and vegetables.

In the afternoon, I call Tim Steele to see how his senses changed with the hack. His country accent lights up on the other end of the line. "Any diet will let you lose weight; you can eat just candy bars, and if you keep the calories low enough, the pounds will melt. But the problem is that there's no nutrition in that. In eating potatoes, you chew and stimulate the vagus nerve. You get fiber and process chemicals that talk to your brain. It has almost everything you need to be a healthy, happy human. You don't need other food experiences, even if you might crave them. Of course, if you fight it—if you cheat and look for exceptions—your mind always wanders to other options. Your mind fights against you and you're miserable. In America, we're surrounded by almost infinite choice and have tasty treats available to us all the time," Steele says with the confidence of a man who has spent a lot of time thinking about food. Indeed, until you've gone without it, it's hard to truly understand how taste and flavor color every aspect of the environment. It's part of the Wedge that's so omnipresent that we don't even recognize how it frames everything around us.

Chronic oversupply of food in the Western world doesn't only mean constant calories, but also near-limitless flavors. Our brains code every nutrient that we've ever had as a flavor and bonds that sensation to an emotion in a neural symbol. Now that emotion is only as far away as a cupboard or grocery store.

For me, the potato hack is surprisingly easy. After a day of cravings, I settle into a routine. I don't leave the house much (except for a run to the grocery store to get more potatoes) and don't actually think about food all that much. Laura's experience is something of a different story. She admits that she fought the hack. And on the third day, she falls into some sort of rut. At dinnertime on the last day of eating only potatoes, she just sits on the couch and can't stomach the idea of eating another one. "I'd rather just not have dinner and wait for tomorrow," she says. For better or worse, she's turning a hack into a fast. I scarf down some bland hash browns and make sure she has at least a few bites.

"The thing is," she says with a philosophical raise of her eyebrow, "potatoes quell the hunger, but they don't staunch my appetite." Our different perceptions might come down to different body compositions. She's usually 50 pounds lighter, with a lot less mass to lose. She also has less tolerance for boredom than I do, a greater drive to exercise, and less experience meditating.

On the last morning, we weigh ourselves a final time and see that we've both lost five pounds in just three days. That's more weight than what you would expect to be possible in that time frame. Humans use about 2,000 calories a day, roughly equivalent to the amount of energy stored in a single pound of fat. We somehow lost more than you would expect from not eating at all. I suspect that at least some of the loss has to do with expelling some of the matter that we typically store in our intestines.

That said, it is the fastest I've ever lost weight outside of climbing up Mount Kilimanjaro without a shirt—where the cold and heavy exertion cannibalized my waistline.

We break our hack with a trip to a nearby diner. Laura couldn't gin up any more excitement if she tried. We order up healthy portions of eggs, pancakes, bacon and anything but a potato. Starved tastebuds wake up to the sensation of ambrosia. No pad of butter ever felt so full before; no piece of pork was ever this divine. As to be expected with an intervention like this, after resuming my ordinary diet, my weight comes right back to the earlier baseline in about a month.

But that aside, there's an insight that comes with restriction that doesn't fade back quite as quickly as the springs that power the scale. I'm a little more attentive to the sensory changes that came along with a bland diet. I try to keep observing how food makes me feel—not only by listening to a grumbling stomach, but through the subtle cravings that permeate every moment of our oversaturated lifestyle. I'm a little more aware of how my body automatically makes associations between sweetness and pleasure, and of my Pavlovian response to the presence of food in my house. It's harder than when I'm not eating only potatoes, but at least I'm aware of how those urges somehow influence my conscious cravings.

Every diet since the beginning of time hinges on our individual ability to choose what foods we put into our bodies. Unless we're consciously *on a diet* with a goal of losing or gaining weight, most of us let our associations between taste and emotions dictate our menu. How often have you asked yourself what you "feel like eating"? That act of looking inward is a wedge that you work unconsciously into your brain to form and reinforce neural symbols. For me, the potato hack is a lens to examine how I let those passive associations control my behavior, and an opportunity to make a change.

There's no question that a potato-hack lifestyle would be a bad idea over time, but it's telling that many spiritual and meditative traditions recommend either fasting or various bland diets before partaking in a new practice. A restricted diet offers a reset to a physical baseline and makes a person more sensitive to the sensations that their body detects. And this goes for any sensation. When you increase the intensity of one signal, others get drowned out. Lower intensities in one area makes the others seem louder. An important aspect of the neural symbols that make up our cognition is that they not only register emotion and sensation together, but also the volume of those signals. An intense emotion or sensation is more likely to get picked up by the limbic librarian than one that doesn't stand out. Insofar as the Wedge requires a person to be attentive to their sensations and feelings, learning to play with the volume levels is another tool we can use to subtly alter the way we experience the world. As counterintuitive as it may seem, sometimes diminishing our senses is the key to connecting outward.

And yet that volume can also go the other way. What happens when instead of reducing stimulation, we try to ramp it up almost to its maximum extent? I've gotten a taste of that with kettlebells, where I tried to stoke up enough fear that I could wire a neural symbol. But the fear of an injured foot still sits on the lower end of the threshold. Ice water will trigger a strong primal survival program. But what happens if we turn up the heat instead? What happens when the volume goes so high that we brush against the upper limits of what we're able to tolerate?

The usual practices of so-called "medicine men" shall be considered "Indian offenses" cognizable by the court of Indian offenses, and whenever it shall be proven to the satisfaction of the court that the influence or practice of a so-called "medicine man" operates as a hindrance to the civilization of a tribe, or that said "medicine man" resorts to any artifice or device to keep the Indians under his influence, or shall adopt any means to prevent the attendance of children at the agency schools, or shall use any of the arts of a conjurer to prevent the Indians from abandoning their heathenish rites and customs, he shall be adjudged guilty of an Indian offense, and shall be confined in the agency guardhouse for a term not less than ten days, or until such time as he shall produce evidence satisfactory to the court, and approved by the agent, that he will forever abandon all practices styled Indian offenses under this rule.

—Regulations of the Indian Office

April 1, 1904

CHAPTER 8

REDLINE

It's 180 degrees, and I'm lying naked on a cedar bench. Peeking out from behind his handlebar mustache, a man in a pointy green hat and a loincloth beats me with a bouquet of flowers. Petals and pollen break apart on impact and drift down to the wet floor. I open my eyes between the lashings to see my wife, Laura, also nude and drenched in sweat, on a bench opposite mine. Birch leaves, sticks and yellow flowers form a pile on her head and chest.

We are dressed like salads. We marinate like steaks.

A woman in a felt hat and a loose nightgown pours water onto a bed of glowing coals in the corner. A column of steam erupts upward, and she deftly waves a branch of spruce leaves like a fan sending a hot cloud cascading down on Laura's prone body. The hot vapor drenches her feet, calves, thighs, stomach, breasts and head.

Laura whimpers.

I make out her pleading whisper. It's too hot. It's too much. Then, just when my wife is about to break, the gnomish woman dips her bundle of branches into a pail of cold water on the floor and shakes it, letting loose a torrent of cold water. The burst of contrast—hot to cold and cold to hot—brings Laura back from the brink.

A cloud of steam obscures my view, and I have to remind myself that this is not a fever dream. This is medicine. This is the Wedge.

And I'll admit, the whole situation is strange and otherworldly.

Laura and I have come to this isolated spot to learn how in-digenous medicine differs from the targeted drug prescriptions and discreet physical interventions that are so familiar back home. The fey couple running the ritual uses the contrast between hot and cold to seesaw our bodies into surrender—ultimately helping to build up resilience to emotional and physical stress. They're feeling the same heat we are, which means that we're all working the Wedge together, communally reaching our breaking points and then walking it back. It's a team effort.

The sauna is tucked away in a dark pine forest about forty kilometers from the post-Soviet capital city of Latvia, roughly ten degrees of latitude south of the Arctic Circle and sandwiched be-tween Estonia, Lithuania, Belarus and Russia. The sauna itself is a fancy affair: half hobbit hole, half upscale spa. Most of the building is tucked into the belly of a hill, but its floor-to-ceiling windows look out on a placid pond.

I can't say exactly what I expected when I signed up for a five-hour ritual of contrasting sensations. All I knew was that this is an old tradition that harks back to a time when people were more connected to the natural world, when conditions were brutal and death was much more present. Most indigenous medicine traditions I know of use sensation and stress as entry points to manipulate the body and build on the principles behind the Wedge long before I ever came along. Still, I figured that the skills I've learned in other parts of my journey would apply in some way to enduring heat. And though I can't say where this is going, I do expect it to be profound.

The people in pointy hats are *pirtnieks*, or, in English, "sauna masters," trained in the art of using contrasting sensations to stimulate psychological and physical changes through intense heat. In ordinary life, the woman, Ivita Picukane, is a nurse at a local hospital. Her part-ner, Vilnis Lejnieks, is a reiki healer. But right now, they're shamans acting as conduits between nature's energy and the people on their cedar benches.[6] While Latvia is ostensibly a Christian country, and the home of the very first Christmas tree, most people I meet here consider themselves part of a pagan tradition that goes back thousands of years. Latvians grow up foraging for mushrooms with their families in the forest and celebrating the solstice with much more enthusiasm than anything you might find in a church. It's probably one of the last stands for Europe's old nature-loving traditions.

Neither Picukane nor Lejnieks speaks more than a handful of English words, but they're communicating through their actions and the tools of the ritual. Under ordinary circumstances, the temperature and humidity in this room wouldn't only be unbearable; it could be lethal without the sauna masters' tricks. They perform a sort of dance with the heat, hitting us with steam and the ambient temperature until we reach the very edge of tolerance, where it feels like we're suffocating, and then they walk us backward from the edge with a splash of cold water, a torrent of sound or the slap of their branches. The goal seems to be to keep us as close to our red line as possible without pushing us over.

The stress is all in service of their goal of pushing us past the emotional and physical limits that we arrived with. And if I'm being honest, the limits they're working on really aren't things that I've pushed too hard on before. Everything is context, and I simply don't have occasion to think about my breaking point with heat all that much. I don't know what passive associations I've locked into my psyche by *not* trying to push up the thermometer's mercury. This is the tricky thing with any new Wedge experience. I simply don't know where it will go. I'm trying to feel how my reaction to heat defines who I am, and how facing it makes me more human.

---

[6] The word "shaman" originates from Tunguskic religious healers who enter into trances to communicate with the spirit world. Anthropologists like me use the term to speak about similar indigenous spiritual healers on every continent who usually have gone through years of training to attain the title. This can be confusing, because in recent years, the term has grown in popularity and has also lost its specificity. Today it has come to mean any priest of a New Age order.

And to really understand what I'm doing and how it informs my understanding of the Wedge, I need to take a step back to try to reconsider what medicine is in the first place. The medicine served in hospitals and doctor's offices back home concentrates on eliminating the symptoms of disease. It's a laudable science that can deliver specific cures to well-defined conditions. In its most ideal form, Western medicine is mechanical, objective and repeatable. But Western medicine's specificity doesn't always account for the vast range of human subjective experience. Western doctors rarely care about how you feel; sensations don't much matter to them. At the end of the day, all they see is pathology.

However, while underlying pathology can certainly cause you to feel bad, you don't go to the doctor to make a mechanical change; you go because you want to feel better. You go because your senses are telling you something is wrong. And sometimes, being myopically focused on pathology can obscure the true causes of illness.

Medicine isn't exclusively a human domain. Every living creature on Earth struggles against the threat of disease. The grinding process of evolution has given us a bewildering array of tools to help keep infections at bay—from cell walls and skin that form barriers to the environment, to highly advanced immune systems that can adapt and respond to danger without any conscious input. But it's also important to realize that many animals take an active role in their own recoveries. They use things they find in the environment to provoke physical responses. Cats and dogs both eat certain grasses to induce vomiting when they feel sick. Chimps, bonobos and gorillas eat tree bark to rid themselves of parasites and reduce fever, moths lay eggs in anti-parasitic milkweed to protect their offspring, and bees brew antibacterial honey and can raise and lower the temperature of their hives to make it less hospitable to invaders. These actions are based on the sensory interactions of the Wedge. The animals don't have a specific plan to alter mechanical processes the way a scientist might; they just somehow know that taking a particular action changes how they feel. And sometimes—especially with chronic conditions—our sensory system has more information to draw on than any medical diagnostic.

Indeed, Western medical interventions—cocktails of drugs, surgeries, etc.—are an often too-narrow way of addressing how the human body heals and recovers. By putting sensation first, indigenous traditions around the world offer other perspectives on chronic illness that in many cases can be more effective than treatments in hospitals and doctor's offices at home. The breadth of indigenous treatments is too vast for a chapter, a book, or, for that matter, the entire field of medical anthropology. However, many practices build on the same foundation as the Wedge as they skillfully manipulate sensory pathways to coax the body into healing itself.

Just about every circumpolar indigenous community has its own sauna tradition that employs extreme heat to usher in transcendental experiences, to heal, to build community, and to foster resilience in the environment. Cold, prayer and psychedelic plants all play a role in many native medicine systems. However, traditions that manipulate heat stress are unique not only because of how our bodies respond to the upper end of the temperature scale, but because of how a skilled practitioner can use those temperature reactions to alter the way another person feels the stress. The doctors of the indigenous world wield the Wedge like a scalpel.

In North America, Lakota sweat lodges, called *inipi*, are sacred spaces where the community comes together for ceremonies, and as a form of indigenous psychotherapy. When I started to research heat training, my first instinct was to sit down with the Lakota, but a violent history of genocide, oppression and bad-faith treaties makes reporting on Native American traditions contentious for an outsider like me. Up until the late 1970s, merely setting up a sweat lodge could land an Indian medicine man in jail. Today there's a well-founded concern about cultural appropriation of their ancient traditions. I approached several tribal groups asking for permission to write about *inipi*, and was pointedly but politely asked to look elsewhere.

The same week that I gave up on the tribes near home, I got an invitation from a man named Maris Zunda, who was trying to organize the first biohacking conference in Latvia. In Scandinavia, the Baltic states and Russia, saunas remain a mainstay of social life. Zunda asked me to deliver a lecture on the principles behind the Wedge and what I'd learned from controlling my body in ice water. He sweetened the deal by saying he could help me experience one of the oldest continuous pagan rituals in the world: *pirts*, the Latvian sauna ritual. That, in short, is how my wife and I ended up at the mercy of two wood elves halfway across the world.

...

Let's jump back in time, to when we arrive at the sauna and meet Picukane and Lejnieks, with Maris Zunda in tow. The pirtnieks take us into a small tea room, and Zunda acts as translator. They say that the sauna is a special place in Latvia, not recreation, and that we need to take it seriously. They are, after all, masters. A traditional *pirts* takes at least five hours. That's a long time to be on the razor's edge of tolerance. They warn me that it will go from pleasurable to grueling and then back again, but we should trust that they're in control.

"Our tool is feeling the same heat that you do," says Lejnieks.

They tell us to stand in a circle and set an intention for the ceremony. I focus on the darkness behind my eyelids and concentrate on health, strength and bounty for the people closest to me. Maris and my wife are close to me, and I can feel everyone's presence echo on my skin. The ritual begins when the shamans start to walk in a circle around our small group while playing what seem like improvised instruments. Since I can't see them, my imagination paints the stage. One shakes a branch of dried leaves in my ear so that it sounds like the patter of a gentle rain. The other starts a steady rhythm on a hand drum. Someone whistles. And the cacophony of sound only grows weirder over time, as I imagine the shamans are dancing around us. The rain morphs into the high-pitched *plink* of someone running their fingers over the hard tines of a pinecone. I hear the whistle of wind through trees and the scent of pine fills my nose. Just as I start to feel like I am weathering a storm in a forest, the unmistakable notes of Beethoven's *Für Elise* come through what must be the plinking mental prongs of a child's music box.

It's not really a song. I can't even say that it all hangs together. I'm not sure that I can identify what instruments are playing or where the smells are actually coming from. And yet because of all the discordance, I miss one critical thing. Sometime at the beginning of the impromptu nature concert, one of the shamans snuck off and opened the door to the sauna. It must have been more than 200 degrees inside. Over the course of five minutes, heat that had been trapped in the adjacent room filled this one. It's only when I open my eyes that I notice we're in a pine-heated oven and I start to sweat inside my clothes.

Outside of the array of branches and tools at the shamans' disposal, they've just shown me the first technique that underpins the entire five-hour experience. There's no English term for it that I can determine, but it's definitely a wedge. I'll call it *distraction*. In the opening of the ceremony, they flood my sensory pathways with unexpected stimuli—sounds, smells and vibrations—so that I'm not actually aware of how my environment is changing. It's like sleight of hand for my nervous system—tricking my sensory pathways by making me focus on the incidental noises they make so that my mind isn't aware of the general context.

After the sound circle, the shamans close the door to the sauna, Zunda excuses himself, and Laura and I sit down at a wooden table. There's a small meal of different teas, waters, honey and a loaf of dark bread in front of us. Over the last few weeks and months, Picukane infused each treat with herbs that she's collected from around Latvia.

I try the tea first. It's a deep and astringent yellow brew distilled from wormwood. It puckers my face into a screw. The honey tastes of pine needles, and, indeed, when I look closely, I can see flecks of green floating in it. The bread smells of lavender. Every taste is familiar but out of place. It feels deliciously exotic, like something out of a fairy tale.

After the meal, we strip off our clothes and head into the sauna, where Picukane has arranged for us to meet all those ingredients again in a different way. Maybe it's an American thing, but Laura and I are both a little embarrassed about the idea of getting naked in front of total strangers. I feel vulnerable and exposed. But the pirtnieks don't bat a lash. They have us take spots on cedar benches. In a matter of minutes, we're drenched in sweat. The pirtnieks start rubbing the same herbs that we just consumed onto our skin and into our hair, then use dried switches of them to beat our bodies. The plants suffuse every sensory portal.

When Lejnieks rubs a spruce frond on my chest, the taste of spruce comes up through my esophagus and floats in the back of my palate. When Picukane puts a bouquet of yellow wormwood under my nose, the smell connects to my stomach. I can feel its astringence in my bloodstream. The ritual induces a sort of synesthesia. I feel smell as one pirtniek grinds a flower blossom into my skin. I smell sound when the shamans shake the flower in my ears. I mull over what to call this second wedge, and I settle on the word *bonding*.

The shamans manipulate neural symbols in ways that I had never really considered possible. The strangeness of the ritual heightens my attention, but there are simply so many sensations to pay attention to at once. Neither I nor my body have a baseline to work from. Instead of emotions linking to sensations the way it normally works with neural symbols, the pirtnieks' bond sensations to sensations. This sensory witchcraft wedges space between what my senses are supposed to tell me and how I actually feel in the increasingly difficult environment. Stressors that I'm used to experiencing in one way—like the taste of tea made from wormwood—I now experience in sound and touch. It's hard to tell exactly why my body starts to mix the signals; perhaps it only happens while also fighting the stress from heat. And all the while, I'm slowly heating up without noticing that the room is more than three-quarters of the way to the boiling point of water.

My senses are occupied well enough that I don't realize I'm withstanding brutally hot temperatures. And yet I know that some part of my brain must sense the temperature. Those areas of my brain stem exist below conscious thought. And I guess that it would have raised alarm bells much earlier if it had known where to pay attention. But the periods of relief between sweltering heat and brief baths of intervening cold keep changing the overall baseline. Before I know it, I breach the point where I *should* have broken, but instead ascend into uncharted territory. And then, before my senses can catch up, the shaman gently brings me back down. This pattern of subtle expansion and retreat is altering my relationship with heat—and, to some degree, stress in general.

Most people associate warmth with love, safety and well-being. At higher intensities, heat gets insufferable. The body responds with a sense of claustrophobia as a sensation that urges the conscious mind to take action and find a safer, cooler environment. This is the way most neural symbols are supposed to work. Claustrophobia conveys bad feelings about the environment and demands that the conscious mind come up with a solution. The conscious mind can override the sensation until the sensory system decides to make itself unbearable. It becomes a conversation between consciousness and sensory-ness. And this is an insight into comfort and homeostasis.

Warmth feels good because our bodies don't need to work to maintain their core temperatures. Heat feels bad when our bodies have to alter the way they function in order to dump excess energy. When we're hot, our central nervous system triggers autonomic programming that relaxes arteries to increase blood flow to the extremities. It lowers the metabolic rate and increases the rate of perspiration. For the most part, you can't feel any of that happening. It's only that sense of claustrophobia that signals our conscious minds to take action or risk cooking our insides.

In ice baths and cold immersions, the sensation we think of as "cold"—that shivering, clenching feeling that seems to start in the shoulders and arcs across the skin—corresponds to autonomic changes in our metabolism and vascular system. Those contrasting sensations between temperatures begin whenever we stray from that narrow band of stasis, where our bodies are in equilibrium with the environment. The discomfort is a signal that your body is doing work that it would rather not have to.

In the modern world, where changing environments is as easy as pressing a button, homeostasis is also an addiction. When we appease our internal sense of comfort by changing environments, over time we feel comfortable in an ever-decreasing range of external conditions. The cycle continues until everything feels uncomfortable. Cold training allows a person to develop resilience at low temperatures. Heat training in saunas is one way to extend comfort's upper limit. This gentle seesaw between hot and cold in the pirts exercises autonomic processes that foster adaptation to temperature variation and increase our overall resilience.

I'm grateful that my wife and I have the advantage of having two guides carefully lead us through increasingly difficult temperatures. They keep us right on the cusp of danger and then skillfully bring us back into the realm of tolerance. Their manipulations help us maintain our own mental orientation to the heat. We're getting stronger with their help.

But I have to remember that training with heat is potentially more dangerous than training in the cold. It's far easier to heat a person up who has been in an ice bath too long than it is to bring their body temperature down from beyond the redline. Frostbite and hypothermia occur far below most people's comfort thresholds, but danger is closer at hand in a sauna. Overheating can sneak up on you.

Proteins begin to unwind if your body temperature arcs above 104° Fahrenheit (40° Celsius) for an extended time. At that temperature, the brain starts to cook and you might well die. It's happened before.

In 2009, two people died and 18 ended up in the hospital at an ill-fated sweat lodge run by Law of Attraction self-help guru James Arthur Ray. They'd spent several hours in a sauna ritual meant to push the limits of human endurance. Ray and the other men urged each other to stay in a little longer until a few of them cooked from the inside. And while their deaths could have been prevented by toning down the macho vibes, it also sounds at least a little similar to what I'm doing here in Latvia. With all this distraction and bonding going on, how am I supposed to know when I've gone too far?

Across the room, one of the sauna masters pours a ladle full of water on the pile of hot stones in the corner. Steam erupts upward like it's charging out from a volcanic vent. The 50-ish man places his hand on my feet to check my temperature; even though both our bodies are surely already running high fevers, the way people feel sensation is relative. If I feel hot to his touch, then it means that my body temperature at that point of contact must be higher than his. This is the gauge he uses for how I must be feeling.

Pirtnieks know that heat is a great leveler and that everyone feels the same sensations when they've had too much of it. Everyone, eventually, will feel the need to get out; everyone gets claustrophobic. It's the pirtniek's job to keep me right on the edge of tolerance and then get me out when I'm hotter than he is. This is what he meant when he said that the heat was his tool. He grabs a fan made out of willow branches and waves it above my head. I feel the steam push down on me like high tide rolling in on a beach. He wafts the steam down my body and past my toes. I open my eyes and my vision narrows, like I'm looking down a tunnel with hazy red outlines in my periphery. My back begins to strain, and he puts his hand on my feet again and nods.

"It's time," he says struggling with his English. "Get up."

I'm unstable on my feet. He takes me through the tea room and stark naked into the brisk April air. He is watching me closely to be sure I don't fall down. With his guidance, I walk into the still pond in front of the pirts, sending waves across its flawless surface. Steam wafts upward off my body, and I slowly submerge.

Relief.

...

Even with the potential dangers of overheating, actual sauna fatalities are extremely rare. We know this because a series of exhaustive demographic studies out of Finland over the past few decades on the benefits of sauna therapy reported that fewer than two people out of every million regular users die during exposure. Similar to Latvians, most Finns keep saunas in their homes and use them at least once a week. They're sauna evangelists. The medical data that Finnish scientists publish show how regular use can radically improve people's health over the baseline. One study tracked 2,315 middle-aged men in eastern Finland over the course of 20 years. The most frequent users, who sat in saunas four to seven times a week, demonstrated a 40% decline in heart attacks and cardiovascular disease as compared with people who sat in one just once a week. Other studies indicate that regular sauna use helps dementia, strokes, Alzheimer's and, as one article put it, improves on "all-cause mortality events."

Yeah, that's right. As far as the cutting edge of Finnish science is concerned, saunas keep death at bay.

This makes intuitive sense to me. If saunas stress the cardiovascular system by dilating arterioles and sweating out whatever toxins build up in the body over time, it stands to reason that it helps anything that afflicts the 60,000 miles or so of tubing in our bodies. Heat stress exercises the entire unconscious biology, and thus has a generalized effect on human health. And it's not just circumpolar scientists who extol the clinical benefits of heat. Researchers in America are increasingly excited about the potential of high temperatures to fundamentally change depression and anxiety, too.

...

Let's go back in time to early April. I'm sitting in a large conference room full of doctors, neurologists and full-time researchers at one of the largest mental hospitals in Oklahoma. This is the same trip where I have a chance to see Feinstein's float set up. We've taken a short break from the tubs in order to peek in on grand rounds at the hospital. There's a lecture that he thinks I absolutely have to see. In fact, the whole institute is on tenterhooks.

Charles Raison, a professor of psychiatry and evolution at the University of Wisconsin-Madison, stands at the front of the room wearing a tweed jacket with patches on the elbows—a nod to the stuffy academic halls that he's used to lecturing in. He's discussing the relevance of ancient medicinal practices in 21st-century psychiatry. And he starts with a simple supposition: Until the modern world, energy was always at a premium, and humans—not to mention every other living thing on Earth—need energy to survive. The first challenge for any living thing is to find a way to produce, store or share heat.

Raison's slideshow settles for a moment on a picture of penguins huddled together on an Antarctic ice sheet. It's a shot that you've probably seen in any polar documentary of tens of thousands of flightless birds in black tuxedos massed in an impossibly large group. They stay like this for months in order to resist the brutally cold weather. "If they didn't have each other, they'd all be dead," he says. *Kleptothermy*, or the practice of sharing body heat, does more than help the penguins survive the ice; it organizes the species' entire social behavior. While it's obvious in penguins, Raison says, temperature affects human psychology just as much.

"One characteristic that most people suffering from depression share is that they run higher temperatures than non-depressed folks. And if you treat their depression, their temperature returns to normal. Not only that, but depressed people typically don't sweat," he says. It's a bombshell of a statement, because if it's true, then Raison is essentially arguing that depression stems from bad thermoregulation as much as from any other factor. I have to admit, it's a statement that I have some trouble accepting on face value. So as he speaks, I open my laptop and log in to an academic database that I have access to. I find a 2003 article in the journal *Neuropsychobiology* by a team of psychiatrists at the Veterans Administration in Georgia that shows that people with major depression tend to average about a half-degree higher body temperature than non-depressed people. The data on sweating is a little more difficult to parse out, because about 80% of depressed people also suffer from anxiety, a condition that causes excessive perspiration. A careful analysis of psychobiological literature by Raison's team indicated that if you isolate your sample so that it includes people who are depressed but not anxious, then they barely sweat at all.[7] Perhaps even more interesting is that sweating is one of the most common side effects of antidepressant drugs. There's a connection. I'm a little surprised.

One way to think about inflammation is that it's heat building up in the body. At a basic physiological level, it's a primary immune response that stabilizes tissue, heats it up, and isolates pathogens from circulating freely. Inflammation isn't bad in its own right—it helped us survive our long evolutionary journey—but it damages tissue in the process. In the world of our ancestors before antibiotics and critical

---

[7]   In that article, titled "Somatic influences of subjective well-being and affective disorders: the convergence of thermosensory and central serotonergic systems," in *Frontiers in Psychology*, Raison and his five co-authors pull from literature dating back to 1890 that correlates decreased skin conductivity with depression. The article lays theoretical groundwork that suggests that not only does temperature affect depression, but that external stimuli in general can generate natural antidepressant effects that are potentially more powerful than current antidepressants—and that one sign that a depressed patient is recovering is if they start sweating more.

medical care, inflammation could be the difference between life or death. But it was also a sign that a person was sick. Raison knows that he is building up to something big, and he smirks as he suggests that inflammation sends ancient signals to our unconscious minds to prepare ourselves for death. While inflammation doesn't correlate with mortal danger in the same way that it once did, our bodies don't have any way to know that. In other words, just as too much heat signals claustrophobia and too much cold triggers clenching up, inflammation causes system-wide depression.

Raison's argument inverts the normal discussion that we have about depression in the Western world. Therapies usually target chemical imbalances in the brain or fractured social relationships, but Raison thinks that maybe treating inflammation would be just as effective. "Is it any surprise that just about every ancient culture in the world has some sort of sweat lodge tradition?" he asks.

Think back to those emperor penguins on an ice sheet: They're sharing heat, and their combined thermoregulation means that the entire community will survive. Heat is life. Indeed, Raison points out, in lieu of pharmaceuticals, indigenous communities around the globe use sensory and environmental stimuli to treat their sick. He flashes a list of techniques culled from ethnographic accounts and ancient texts on the screen: sensory deprivation, breathing, fasting, extreme exercise, meditation, hyperthermia, hypothermia, and psychedelic plant medicines. All of these interventions aim to wedge space between the way we experience stress and how our bodies respond to difficult environments.

Someone should write a book! I think to myself.

Most people today rarely reflect on the subtle ways that the environment frames their mental state. If we're depressed or angry or anxious, we tend to look first for events around us as a trigger. Maybe we're off-kilter because of an argument with a friend or an awkward comment or misstep in etiquette. We're less aware of things that don't change rapidly—unaware of our breathing, for example, or the million environmental signals that reinforce how we feel. Outside of a sauna or an ice bath, when was the last time you noticed how the environment altered your mental state?

As Raison writes in one of his many articles, "It would seem that the most important cause of [any mental condition] is not the normal evolved brain response to the environmental stimulus, but the stimulus itself." This is the Wedge in action as it separates stimulus from response. The brain *is* the environment. Evolutionary programming matters, but context matters more because human physiology knows how to adapt. Raison does more than just philosophize about depression and heat; he designed an experiment to test the hypothesis.

He flips through slides and shows an image of the basement of a hospital in Switzerland where he found an abandoned 70-year-old infrared sauna from an era when the idea of environmental medicine was more in vogue. The machine was essentially a human-sized box of water-cooled infrared lights with a hole cut out at the top so that the patient's head would stick out. This setup allowed doctors to heat up someone's body without worrying about boiling their brains. It was a revolutionary treatment at the time and garnered acclaim for managing a wide variety of psychiatric conditions. However, in the intervening decades, the pharmaceutical approach to psychiatry became more popular, and the sauna ended up gathering dust in the basement. Raison resurrected and refurbished the device, then made an identical copy with one key difference. Instead of infrared bulbs, he used ordinary incandescent ones that didn't give off much heat. He reasoned that this sham device wouldn't heat up nearly as much as the real one, but might provide a convincing enough placebo for a clinical control.

Raison deposited two groups of depressed patients in the different saunas and heated the active group for almost 90 minutes until their core temperatures hit 101.3° F (38.5° C)—the equivalent of a mild fever—then cooled them off for 60 minutes. The patients in the sham device heard the same sounds and saw the same colored lights, and completed a questionnaire whose answers showed that 10 out of 14 of them believed they were getting the real treatment. Clinicians assessed both groups' levels of depression over the next six weeks, and astonishingly, the people who had the real sauna showed significant improvement compared to the folks in the sham setup. The effect was so powerful that it matched treatment with ketamine, one of the most promising therapies for depression.

Simply heating up someone's body was enough to make depression go away.

A few weeks after meeting Raison, I ask one of his co-authors on the paper, a neuroscientist at the University of Colorado Boulder named Chris Lowry, why he thought the heat therapy was so promising. "At the largest level, depression is all about a person pulling inward, so that they only think about what's happening inside their own minds, usually in negative ways. But external stimuli like heat and cold force a person to reckon with their environment. It pulls you out of yourself," he explains. The heat is a wedge that interrupts the things that reinforce feelings of depression. And maybe that is all a depressed person needs: to have a reason to look outward.

...

Back to the present, and underwater somewhere in the Latvian wilderness just a few steps away from the sauna-hobbit hole. I blow out a small stream of bubbles and feel them roll upward past my nose and forehead on their way to the surface of the pond. The water is brisk, maybe 50 degrees, but I've been in the blistering sauna for the past couple of hours, and the cold water feels like coming home. I stay under the surface for a few more seconds, and my skin cools rapidly. My core temperature is still high, though, and I have no idea what sort of fever I'm running.

When I come up for air, Laura is naked next to me, her head below the water. I dunk under again. The man and woman in felt hats motion for us to go under a third time. When we're up again, a small frog pops its head out of the water between us and blinks. The woman smiles and says it's good luck. Then they usher us back to land and point to two small mats outdoors. They're stuffed full of local grasses and herbs and crunch pleasantly beneath our weight. The shamans then cover us up with blankets. The man wraps a towel around my head so that the only thing touching the outside air are my mouth and nose through a little hole. He tells us to get up only when we start to feel cold.

So to recap: I've been steamed like a potato, then blanched in cold water. It's a procedure similar to the one that chefs use to remove the skin from tomatoes. The quick underwater dunk was too brief for the laws of thermodynamics to allow my core to cool. At best, the blanching just sealed the heat in as my veins constricted around my hot core. Even so, my skin is icy to the touch. I close my eyes and try to focus in the way that I would at the end of a long Hof breathing session—at a point between my eyes where I often see colors. My mind is unusually clear, but my body is confused. I feel a shiver rock up my spine and out through my arms. I have a few short convulsions, but it's not because I feel cold. I'm shivering from the heat.

Synesthesia again.

The contrasting temperatures have confused whatever software my body uses to control thermoregulation. It's trying to dump heat from my core into my hands and feet, but my extremities are pulling inward. Up is down and down is up. The two opposite bodily reactions bring the taste of pine from the branches or honey that I'd eaten earlier into my mouth. I feel clean inside and out. Soft convulsions rock my body for a few minutes before Lejnieks puts his hand on my shoulder and asks if I'm okay.

I am. In fact, I feel great.

Despite the contradictory sensations and physical responses, I feel connected and grounded in my body in a way that I haven't for a long time. The sensation is similar to the diminished brain functions from intense breathwork in Elee's class that helped me connect to that feeling of universal consciousness. My body is so confused that my mind has nowhere to go but inward...and, paradoxically, outward at the same time.

I lie there for a few more minutes before I feel ready to go inside and start another round of heat. Laura is already on a chair inside, wrapped in a brown sheet. She's sipping a cup of bitter wormwood tea out of a clear glass.

The secret is in the contrast between hot and cold, between sound and silence, taste and smell. When they confuse and alter the sensory pathways, the pirtnieks aren't really sauna masters: they're *contrast* masters.

For thousands of years, philosophers have argued among themselves whether or not it's possible for two people to experience the world in the same way. While we can agree on words—it's not controversial to say that bananas are yellow, for instance—how do we know that all people experience that color in the same way? What looks yellow to you might well be red to me if I saw it through your eyes. How you answer this question ultimately depends on how much you trust your senses and the existence of an objective reality.

Pirtnieks don't struggle with such arcane questions, because they know from the experience of a thousand saunas that everyone feels the claustrophobia and panic from extreme heat in the same way. They know that cold brings relief to people on the edge. For them, the ultimate question isn't about the nature of hot or cold, but is perhaps better understood as the contrast between opposing sensations. In this superheated chamber, they don't need language to communicate with the two Americans on their cedar benches. Sensation is everything. They're shamans because they feel what we feel.

...

Three years before I came to this sauna, I ran a race in England called the Tough Guy that was supposed to be the coldest obstacle-course race in the world, yet I ran it wearing just a bathing suit. Most everyone else on the field that day wore neoprene wetsuits. After the first few minutes on the course, I felt hot. While I was far from the fastest person in the lineup, every picture that course photographers shot of me caught me wearing an ear-to-ear grin. I'd practiced the Wim Hof Method for months before the race and was conditioned to the cold. But why was I so happy? When I started to run over obstacles and dunk nearly naked into muddy pits of water, I felt the sensations of frigid cold on my skin, but I was also having an absolute blast. At some point I told myself that it wasn't cold that I was feeling on my skin; the muscle-tensing sensation caused by my environment was joy itself. This mental trick transmuted the entire experience. I consciously assigned a meaning to my sensations, and that alone made me more resilient.

Somehow I'd managed not only to maintain my body temperature through my training, but I'd also triggered a change in the emotional valiance of the cold and reprogrammed the sensation as a full-body experience of happiness.

There's an anatomical explanation for how that works. When we sense heat, the signal first comes in through the skin, and the nervous system sends the information from the outside world through the thalamus, where it branches off into two main directions. First into the *rostral insula*, an area in our gray matter on the periphery of our brain that deals with the intensity of a sensation. The second path heads to the *anterior cingulate*, a brain region that assesses the quality of a sensation. The anterior cingulate is the part of the limbic system that controls the emotional resonance of the signal as well as other higher brain functions. I believe that when I chose to focus on the joy of running the race instead of the pain of cold on my skin, I allowed my brain to give preference to one neural symbol over the other. This split in the sensory pathways creates an opportunity to change how we react to environmental sensations. I'd created a new neural symbol in the moment of stress.

The same technique works in the sauna. When the intensity gets too high, I can focus my mind on the thrill of the challenge instead of the walls closing in around me. And the shaman can help when I start to lose control.

Back in my position lying face down on the cedar bench, I'm doing something similar to what I did when running the Tough Guy. The man in the felt hat starts beating me again with willow branches. These are the same sticks infusing the tea in my stomach and the branches I laid on outside. The sensations from the natural world are all around me. And I can't tell if the lashing is pleasurable or painful. I realize that, just as when I was running the race three years ago, my reaction to the branches, to the funnily dressed sauna masters, to the heat, the food and the cold, are all a choice. I can be embarrassed by my nakedness. I can cringe at the heat or retract from the branches. Or I can embrace the experience and realize how unique and special it all is. My mindset is a choice where I get to decide what my sensations mean.

Someone pours another cup of water on the scalding stones, and steam erupts again throughout the room. The shaman is bringing me to the edge of tolerance, but it's my choice as to when I feel that limit. Even though the pirtnieks are doing the physical work, Laura and I can manipulate our reactions. We're letting the heat flow through us like water and trusting that nothing here is going to push past any hard limits—past the so-called redline, where we'll start to hurt ourselves. The Wedge is our ability to surf that sensation, and the pirtnieks aid our journey by redirecting our attention away from the most difficult sensations.

Perception is key. Whatever heat tolerance I build in this moment also stretches into more mundane stresses once this is all over. It's the same concept of resilience that Mackenzie finds when using parasympathetic breathing during high-intensity workouts. I'm learning a new way to be comfortable in uncomfortable surroundings.

The pirts slowly winds down over the next hour. The contrasting sensations level out into our normal ranges, and I feel a full-body sensation of happiness. I'm also exhausted. The sauna was difficult and deeply rewarding. I've connected in my body how sensation can manipulate my mental state, and I'm eager to apply that knowledge to other aspects of my life.

I notice one change almost immediately. Normally I keep the temperature of my house pretty cold in the winter, below 60 degrees. This forces my body to increase its metabolic rate and switch to burning fat. This is what I call *slow cold* (in contrast to the *fast cold*, when you jump into ice water and feel the contrast immediately). The problem with slow cold is that it can make you feel achy and tired over time—maybe even a little depressed. But brief bouts in a sauna change the game. Now, instead of only being cold, I give myself some variation of extreme heat. So I when I came home, I bought a sauna. I've never been happier.

If heat can alleviate depression, then maybe there are other sensations that trigger beneficial changes to human health. Maybe in our search for ever more efficient medicinal chemicals, we've left other healing pathways off the table.

And this is how a trip to a Latvian sauna made me question a fundamental process of human healing that functions in the background of all medical research and medical miracles. While indigenous traditions use sensations to manipulate the body, Western medicine aims to treat the body as an object without any subjectivity of its own. The two systems are at odds. But lurking underneath every drug, every diagnostic technique and in the back of the mind of every doctor is the fact that most of the time, the body knows how to heal itself. And the most derided words in medicine might just be the key to shifting our medical paradigm to accept the Wedge: the placebo effect.

Human psychology and physiology are too complex for us to trust that the medical world is infallible.

—Ellen J. Langer, *Counterclockwise*

Normal science, the activity in which most scientists inevitably spend almost all their time, is predicated on the assumption that the scientific community knows what the world is like.

—Thomas S. Kuhn, *The Structure of Scientific Revolutions*

CHAPTER 9

THE PLACEBO PARADOX

A fascinating article lands on my desk while I'm trying to understand what sorts of wedges might be able to interrupt the feedback loops of an out-of-control immune system. For decades, best-selling pop books have made big promises about how the power of positive thinking can reverse disease and make a person healthier. But the paper in my hands offers another perspective, told through the eyes of a patient known only as "Mr. A."

It's not clear what was going through Mr. A's mind when he took all 29 capsules of an experimental antidepressant—other than, of course, the argument with his girlfriend. Mr. A always had trouble making decisions, but tonight he gave in to impulse. Perhaps he thought the pills would course through his bloodstream and turn off one organ system after another until he died. Perhaps he figured that if one antidepressant wasn't enough to cure his blues, maybe a whole bottle might do the trick. Either way, a few hours later he showed up in the emergency room of a Virginia hospital. He stood at the front desk just long enough to stammer the words "Help me, I took all my pills" before collapsing on the floor.

Nurses and attendants rushed to his aid, and their notes from that evening recorded that he was drowsy and lethargic. They found an empty bottle of pills in his pocket, but the sticker didn't reveal any medication that they'd heard of before. It was just a string of numbers and codes indicating that it had come from a nearby clinical testing facility. All they knew for sure was that Mr. A was in trouble. Sweat beaded on his brow, his heart rate spiked, and his blood pressure plummeted to 80/40. Nurses threaded a saline solution into his trembling arm as the office staff scrambled to get ahold of whoever ran the clinical trial to figure out what chemicals might be causing the reaction. When they finally made contact with the researchers running the study, the doctors on the other end of the line were puzzled. It's true that Mr. A was part of their experiment, but he was part of the control group. The bottle contained 29 sugar capsules.

Placebos.

When the staff at the ER told Mr. A that he was taking inert chemicals, his demeanor changed almost immediately. Within 15 minutes he was fully alert, blood pressure back to normal, and probably slightly embarrassed by the whole affair. Rather than a life-threatening condition brought on by a chemical reaction, Mr. A's story showed up in the journal of *General Hospital Psychiatry* as a dramatic instance of the nocebo effect—serious symptoms caused by belief alone. The nocebo effect is the evil twin of the placebo effect—or, what happens when simply believing a medicine will work ends up making someone better. A skeptic might say that Mr. A's blood pressure, heart rate and fainting were all in his head, but that doesn't explain the very real symptoms that hospital staff recorded when he entered the hospital.

The medical community often pillories the idea that the mind can overcome biology. But the Wedge has made me think of the division between mind and body in different ways. If we are *the* environment at the same time we are *an* environment, then what we think of as health has to take into account those different layers of perspective at the same time.

Our minds don't have direct control over every autonomic process. We can't just think the word "adrenaline" and trigger the hormonal release we want. But we can put ourselves in situations that trigger that same predictable hormonal release. When we choose stressors, we choose our biological reactions. The same goes for the immune system: We can't think it into action, but we can certainly change the environment that the immune system responds and reacts to. I believe that this explains what happened to Mr. A—and that has implications for the entire medical system.

The nocebo and placebo effects are the most mysterious phenomena in medicine. Their very existence calls into question the underlying mechanics of how the body tackles illnesses, the function of the immune system and the power of the mind to control biological processes. Every clinical trial approved by the U.S. Food and Drug Administration has to control for the healing power of the placebo effect, and yet medical research almost never directly studies it. With just a few exceptions, pharmaceutical companies treat the body's in-built healing mechanisms as an obstacle to overcome rather than a system to bolster.[8] The remedies of the past half-century tend to try to circumvent the immune system with targeted chemical therapies that attack pathogens or intervene directly in biological processes that have gone haywire.

The Western approach has certainly generated a boon in life-saving therapies and radically improved human health and life expectancy. That said, when an "incurable disease" spontaneously goes into remission, most medical practitioners chalk it up to chance. However, it's likely that the healing power of the body isn't just dumb luck, but at least in part a physiological response to the environments that we inhabit, our sensory pathways and the mindset that we give to medical treatment. In other words: The placebo effect might actually be the Wedge in action.

---

[8] One interesting exception to this is promising new cancer treatments that train the immune system to directly target cancer cells and destroy them. These groundbreaking therapies bolster and improve immune function. Another exception are vaccines that train the immune system to recognize and destroy specific viral pathogens. Yet calling vaccines "Western medicine" fails to recognize that Chinese doctors used smallpox inoculations as early as 1000 A.D., and that the first true vaccine arrived in 1796 in France, when the medical paradigm was based on the four humors. Even though it was in Europe, the medicine of that era wouldn't be accepted in modern hospitals.

...

I got my first canker sore back when I was a toddler—so long ago that I only have my mother's memories of it. She tells me that it made my whole tongue swell up and that I wouldn't stop crying. For those fortunate enough to never have had one, let me explain. A canker is a white raised disc of an ulcer on the inside of your mouth. Cankers start after one of a hundred strains of herpes that humans have toted with them since prehistory enters the body. But the virus doesn't cause the sore; the immune system does. The immune system sniffs out something that reminds it of the virus and then wages a scorched-earth campaign to get rid of it. The sores are painful, horrible, and pretty much ruin everything for a week.

For roughly thirty years, I'd get one sore a month, and it would take a week to go away. I tried everything to get rid of them—different toothpastes, supplements, ice, salt (really bad idea), steroids, goops, gels and herbal coverings. Nothing worked. Some things made them worse. I started to consider myself a canker survivor. I figured that when I die, I'd have a canker in my mouth.

And then I started practicing the Wim Hof Method and learned how to manipulate my own reactions to the environment. I practiced the breathing regularly and felt myself getting stronger. It wasn't until about five months after coming home from Poland for the first time that I realized I wasn't getting cankers anymore. Sometimes I would feel them starting—a rough spot on the inside of my mouth that I learned to associate with impending pain—but redoubling my efforts with the Wim Hof breathing makes them go away before they progress. While this is by far the least interesting immune-system remission story in the annals of medicine, I've only had one canker in the last decade.

Now, here's the question: Was the Wim Hof Method medicine, the placebo effect or something else?

...

Until the invention of antibiotics in 1928, Western medicine couldn't deliver much better results than indigenous medicine anywhere else in the world. In many cases, going to a shaman or witch doctor offered just about the same likelihood of recovery as seeing a Western doctor. As for hospital stays, the general lack of hygiene often meant that the risk was actually higher.

Antibiotics were miracles because they reliably took care of the root cause of infections—the bacterial growth in the body. Later, anesthesia helped our surgical prowess to achieve a similar level of success. Now we are masters at repairing physical injuries. Break a leg or show up in the emergency room with a gunshot wound, and you're pretty likely to survive. Yet for all those achievements, Western medicine is pretty darn bad at managing chronic illness.

The majority of drugs that appear on the market today—to manage autoimmune illnesses, psychiatric conditions, hormonal deficiencies and even cancer—have rather dubious records. Most drugs tested for chronic conditions barely perform two or three percentile points better than the healing power of the mind. While placebo response rates vary drastically, it's common to find drugs where placebos account for between 20% and 85% of the healing power of any given medicine. This is particularly true for drugs targeting pain, anxiety, depression, coughs, erectile dysfunction, irritable bowel syndrome, Parkinson's and epilepsy. While that 2% or 3% is statistically significant across millions of patients, more often than not, when we think a pill is curing our ills, we're actually healing ourselves. This open secret has huge financial implications for the pharmaceutical business. Clinical trials for a successful drug can cost billions of dollars to run, but no patient is going to want to pay for a therapy that their body already provides naturally. And since it's impossible to separate economics from modern medicine, it's also important to note that Western treatment for chronic illnesses often requires that patients continue to take expensive medicine their whole lives. In these cases, the disease is much more profitable than a cure.

One way to think about the placebo effect is the basic principle of statistics known as *regression to the mean*, where any sort of complex system will return to its baseline over time. To illustrate this concept, think about the weather in Los Angeles, a city typically bathed in sunshine and pleasant marine breezes. On any given day, you can bet that L.A. will be pretty nice. Sometimes the heat can spike to insufferable peaks, and other times it can even rain. But wait a few days, and L.A. will likely regress to the mean and be nice again.

Your body is a little like L.A. Illness tends to go away over time whether there's a medical intervention or not. Think back to the last time you had a cold. Your eyes might have itched. Your bones ached, and you might not have been able to stop from sneezing.

When you reached for standard-issue cold medicine, the directions on the package probably stated that once you started on the medicine, your condition would go away in a few days. But guess what? It was going to do that anyway. Cold medicine will help you feel better in the short-term—stopping the mucus, helping you breathe—but even without it, your body should eventually fight off the viral infection and leave you right as rain. Like L.A., you'll regress to the mean—in this case, back to being healthy.

Now, it's true, we feel better when the innate immune system is dormant, but it's important to realize that "feeling sick" often isn't the sensation of a pathogen, but the sensation of our body fighting back. All of those cold symptoms are actually evolutionary in-built actions of the innate immune system to help kill cold viruses. Mucus membranes make it hard for viruses to propagate, while fevers raise the body temperature to a degree that makes it harder for them to survive.

It's fair to assume that much of what we call the placebo effect is in reality the work of the immune system acting behind the scenes. The body returns to its normal homeostatic state because the immune system rooted out the cause of the illness all on its own. Evolution has gifted humans (and vertebrates in general) two immune systems: the innate immune system and the adaptive one. The innate immune system is the front line of defense and has a standard set of responses—fevers, inflammation, mucus generation, attack cells—to biological threats that are quick and easy to deploy. The innate immune system is a blunt instrument that has a pretty dramatic effect on how you feel. It alters your internal environment to make it hostile to invaders. The adaptive immune system is more selective (this is the Special Forces rather than the regular Army); it identifies the specific threat to the body, learns its weaknesses, then deploys a very targeted response. The adaptive immune system remembers the weaknesses of what attacked you so it can deal with the invader more efficiently in the future. In contrast to the innate immune system, you almost never feel the adaptive immune system doing its work.

In terms of your cold, the first time you encounter it, your body responds with mucus, fever and achy joints—the innate immune response. Meanwhile, your adaptive immune system starts learning the virus's weaknesses and storing that information for later use. The next time you meet that same virus, your adaptive immune system responds without you ever even knowing there was a threat.

We like to think that most medicine works like a substitute for the adaptive immune system—that scientists in a laboratory have discovered the root cause of an illness and developed a chemical that can eradicate the pathogen with a surgical strike. While a few classes of medicine do work like that, most of our go-to therapies actually suppress the activities of the innate immune system in order to buy time for the adaptive immune system to learn about the threat, ramp up against the invaders and neutralize the infection.

Our immune system is the best weapon we have to root out the source of most illness. While not perfect, it's been successful enough to allow our species to survive in a world of things that want to kill us.

While I would never discount the great achievements that Western medicine has given overall to human health, if we spent half as much money and time trying to invent a better placebo—or, maybe more accurately, better ways to train our immune system to protect our bodies—we'd likely discover entirely new ways to treat disease. This is, of course, where it's beneficial to consider the relationship between the environment and human physiology as a wedge to help control and strengthen the immune system itself.

...

A few years ago, I took a fellowship at the University of Colorado Boulder that gave me the opportunity to audit any class in the institution. I sat in on courses on astronomy, abnormal psychology, creative writing and an immunology class designed for medical students. Over the course of the semester, two things stuck with me.

First was the discussion of autoimmune diseases—the sorts of conditions where the immune system turns against the body that it's supposed to protect. Such conditions are some of the hardest for the medical community to treat, and are growing faster in the first world than they are in the third. The professor stood at his lectern and noted that all autoimmune illnesses conform to a similar pattern. They all start with an insult to the body's sense of homeostasis. That insult could be a virus, bacterial infection, splinter, transplant organ, whole-body hypothermia, fever or allergen that triggers an immune response, and, for reasons we barely understand, that immune response never turns off. The insult is a negative wedge—an environmental intrusion that interrupts our homeostatic feedback loops. Long after the insult is over, various immune cells continue their fight and, instead of going dormant, start attacking the body—apparently confused into thinking that the threat isn't around anymore. In rheumatoid arthritis, the immune system eats the connective tissue in joints. In Crohn's disease, it's the lining of the intestines, while multiple sclerosis consumes the mylar sheath along our nerves. Lupus triggers inflammation throughout the body. The list goes on, but the concept remains the same: The immune system is out of control.

There's a parallel here to anxiety. Think back to Feinstein's lab, where he explains anxiety as a feedback loop that interprets every environmental signal as a reason to go into fight or flight. Chronic anxiety redefines what "normal" means, so that everything is a threat. The new normal was called allostasis.

In this way, auto-immune illnesses share a trait with cancer. Cancer is essentially the uncontrolled growth and replication of cells until it overwhelms the host.[9] In both cases, the body fails to issue an off-signal to a process that is usually beneficial.

My professor's interest in immunology probably stemmed in part from his own condition. A victim of *alopecia areata,* his immune system took issue with the tiny cells in his skin that sprout hair and destroyed them. Without follicles, he has no body hair at all. As the class proceeded through the semester, he delved into the mechanics of the myriad of ways that the body attacks itself. He dissected the role of cellular receptors, hormone releases and transcription factors until the class had a molecular map of the immune system. The details were fascinating—all these cascading effects in the body that kept it attacking itself—but one day when I asked him what *caused* autoimmune illnesses in the first place, he just stared blankly at the class for a second.

Then he shrugged.

---

[9] Autoimmune illnesses and cancer share other similarities. They both seem to arise out of environmental mismatches. Citing the work of Yale immunobiologist Ruslan Medzhitov, Siddhartha Mukherjee wrote in the *New Yorker* that cancer is best understood by dissecting cellular environments and inter-cell relationships. He writes: "What Medzhitov calls 'new rules of tissue engagement' may help us understand why so many people who are exposed to a disease don't end up getting it. Medzhitov believes that all our tissues have 'established rules by which cells form engagements and alliances with other cells.'" Physiology is the product of these relationships. So consider our internal-denominator problem. There are tens of trillions of cells in a human body; a large fraction of them are dividing, almost always imperfectly. There's no reason to think there's a supply-side shortage of potential cancer cells, even in perfectly healthy people. Medzhitov's point is that cancer cells produce cancer—they get established and grow—only when they manage to form alliances with normal cells. And there are two sides (at least) to any such relationship.

"It's got to be some sort of environmental factor," he said. Then he returned to examining the specific role of a chemical that facilitates how two cells locked together and exchanged information.

The response was troubling to me. Almost myopic. Locating the cause of a condition seems at least as important as understanding the chemical process that perpetuates the illness. It's as if immunology is so focused on looking inward to the body that it forgot that the body lives in an environment. Why not try to treat autoimmune illnesses in the same way that we do anxiety—by interrupting external feedback loops and allowing the body to return to its original baseline? Just because autoimmune illness takes place in the body doesn't mean that's where the conditions start. If we can find the right way to interrupt the cycle, then we will have found our wedge. In a perfect world, we might even discover ways to treat some autoimmune illnesses just by manipulating the environment around us and eschew drugs altogether.

My second realization came a few weeks later, when the projector above my professor's head illuminated the amorphous image of one specific immune cell called a macrophage. The macrophage derives its name from ancient Greek and translates, literally, as "big eater." It's a special type of white blood cell that wanders through the bloodstream, seeking out harmful bacteria and then gobbling them up. The professor screened a video of a live macrophage under a microscope. It oozed along the glass slide poking and prodding the other cells in its vicinity. It touched one red blood cell, paused, and then examined a platelet, both to no great effect. Then it came across a tiny bean-shaped bacteria, and something about the blob changed. Once it sensed the foreign intruder, it sprang into action and brought its elastic walls around the bean, absorbing it in a matter of seconds.

To my eyes, it looked like the macrophage was hunting. It sensed the environment around it and then decided what was dinner and what wasn't. The professor looked up at the giant killer cell above him and noted that macrophages and amoeba look almost identical.

He went on to note that the only obvious difference between them from a morphological perspective is that the macrophage comes from our own DNA while amoeba live out in the world on their own.[10] This statement stunned me. Why would a part of our body look and act like something that evolved outside of it? When I dug into that question in the secondary literature, it got even weirder; some evolutionary biologists argue that the amoeba and the macrophage share a common ancestor. Several articles from across the research spectrum note that bacteria that interact with amoeba in the wild learn ways to effectively combat macrophages in the human body. Other papers suggest that macrophages came into existence in the first place through ancient gene transfers. Indeed, this isn't as strange as it sounds: lots of other life forms have participated in building our immune systems. A 2016 paper in *Science* magazine by computational biologist Edward Chuong showed that ancient viral DNA makes up about 8% of our total DNA, and several genes we inherited from viruses actually regulate our innate immune system. Whatever the mechanism, macrophages and amoeba are eerily similar.

If you hold these two thoughts in your head at the same time—first, that the environment triggers autoimmune illnesses, and second, the physical resemblance between our immune cells and ones in the wild—it's reasonable to conceive of the immune system not as a component of our bodies, but rather as an independent entity for which our bodies are just environments. That is to say, when attempting to understand the healing power of the placebo effect, it's important to understand the subjective world of the immune system. If we treat autoimmune conditions as a type of bodily anxiety instead of a broken link in a chemical chain, we might have more success with our treatments—or at least another avenue to explore.

By this point, I've written a lot about how humans are part of a great superorganism of life on the planet and that our actions

---

[10] "Morphology" is just a fancy word for the form and structure that a living thing takes. Morphologically identical animals look identical even if they come from different evolutionary lines.

contribute to an immeasurably larger whole of the biosphere. The sum total of all human actions creates larger patterns of which we are only dimly aware. In other words, the whole is greater than the sum of the parts.

The same perspective holds when we look downward into the smallest parts of our physiology. The macrophage has no idea what is happening to the human it's part of, but it has the ability to sense and interact with its immediate environment. When a bacterium enters into its territory, the macrophage knows how to neutralize the threat. In this way, even though it doesn't know what's happening to you as a person, it still interacts with the outside world. When the macrophage neutralizes the bacterium, it fulfills its evolutionary and ecological role.

Throughout our evolution, humans have always been exposed to a certain number of pathogens, and the macrophage always had a certain amount of work to do. Let's use a metaphor: Think of the macrophage—and, for that matter, the entire diverse assembly of immune cells—as a pack of friendly wolves patrolling the area inside our skin, attacking the things that might hurt us. What happens when those wolves no longer have regular prey? They go stir-crazy. They get bored. And they might turn on themselves. While macrophages pull nutrients from the bloodstream for survival, their entire evolutionary purpose is to hunt and kill invaders. They don't have secondary jobs. Once they run out of prey, the macrophages (and for that matter, other immune cells) sometimes continue the fight, and the immune system turns on itself.

This is the clutch of what evolutionary biologists call the *hygiene hypothesis*. According to this hypothesis, the reason autoimmune illnesses are more common in the first world than in the third is because our efforts to clean every surface and eradicate germs from the environment have altered our internal microbial environments. But when we sterilized the places we lived, we never took into account how our own bodies might react. We never considered how the ecology we influence outside of our bodies reflects on what happens inside us. Our immune systems don't face the constant battle that they evolved to fight and don't respond to the body's signals to end their watch.

The immune system isn't a mindless machine. It has a sort of intelligence all its own. Macrophages and other immune cells don't just respond to bacterial and viral threats; they also bathe in the wash of chemicals—hormones, neurotransmitters and everything else—that courses through the various channels of our body. Just like a human, they need to monitor their environment to survive. And just like a human brain, the immune system uses a similar set of neurotransmitters to reinforce their behavior.

Take, for example, dopamine. It's one of the most important neurotransmitters for human cognition, and the foundation of any feelings that we have for joy or reward. When you feel excited and euphoric, dopamine is the reason for the buzz. The bliss that comes with cocaine and gambling comes back to dopamine. So does any sense of accomplishment that you might feel from learning a new skill. Dopamine is such a powerful reinforcer that not only can it change your personality, but high levels of it can actually hijack your behavior.

For example, patients with Parkinson's almost always have critically low levels of dopamine in their system, which results in their muscles no longer working correctly. In order to counter those deleterious effects, doctors prescribe drug cocktails that ramp up dopamine production to keep their systems working. However, the practice comes with important risks. In 2006, a research team in Scotland discovered that these dopamine-enhanced patients had a radically increased likelihood of developing pathological gambling problems. The emotional and neurological rewards they received when they hit jackpots reinforced addictive tendencies and altered their consciousness.

And it turns out that immune cells also need dopamine.

Generations of immunologists already knew that the immune system could learn to defeat different infections and then store that information as a blueprint to combat future infections. But the addition of neurotransmitters into the picture gives insight into the reward system that motivated immune cells to learn and evolve. In 2017, the journal *Nature* published groundbreaking research that showed B-cells, the immune cells responsible for producing antibodies, take up, release and respond to most neurotransmitters, including adrenaline, noradrenaline and dopamine. T-cells (specialized killers of the immune system) produce dopamine in part to assist and teach other immune cells to select targets once they've learned to kill them. These are all the same neurotransmitters that neuroscientists identify in the brain that underpin human cognition and behavior. You wouldn't be conscious without them.

So if the immune system uses the same chemical hardware that creates feelings in our brains and influences our behavior in the world, then how much of a stretch is it to say that our immune system is conscious? What if instead of assuming that the immune system is just a machine, we give it a chance to have a semblance of cognition? Obviously the immune system can't have the sort of complex emotions or thoughts that you or I experience, but even a shard of that subjectivity is powerful.

It doesn't stop with dopamine. Immune cells also take up and respond to adrenaline—the signpost of the sympathetic nervous system and the very hormone that gets a person ready to fight or run from an external threat. When we bathe our insides with adrenaline, we also bathe the immune system, making a pretty clear chemical connection between the mammalian stress response and how some immune systems go haywire in the modern world. Threats in the ancient past almost always required some sort of physical exertion—fighting or fleeing—that provided a physical outlet for the energy boost. But when we release copious amounts of adrenaline into our bodies today and just sit and try to think our way out of a problem, that extra energy boost has nowhere to go. Stress needs a physical counterpart.

Together, this all at least partially explains how people who learn to control their stress response in ice water and hold their breath for long periods of time can show near-miraculous reversion of Crohn's disease, accelerated healing, remission of rheumatoid arthritis and management of Parkinson's symptoms. It also explains my own experience with the sudden disappearance of canker sores. These environmental triggers can pacify and redirect the responses of the sympathetic nervous system. And so by altering the environment, practitioners learned a back door to directly communicating with the immune system. In other words, if the immune system is a pack of wolves attacking the body's invaders, and maybe even *motivated* by the sympathetic nervous system, then managing physical stress and doing breathwork gives those wolves chew toys.

That's the placebo effect in action. There's no medical intervention that a doctor might recognize, but the therapies work by utilizing the body's own in-built healing mechanisms. Another way to look at it is that the placebo effect is what happens when the different levels of our Russian-doll consciousness synchronize together, so that the distinctions between individual and environment all react appropriately to their environmental position. In this way, the placebo effect isn't so much about an individual body finding its innate healing power as it is about experiencing flow between different layers.

To be clear, this interpretation of the immune system is not going to endear me to the medical mainstream. The standard view of the immune system is that it is a sophisticated machine that operates on well-established—purely mechanical—principles. My professor would say that macrophages aren't *hunting*, but that the chemoreceptors on their skin are mechanically detecting cytokines on bacterial cell walls and responding according to an unvarying program. Suggesting that the immune system has some level of subjectivity, or its own independent consciousness, goes against everything in medical textbooks. Following me any further is at least a tacit acknowledgement that the medical world might need a paradigm shift. Then again, it's a paradigm shift that has been a long time coming.

...

A little over a century ago, an Estonian-born philosopher named Jakob von Uexküll coined the term *umwelt* to make sense of consciousness in the animal kingdom. Translated as "self-world" or "environment," umwelt is the way that an organism's senses frame its experience. Using umwelt means putting yourself in that organism's shoes (or paws, flagella or tentacles, if you prefer). Every living creature has an umwelt of its own based on how it senses the environment. Perceiving that umwelt requires a level of empathy usually absent in hard sciences.

For instance, I have a small gray tiger-striped cat named Lambert who spends an inordinate amount of time meowing at my feet, chasing bugs and napping on my sofa. While we both inhabit the same space, we have radically different assessments of what's happening around us. He sees the world from about a foot off the ground but can alight on the roof of my house in three small leaps, showing that he can think about vertical space more dynamically than I ever would. He's aware of a million different scents and markings from other animals that I can't detect. He knows his name; that's the sum of his English abilities. Even so, he seems to know if I'm happy or sad. His purrs rumble through his body when he's happy and comfort him when he's sick. These are just a few parts of Lambert's umwelt.

Von Uexküll applied the concept to try to understand how insects saw the world. He writes, "Take for instance the eyeless tick who is directed to [her] watchtower by a general photosensitivity to her skin, the approaching prey is revealed to the deaf highway-woman by her sense of smell. The odor of butyric acid that emanates from the skin glands of all mammals acts on the tick as a signal to leave her watchtower and hurl herself downwards." And thus the tick had motivation. But why stop there? Why not go further down the microscopic ladder into the tiny cells that make up our immune system? This is the sort of thinking you need to use to start contemplating the Wedge for the Russian dolls inside of you. Instead of thinking about how *you* feel the environment around you, instead consider how your actions change the ecosystem inside your skin.

If you want to talk with a macrophage, you first need to think like one. Of course, this offers more than a few challenges. While I think a macrophage has some semblance of consciousness and subjectivity, it has such a minute form of it that human words could never do it justice. We do know that it (and every other semi-autonomous cell) senses and responds to its environment. There are baths of neurotransmitters and hormones, changes in blood pressure, and maybe even sounds that vibrate through the body from the outside world.

The environment that we as humans inhabit, the world that influences our actions, thoughts and stress levels, translates into chemical signals that make up the umwelt of the immune system. These chemical and physical signals are the immune systems' lens to what's happening outside the skin. I like to think of our bodies as jumbles of concentric and constantly interacting bubbles, where each bubble is an umwelt of another subjective experience: The skin senses the environment, the muscles sense the skin and brain, the gut senses food, and bacteria in the gut break that food down and release energy and nutrients that are resources for the body to use. Somehow all these different parts form the great mass of interactions for a single animal. Humans are superorganisms.

The trillions of cells that make up our bodies are an ecosystem regulated by complex relationships and innumerable interactions. While it may never be possible to reductively compute every single connection, we can understand the overall tone based on whether or not the system is in equilibrium. When an ecosystem functions well, it's *homeostasis*; if it's in decline or in the midst of unsustainable growth (as with cancer), then it's heading into trouble. The system could end up in a state of constant vigilance and, to use Feinstein's term, become allostatic and never return to normal.

In the modern world, real life-threatening events are few and far between. Instead, we use our sympathetic nervous system to tackle mundane challenges.

There's almost no chance that I'll confront a dangerous animal any time in the next few months. Instead, it is far more likely that I fret over my rising health insurance premiums, worry about taxes or burn through an all-nighter to meet some deadline or another. I'm stressing against obstacles in a remote future. These sorts of existential threats have no biological precedent. I deal with stress by mashing away at a keyboard or quietly strategizing in my mind. There's no physical output to match.

Now, look at this from the perspective of the macrophage and B-cells in my bloodstream. When my credit card company calls and tells me that someone in Nigeria has just charged a couple thousand dollars to my account, the cells receive that message as a bath of adrenaline. They're being primed to fight, but there is no fight to be had—no person to punch or lion to run from. They're confused. It's no wonder that stress leads to illness: This type of stress is an evolutionary mismatch.

However, if I match those same stress sensations to actual physical stresses, then my immune system would have something to do. The wolves would have their chew toy.

The Wedge has shown me that it's possible to reconcile the way that our external environment affects our internal one. We can use our sensations of the stresses of the world to consciously send signals to the unconscious parts of our bodies.

But I'm also a realist. Even though many medical conditions we suffer from today come from evolutionary mismatches, few humans alive today will actually return to an ancestral lifestyle that gives us exactly the right external inputs to harmonize our internal ecosystems. Indeed, if we traveled back in time a few thousand years, we'd probably agree that our ancestors didn't have it half as good as we have it now. And for all the failings of Western medicine, it offers evolutionarily unthinkable powers to treat acute illnesses. That doesn't mean that we can't at least try to be mindful of the sort of signals that we are sending our bodies and try to develop a more robust concept of human health.

Broadly speaking, working with the immune system and our inner worlds means paying more attention to the bounty of sensations that are available to us. This includes the five main senses—sight, smell, touch, taste and sound—but also the interoceptive sense that we develop when we quiet the outside world and look inward.

In the face of an illness, the first thing we should ask is what practices make us feel better. What things make us feel worse? These are basic tenets of what Harvard psychologist Ellen Langer calls "mindful health."

Practicing mindful medicine doesn't require a totally new worldview. It's safe to say that every patient suffering from a chronic disease that's resistant to medical intervention is already practicing mindful medicine. Let's say you suffer from irritable bowel syndrome, or chronic back pain. Both conditions are notoriously difficult to treat, and you can expect numerous unhelpful doctor visits on your path to recovery.

When a treatment doesn't solve the problem, you head to another doctor and try a new therapy. That search mandates a certain level of attention to your body. This is a version of the interoception that Feinstein tries to train with float tanks. Eventually, by modulating different inputs, you figure out what makes you feel better. This is the human process. It's just as much a part of the scientific method as it is the wellness revolution. In many cases, the recovery has as much to do with the healing power of the body itself as it does with the treatment. Recovery might well be little more than regression to the mean: the mighty placebo effect.

In previous chapters, I used the concept of "flow" to describe how the sum total of individual actions can form a system far greater and more complex than the sum of its parts. I also note that flow states use the sensory information available to a person to choose the most optimal physical response to a given action. To my mind, equilibrium in a healthy body means that all of the pieces that make us up are in a state of flow. The inside world and outside world communicate harmoniously and tune the entire physical system. This is what homeostasis should be: communication through flow.

It's the same skill of cooperation that allows me to throw kettlebells with a partner and feel a connection to something greater than myself. Working with the placebo effect means finding flow with your interior self—using careful application of stress and recovery so that all the parts work together. The Wedge works on all those levels.

In many indigenous traditions around the world, the concept of "medicine" doesn't depend on a chemical agent or physical intervention. For those traditions, medicine is often a much broader concept that incorporates anything that changes our bodies or perception of the world for the better. Sensory stimuli, environmental variability, meditation and even prayer all have a role to play in generating and maintaining human health. These all correspond to the key frames of the Wedge: stress, sensation and orientation.

Whatever the placebo effect actually is, the medical community agrees that its results are subjective. And while that subjectivity is often cast as its most critical weakness, there's a case to be made that subjectivity is also its greatest strength.

Of course, none of this is to say that medical interventions and drugs prescribed by Western doctors are bad, or even that they are wrong. Nothing in this book should make you eschew your doctor's prescription for a sauna. What I *am* saying, though, is that Western medicine often loses the forest for the trees and often lacks the vision to see the larger picture. We should try to understand any chemical we take from the perspective of the superorganism and from the umwelt of our insides.

As we will see, sometimes a drug that causes a chemical change in our sensory system can be exactly the type of psychological stress we need to wedge a deeper look into our own biology.

Empathy is a tool for building people into groups, for allowing us to function as more than self-obsessed individuals.

—Neil Gaiman

CHAPTER 10

TRUTH SERUM

Two board-certified relationship counselors are trying to get a handle on whether or not my wife and I can be trusted. They look skeptical: There's a cocked eyebrow on the man, and the woman has her arms crossed across her belly in what might be a defensive posture. We've shown up at this office to ask them to break the law and guide us through a chemically assisted couples therapy session. We believe that a drug best known for fueling night-long raves in the electronic dance scene might have a more legitimate use in a clinical setting. MDMA—or methylenedioxymethamphetamine, for people who prefer chemical tongue twisters—also has a street name: ecstasy.

Laura and I don't fight often; we are both generally game for working through the issues in our relationship. Like all couples, we have some hangups and tension points that are easier to avoid than talk about directly. We are so close that we can finish each other's sentences, and sometimes we just know what the other one is thinking. In other words, at times we work like a single unit. So the reason we're here is to see if we can treat the space between us as a point to work on the Wedge and take a little control over the unconscious bonds between us.

It has taken us a long while to get to this meeting. For the last month, we've exchanged messages on encrypted applications as we delicately went over risks and rewards. On the one hand, these counselors could lose their license to practice or even face jail time. On the other hand, they have a chance to examine a revolutionary new type of therapy that will probably be legal—or even standard—in America pretty soon. In order to protect their careers, the two clinicians use pseudonyms: Dr. Clark Kent and Dr. Lois Lane.

Dr. Kent's bookshelf brims with dense-looking psychological manuals and pop-culture-inspired self-help bestsellers. One shelf nods to his expertise in helping couples get over infidelity, with one title asking what happens *When People Cheat*, while a second shelf caters to open relationships, sex and bondage: *The Ethical Slut*, *The Multi-Orgasmic Woman*, and *She Comes First*. It's quite a reading list. There's also a wall for diplomas, and another dedicated to non-threatening floral paintings.

We're not here today to actually take the drug; this is a preliminary meeting for Kent and Lane to go over ground rules and figure out if we're good candidates for MDMA-assisted therapy. They also want us to sign a multi-page agreement that acknowledges the risks we know we're taking, and asks us to commit to further psychiatric treatment if we have trouble integrating the session when it's over. The goal is to make our relationship stronger, with the assumption that the chemical will facilitate our ability to empathize with each other's problems during the session.

"One session with MDMA has the potential to replicate months, if not years, of in-person therapy. It confers the miraculous ability to completely deflate a person's fight-or-flight response, so that while you can still feel sadness or anger, all sense of defensiveness evaporates. It lets a person empathize with their partner without any boundaries," says Dr. Kent. This is a sort of therapy Holy Grail.

MDMA floods your senses with chemically induced euphoria. Taken recreationally, it might just be a good time, but under the guidance of a therapist where the goal is healing, MDMA can change lives. There's no need to dance around stressful topics. When two people take it at the same time, the shared bliss becomes a wedge that operates at the level of their interpersonal relationship. The therapist only needs to guide their conversation to what would ordinarily be pain points and watch the patients work through their issues.

"It's like the therapy version of autopilot," he says.

The words "mind-altering drug" don't sit well on the American palate. When a person seeks out an altered state, we reflexively think of it as a moral failing. But what happens when feelings and sensations *are* the goal? In cases where altering the external stress is impossible, our mindsets can get reflexively fixed, and sometimes the only place to insert a wedge is in the sensory pathways themselves. This is the promise of MDMA: The side effects are the point. We can feel those side effects as a wedge into the unspoken patterns that reinforce relationships. MDMA is an *empathogen*, meaning that it's a chemical that creates feelings of empathy and connection.

This is somewhat similar to what we just saw with the curative potential of the placebo effect. When an attentive person carefully calibrates external stress, they can influence the internal environment of their body and guide their immune system to healing. MDMA turns that communication outward when it eliminates emotional reactivity at the personal level. Since they're feeling the same set of sensations, a couple can work together on the level of the issues brewing between them. They gain perspective. It's almost like they're in flow.

Doctors Kent and Lane both tried MDMA recreationally years ago, though neither therapist has ever seen it used in a clinical setting before. Part of the reason they entertained my offer was so they could see for themselves if the clinical promise lives up to the reality.

Like the doctors, this is not my first rodeo with the love drug. I experimented with a few mind-altering substances in my 20s. Once at a flat in Boston, I poured a white powder of crushed ecstasy into tea with three friends and then we danced. We howled barbaric yawps into the alley behind the flat, bore our souls to one another and felt expansive. But I never sought it out again until the year that my wife and I started dating. We holed up in a cabin deep in the California wilderness, took a healthy dose of MDMA, and for five or six hours spoke to each other about our deepest, darkest fears and hopes for what the future could look like. Eventually we found ourselves hugging each other and swaying to the soft sound of snow falling outside. I look at that time as a moment that cemented us as a couple, where the barriers broke down and our words always rang true in each other's hearts. And though it was chemically induced, the sentiments weren't any less real. Ecstasy keeps you lucid. However, as with any drug, the high didn't last. The comedown was hard, especially for Laura, whose hangover was probably intensified because she had been taking an antidepressant, a Selective Serotonin Reuptake Inhibitor, or SSRI—a class of drugs that includes Prozac, Lexapro and Zoloft.

Dr. Lane leans forward and asks us pointedly if either one of us is on an antidepressant now. Since both MDMA and antidepressants modulate serotonin levels, mixing the two can lead to serious drug interactions. This often means it makes hangovers worse, but in some cases it can lead to a dangerous condition called "serotonin syndrome," which, in rare cases, can chemically lock a person's brain chemistry into permanent depression. We tell her that neither of us have taken them for years, and the doctor smiles.

The rule for most drug experiences is that whatever high notes you feel come with an equal and opposite down. The experience follows the delicate balance of a sine wave as the body tries to return to homeostasis. We're all familiar with the hangover that comes after a night of alcoholic bingeing, or perhaps the mental fog aftermath from smoking marijuana. Most people pay for MDMA's heightened state with a few days of mild depression as their bodies restock the depleted neurotransmitters. And though she has been off antidepressants for several years, the memory of the prolonged hangover makes Laura hesitant to try ecstasy again.

In the 1970s, a Jungian psychiatrist named Leo Zeff trained 4,000 therapists to use MDMA in their practices. It was a revolutionary new treatment that saw many early successes, but things fell apart once the drug found its way into the discotheques of New York, L.A. and San Francisco. In 1984, banning MDMA became a cornerstone of Ronald Reagan's War on Drugs, and the chemical was off limits for even clinical research. The ban has only recently begun to thaw. In the last few years, the efforts of do-it-yourself biohackers and podcasters like Joe Rogan, Russell Brand and Tim Ferriss have brought the chemical into the spotlight again. New clinical trials under the rubric of the Multidisciplinary Association of Psychedelic Studies (MAPS) out of UCLA, CU Boulder and Johns Hopkins show that MDMA is useful for treating people with post-traumatic stress disorder. Even more promising, at the time of writing, the Food and Drug Administration has indicated that it might consider taking MDMA off of the restricted-drug list. A change at the government level would open up the floodgates for new research into the drug and clear the way for new uses in clinical settings. Perhaps it's all a sign of a cultural shift that gained traction when the clubbing teens from the '80s and '90s made it to adulthood. Now they're looking for salvation from maladies of middle age using something they discovered in their youth.

By day, Dr. Kent's practice focuses on the imponderable problems that arise between two people in whatever sort of marriage structure they have. Dr. Lane's practice centers mostly on individuals struggling with addiction and anxiety; Dr. Kent wanted her here because she ran a psychedelic integration program in Brooklyn for several years in which patients used mind-altering drugs to explore their inner lives. These mental explorers are chemically interested soul-searchers. Raised on science and psychedelics, many psychonauts look for ways to objectively assess their transformations. After all, simply thinking your life is better because of a mind-altering drug doesn't mean that it actually *is* better. And not all drug-induced realizations are worthwhile. Dr. Lane sees herself as a critical stable foundation in her patients' lives, helping steer them away from more dangerous paths.

She offers that, in her experience, MDMA widens the gap between stimulus and response. Rather than simply reacting to an emotionally charged statement in a therapeutic setting, instead you have a chance to receive the words in the most positive light possible. As long as we're both in the chemical's sway, neither of us will be able to judge each other negatively.

The thought of that much openness is a little unsettling. I wonder what it will be like to suddenly feel so open about my deepest secrets and fears—not just to my wife, but also in front of two counselors whom I've never met before. They've assured me of the sanctity of the doctor-patient covenant, but in an ordinary therapeutic setting, we always have a mental governor that lets us restrict information as we build up trust. MDMA strips away that governor. What will happen when all my secrets come out at once? What judgments secretly lurk in the hearts of therapists? I can't say for sure, but the project means I will just have to trust them.

And finally, our introductory meeting settles on the tricky question of procurement.

Acquiring the drug crosses certain lines that they're just not comfortable with. Dr. Lane says she doesn't have any way to get us any. But she adds that once I do locate a source, I can order chemical tests online that will identify common drug adulterants—from amphetamines to rat poison—that dealers sometimes put into pills to make them stronger or make their supplies stretch a little further.

This is a problem when the wedge between stimulus and response is a chemical and not a technique. With a kettlebell, sauna, ice bath or breathing program, I always have the option to stop the ride and find my bearings. I can jump ship at any time. But once I've taken the drug, there's no way out of the experience except through it. So testing what we're going to put into our bodies makes a lot of sense.

I started making inquiries a few months ago with a friend of mine who "knew a guy" who "gets it straight from the lab." Without any better recommendations than that, I decided to buy 400 milligrams, which eventually arrived in a one-inch-by-one-inch plastic bag with red hearts stenciled across its face. It was as sketchy as it sounds.

The following Sunday morning, I need Laura's steady hand to run an experiment on the unknown powder. The testing kit arrives in a black cloth bag that contains several small eye droppers full of chemical reagents. Back in the 1990s, a company called DanceSafe emerged as a harm-reduction nonprofit that would test the purity of drugs at raves, concerts and parties in the hopes that fewer people would die on the dance floor. The kit is fairly straightforward to operate for anyone who has ever had to test the levels of chlorine and pH of a hot tub or swimming pool. I pour out the contents of the plastic bag onto a dinner plate and place six individual grains in separate piles. When Laura drops a dot of reagent on a grain, the liquid instantly changes color on contact. We match the color to a key that comes with the kit to see if the change indicates something chemically fishy. The contents of the mystery bag passes with flying colors. The bag is 100% pure and unadulterated MDMA. All we have to do now is wait for our appointment.

...

In the next two weeks, Laura and I talk a lot about the plan to hack our minds with an illicit drug. I've never had a bad experience on MDMA and am excited to be able to use it under guidance. I've felt how two people can throw kettlebells to build trust, how a sauna removes depression and how sensory deprivation can help me look inward to my own body. But MDMA promises something even more fascinating: the ability to feel no emotional stress at all. Any neural symbol we form will have to bond with a positive emotion. We will be free of inhibitions, which I assume will only make us closer. Laura chews on that idea and is less sure. Yes, MDMA feels great in the moment, but what about the hangover? And will it really make lasting change, or will the lessons vanish with the euphoria? I'm grateful that she trusts me enough to try so much with me.

And then, before we know it, the day is here, and Kent and Lane arrive at our door. They offer us warm smiles and, after a few pleasantries, ask us once again what we want out of the experience.

"Your intentions matter a great deal in any therapeutic session, but they're even more critical when there's a chemical involved," says Dr. Kent. They remind us that Laura and I are the ones in control and that we're free to leave the room at any time if we want. I mention that it's a little weird to have witnesses to what is likely going to be an intimate moment between Laura and me. Dr. Kent responds with what sounds like stereotypical therapist speak: "Thank you for naming that," he smiles respectfully. He says that if they make us uncomfortable, they're comfortable with waiting outside. "This is supposed to be for you two," confirms Dr. Lane.

Laura and I are nervous. But the therapists exude different energy: They're excited. While they've both sat in on hundreds, if not thousands, of couples therapy sessions over their careers, and both have independently tried MDMA and other psychedelics for personal use, they've never brought those two experiences together. This is going to be their first time using MDMA as a tool for therapy, and I can tell that they're more than simply curious about how it will play out. Could this be the tool they need to save marriages?

We sign the waiver that they gave us earlier and then divvy up the bag of white-ish powder into two unequal clumps. Since I'm larger and have more experience with psychoactive substances, I take what we calculate to be 150 milligrams of MDMA. Laura takes 100. We pour the powder into two mugs of mint tea and drink the brew down while making small talk with our guests.

In some ways, the worst part is the anticipation of what we're going to feel between the time we take the dose and when the feelings actually kick in. We've crossed the Rubicon—the point of no return. We know that MDMA usually takes between 30 and 45 minutes to start working and are trying to pay attention to the first signs of it coming on. *Do shadows look any different? Are Laura's eyes more dilated than usual? Was that joke unusually funny?*

Just as I'm beginning to get concerned nothing is going to happen, Laura stiffens up with a rigid back and puts her hand down on the couch. "Oh. It's coming on now," she says, like she's being pummeled by a wave. A look of sudden seasickness overcomes her face and she gets up and heads to the bathroom. There's a rush of nausea as she begins to lose control. It's hard to say if this is a symptom of the drug or her own anxiety unwinding. After a minute sitting with the doctors, I get up to find her sitting next to the bathtub with her legs out in front of her. She doesn't look like she's going to vomit, but her eyes flit back and forth, slightly unfocused. I ask her if she'd like to lie down, and she answers *yes.*

By now I'm starting to feel something, too. It's not anxiety; it feels amazing, like a silky wave of comfort and peace. I lead Laura to the bedroom, and she lies down on the bed with her arms bolted down next to her. It's as if she's lying down on the sort of backboard that medics use to secure a patient with a neck injury. Her blue eyes dart around the room, and I worry that this might not have been a good idea. What have we gotten ourselves into? I'm at a loss for what to do next until I get the urge to make some sort of physical contact. I reach down to grab her sock-covered right foot and ask if it's okay if I give her a massage. It's warm to the touch. In a matter of seconds I watch her wave of high tension melt away. Her body relaxes as she turns her attention to the rub and lets out a long, audible breath. We look into each other's eyes—both sets of which are dilated into black saucers—and I tell her I love her.

That's when the floodgates open and words start to spill out.

"It's so strange that there are therapists watching us do drugs," she says to me.

"*I know.*" I say. But It's an opening into what would ordinarily be a difficult discussion of the state of our relationship. Every couple, no matter how strong their bond, has habits, routines and verbal short-hands that constrain communication. There are always subjects that we avoid—not necessarily because they might spark an argument, but because we know how that argument might play out. Most people live in a sort of detente, inside carefully mapped-out boundaries that no one wants to cross. But now, here on a bed in the back room of our house, the borders break down and we just start to talk like we haven't since the first days of our relationship—when everything was new and transgressions were overlooked in the excitement of the moment.

On a neurological level, the part of our brains that produces and retains serotonin—the chemical responsible for anxiety, happiness and mood modulation—floods all the synapses in our brain. We've begun to release oxytocin, the chemical that helps two people bond—the very neurotransmitter that floods a mother and child's brain when they first meet, and among lovers just making their feelings known to one another. In these moments on the bed, every chemical in our heads is making us closer, and there is no sense of defensiveness.

It's strange to say this, but the state we're in now is a little related to what it feels like to learn trust while throwing kettlebells. In those exercises, the threat of the bell forces both partners to focus on the threat of injury, and the shared focus puts them both into flow. MDMA tricks our nervous systems into emotional openness that might otherwise feel dangerous. Since the chemical works on our bodies in the same way, it creates a shared emotional environment: chemically induced flow.

The details of what we say are deeply personal and private, but suffice it to say we both bathe in feelings of absolute openness. Eventually I crawl into bed next to her, and the warmth of her body sweeps over me like liquid pleasure. Or perhaps this is the physical sensation of love itself. We stay there like two spoons, me talking into her hair, and her into the air in front of her. We're there long enough that we realize it's a little rude to leave our therapists alone with only a cheese plate for company.

At times the drug makes it too intense to talk. My eyes flit around the room without a lot of control to focus on any one thing. But those peaks only last a few minutes before the intensity settles into a valley of a calmness. We use those interludes as time to speak deeply about our feelings. Our journey out of the room has lasted maybe fifteen or twenty minutes. But when we return to the couch, we are in a stronger place than when we left it.

Dr. Kent and Dr. Lane ask if we're feeling more stable; we say we are and then turn toward one another and lock eyes. Both psychologists scribble in their notepads the same phrase: *The eye contact is amazing.* There is something intense about the eyes of a person on ecstasy. It's not only that the pupils dilate so that the blue of Laura's irises almost vanish into space. It's also that there doesn't seem to be anywhere else to look but at each other. Why would we want to look anywhere else? There's something almost alien to it, and it forces me to remember that for the past few months, even though the relationship feels stable, we've fallen out of the habit of actually looking at one another. When we talk, our minds connect through the sentences and paragraphs we speak, but we've abandoned the visual tether that speaks an entirely other language.

At one point, Dr. Kent asks a question. It's a typical therapist line about how patterns in the past might play out in the future, and as he speaks, we both turn to listen. When we break that focus, my eyes start to search the room again like they're unhinged. It feels like there is a low, annoying flow of electricity in my field of vision. Laura looks anxious. It's not because of the question, but from being pulled out of our concentration on each other.

"Look at me, not them," I say to Laura. The two therapists nod accession, and we lock our eyes back into the comfort of mutual connection. Windows to the soul or not, the way we look at each other is just as powerful as the drug's chemical rush. Our conversation meanders through hard topics: health, the hostile political environment, our relationships with our parents, and whether our previous marriages predict the ultimate demise of what we are building together. We talk about sex. We examine our careers, and how both of us working from home might make us too close sometimes. How, we wonder, do we branch out with friends and family so as not to overload our relationship with too much pressure? The session lasts for about three hours, reaching peaks and crescendos of palpable intimacy, then drifting back to what feels like a normal state. Each peak gets progressively smaller until we are close to where we started.

The conversation flows so naturally that part of me feels that the therapists didn't have enough space to help guide it. When it feels okay to drift my attention away from Laura, I ask them how what they just watched differs from an ordinary couples therapy session.

"I've never seen anything like it," starts Dr. Kent. "It was like the two of you just went through eight months of weekly therapy in just the course of two or three hours," he says.

Dr. Lane nods in agreement, adding, "There are things that you said to one another that I was sure would start an argument. When you started talking about your relationship with your families, I actually cringed inside. I expected a fight. In any other context, someone would snap—anyone would—but you just accepted it and then delved into the roots of the problem. Frankly, this has been amazing," she says.

Most discussions between two people operate on predictably safe scripts. In the same way that we initially form neural symbols with strong stimuli—like cold, heat or exercise—we also encode reactions in relationships based on our emotional state during the first time we experience a conflict or pleasurable moment. We forge reactions to difficult topics at a neurological level and re-access emotions from the past when they come up again. For example, when we see a contrary political view on social media, we generally react according to scripts we've already arranged in our mind. And when those reactions are already ingrained, we miss the opportunity to form new emotional bonds. MDMA breaks that tether and allows for new associations based on the emotional state we're experiencing while on the drug. Done in a safe and responsible context, it allows a person or couple to attach positive emotional values to difficult subjects.

This doesn't mean that you mindlessly accept any new idea as inherently positive on MDMA, but rather that you're able to evaluate new information from the most optimistic perspective possible. Not only that, but the notes that the therapists scribbled on their respective yellow legal pads record that, more than simply listening with empathy, Laura and I automatically started looking for solutions.

Take, for instance, the issue of shared space. Since we work together from home, the way we share space can lead to conflict. As someone who has been diagnosed with attention deficit disorder and dyslexia since childhood, I'm easily distracted. If someone breaks one of those rare moments of focused flow on my work, I can snap without thinking. I can be mean. And rather than continue that pattern, we suggest closing my office door to lessen any tension. This is the sort of realization that might easily come up in a therapy session, of course, but this, and about a dozen other small fixes, appear almost automatically when we process our relationship on the drug. The conversations naturally flow from empathy with the problems we see arising in our relationship to solutions for how to deal with them down the road.

Dr. Kent and Dr. Lane eventually leave, but we make a follow-up appointment with them for the following week, to see how much of the experience turned into practice. For the next few hours, Laura and I ride the wake of the diminishing chemical wave. The high goes away, and in the hours afterward, our feelings balance out into a post-buzz sort of numbness. Rather than succumb to the depression, we decide to go outside on a walk around a lake near our house, with the idea that sensations from the world will help build back whatever neurotransmitter reserves we've burned through. By the next morning, we feel pretty much normal.

...

Over the next few months, we learn how effective a wedge MDMA really was. Things feel smoother between Laura and me. It turns out that the flow afterglow (*afterflow?*) is real. I'm less inclined to myopically snap if she interrupts my work. We have more open communication about our feelings on family matters, and even manage our time with each other with a little more élan. Our sex life improves. We might be 10% happier overall. It's not a complete paradigm shift, but certainly worth the experience.

MDMA is a promising drug for a wide range of therapeutic uses. Currently, clinical trials at the Multidisciplinary Association for Psychedelic Studies won accelerated FDA approval for post-traumatic stress disorder. Depending on how those trials go over the next few years, therapist-assisted MDMA sessions have the potential to become a new standard of care across the country. The chemical's ability to drive a wedge between stimulation and reaction could alter the way that we approach any sort of anxiety disorder or foster bonds between parents and children and husbands and wives. Hell, we might even find a use for it in business negotiations (though one wonders what that might end up looking like).

Of course, there are potential dangers. Most obviously right now is that MDMA-assisted therapy is illegal. Drs. Kent and Lane cloak their identities for good reason. A well-placed tip to the police or regulatory board could ruin their careers, and patients could end up in jail just for seeking treatment. The fact that it's illegal also means that quality control is a major problem. It can be difficult to know if any chemical you purchase off the street is legitimate. While some countries like the Netherlands test drugs for free at harm-reduction programs, similar services in the United States are rare. Outside the legal ramifications, MDMA is probably not for everyone. Underlying mental disorders, including excessive paranoia or schizophrenia, could make the condition worse. And since MDMA releases serotonin into the neural pathways, people on some antidepressants could find themselves in actual physical danger.

Some people might not be great candidates for this sort of therapy for other reasons. In some ways, traditional therapy sessions offer a predictable slow pace where the relationship between therapist and patient follows a predictable rhythm. MDMA's speed is also its liability. Imagine a case of a person who was sexually assaulted as a child and who had never told anyone about the experience before because of the deep shame that it brings up. While an MDMA session could provide an environment where they feel safe talking about those circumstances for the first time, what happens after the session is over? They might think back to the session as painful instead of as a path to recovery. In those cases, aftercare is critical. Alternately, if two people use MDMA together and one of them has a manipulative personality in general, information that comes up during the session could be used against the partner in the future. In other words, it's a good idea to assess how it all could play out with a therapist before you actually try the drug itself.

On a more profound level, people thinking of trying MDMA need to realize that it's not a one-stop shop or magic pill that makes all of a person's problems go away. While the chemical provides an environment for productive conversations, patients need to provide the presence of mind to make the best of their time. Intentions matter, as does taking the session seriously, with a clear desire for a positive outcome.

As an intervention into the sensory pathways, MDMA is a more radical iteration of the Wedge than I've explored before. Chemicals can change the way that our minds experience the world and help us sink deeper into the unconscious psychology that forms our behavior. MDMA creates very specific chemical changes in the brain, but it only works as a medicine when the environment reinforces a positive experience. So when thinking about the Wedge while using a chemical, it's important to control all sides of the experience; the stable and supportive environment impacts your chemically altered sensory pathways in order to create an orientation that is more positive. Together this sort of treatment forms new neurological connections that will influence your life down the road.

But there are other chemical interventions that don't just alter sensory experiences; they actually create entirely new perceptions of the environment whole cloth. Where MDMA is an empathogen—meaning it creates feelings of empathy—other classes of psychedelics create neural environments that radically alter your perception of the outside world. Used recklessly, they are no doubt dangerous, but in the hands of experienced practitioners and guides, the new chemical environments and the experiences that come with them can get to the source of ingrained psychological and physical problems in ways that no other class of medication can.

For the past year, I've built up a skill set with the Wedge that has allowed me to re-evaluate my relationship with my environment and stress in general. I've seen how pushing myself to a physical threshold defines who I am. I've also learned to look inward. I've played with fear, focus and flow. Now I feel ready to take on a new challenge that pushes me into entirely new terrain. Instead of using one stress at a time, I want to dance with an entire world of stimulus and reaction all at once. I want to use chemicals, sound, sensory deprivation, indigenous medicine, fear and breathing in a grand ritual where the barriers of consciousness will begin to break down.

An indigenous shamanic medicine tradition from the Amazon jungle uses a psychedelic ritual brew that facilitates feelings of connection to nature and even god itself. The potion is part of a class of drugs called *entheogens*, meaning they create transcendent experiences. But the ritual of taking the medicine also incorporates all frames of the Wedge at once—with a novel environment, challenging emotional terrain, music, and a shamanic guide through the entire experience—to rebuild the human psyche from the ground up.

*Under certain circumstances one is actually better
informed concerning the real world if one has taken a drug
than if one has not.*

—Terence McKenna, *Food of the Gods*

CHAPTER 11

STRANGE BREW

The lush and verdant jungle outside the plane window extends forever. A dark brown river winds its way through the canopy with no sign of houses, roads or civilization in any direction. I reek of eighteen hours of international travel and looming dread and excitement of a journey into the unknown. And then there it is, emerging with no warning: a sprawling and disorganized maze of a city belching black clouds of smog into the greenery. We touch down in Iquitos, a city born during the colonial rubber boom, as a staging point for expeditions and a necessary supply depot for the plantations and missionaries who transformed the Amazon a hundred years earlier. It holds the distinction of being the only landlocked city in the world that is completely cut off from terrestrial transportation networks. The only way to get here is by plane or boat. No roads or railways connect it to the rest of Peru. It's an island surrounded by a sea of jungle. Or, less charitably, Iquitos is a tumor on the lungs of the world—a cesspool of third-world squalor that mars the most diverse ecological habitat on Earth. Every year its borders expand a little farther into virgin territory.

From the airport, my photographer, Jake Holschuh, and I pile into a compact taxi stuffed with five or six other people. The radio blares Spanish ballads. Jake draws a long drag on a cigarette. Someone in the front seat shares a sweaty plastic bag of sliced guava and chili. I pick at the fruit. My head bobs along with the ruts in the road as I fight to stay awake. Part of my brain is a little concerned about my level of fatigue. It's been a long day already, and I know it's going to be an even longer night. In about an hour, we arrive at a white iron gate with the words "Trocha Amazonica" spelled out above it.

I peer into the property to glimpse a woman in a white translucent dress and a wild mane of black hair walking toward us from behind a tin-roofed hut. She beams a wide grin and chirps out a greeting in her Peruvian accent. "Es-cott, yes? We have been waiting for you." She spills over with musical optimism and excitement, like an old friend, even though we've never met before. There's a crackle in the energy about her; she feels alive and expansive. If I were sailing on a small boat in a gale, she'd be a spit of solid land that I would head toward. Equal parts safety and ferocity, in her presence I feel as if I've come home.

I feel safe. And I'm glad, given what I'm here to do. Luz Maria Ampuero—or Luzma, as she prefers—will be by my side for what I'm guessing will be one of the most difficult journeys of my life. I'm here to imbibe the traditional medicine and hallucinogenic brew known as ayahuasca.

I've waited a long time to try ayahuasca. I first read about the spiritual brews used by Amazonian shamans in graduate school, where pasty-skinned authors explained the strange effects of plant medicine. I'd pored over travelogues from the fringes of the psychedelic revolution, where sunburned pioneers traveled to Peru, Colombia and Brazil on the hunt for chemical-induced transcendence. They drank bitter concoctions and vomited. They had visions of other worlds. They met ancestors and aliens. They watched as jaguars devoured their bodies. And then reported meetings with dark gods. They spoke of reliving trauma from their pasts and coming out stronger for it. The stories were as powerful as they were strange.

And I'm not the only one fascinated by the tales. Today, ayahuasca holds a special place in the minds of many people. Spiritual adventurists believe the psychoactive potion evokes spiritual transcendence and destroys addictions. They claim an ayahuasca journey is capable of reorienting our perspective to the world. It's the go-to transformative drug of the moment. And while it's definitely not mainstream, it's not on the fringes anymore, either. The medicine gets name-checked in celebrity memoirs, in the pages of top-tier scientific literature and on experiential podcasts all over the world. The hope of ayahuasca is simple enough to explain: If the lifestyle that has kept us indoors and away from nature has failed, then maybe the best way to connect with our ancestral roots is through one of the few remaining unbroken rituals to our pre-modern past. Ayahuasca fills the bill not only because it's so unfamiliar, but because the experiences it delivers are so often life-changing.

But since I've never experienced ayahuasca for myself, these stories ring empty; they're only words. I'm here because I think it could be a wedge into my own psyche. I suspect ayahuasca has much to teach me about hacking our nervous systems and living a bolder life. Time and again, I've found ways to use environmental stressors and sensory pathways as wedges that orient my mind in new ways to the outside world. I've seen how altering any one of those frames creates corresponding changes in my underlying biology. Ayahuasca offers something even more radical. It isn't just a chemical intervention, but a fully immersive experience. I feel as if all my Wedge exploration has led up to this moment. I anticipate that this ceremony will pack it all into one. It will have the ritualistic elements of the Arctic sauna, the sensorial muting of a float tank, the altered chemical channels of MDMA, the anticipation of a potentially dangerous experience, and a healing pathway far outside the bounds of the medical mainstream. This trip is the culmination of years of striving to isolate different interfaces with my nervous system. If each of those frames were notes

I was learning in a song of my own body, this ceremony is a symphony. This is big.

Wedges will be everywhere—from the change from first-world comforts to third-world spartanism, the reduction of my ordinary sensory palate in favor of the sounds of the jungle, the fear of the unknown, the rhythmic drumming of a shaman's drum, the ícaros he sings to invoke spirits, and my own response to a hallucinogenic compound in a ritual brew. If the training I've done with the Wim Hof Method, breathing, kettlebells and heat was learning to walk, ayahuasca means learning to run. It's not a path for everyone. Hell, I wasn't even sure this drug was on my path.

That is, not until I had a dream.

The dream came about six months ago. I'd been reading and researching ayahuasca, and along the way contacted everyone I knew who had ever been to Peru. I found resorts and shamans who advertised their authentic rituals online. They all said that *they* were the real thing and other shamans were suspect. Nothing felt quite right. In June, I reached out to Javier Regueiro, who'd written a book called *Ayahuasca.* He gave me Luzma's email, and I wrote to her immediately. But all I got in return was an auto response saying she was "in the jungle" and too hard to reach. Months passed, and I gave up on her.

Then, one cold winter night, I fell asleep in a shabby hotel room in a Colorado mountain town after giving a lecture on the Wedge. While unconscious, this dream arrived:

I was in a cabin surrounded by lush and verdant jungle. A beautiful, dark-haired woman stood at a table in the kitchen with a knife in her hand. Later I'd realize that this was the same woman that I thought I met during my vision while I was pushing the limits of breathwork in Elee's class earlier that year. Now she was cutting something brown and plant-like. I watched as she put the cuttings into a black sticky liquid. Then she looked up from her work and locked her dark brown eyes with mine. She invited me to drink ayahuasca with her. But before we could begin, she told me that I first had to prepare my body for the medicine. I'd have to change my diet and eat only the blandest foods. So I ate a potato. And she smiled. She said I was ready.

Then I woke up and looked at the ceiling for a minute, the dream still strong in my mind. I thought the woman in the dream was the same woman my unconscious had conjured during Elee's Wim Hof workshop in Denver. Then I rolled over and grabbed my phone off the hotel nightstand. I had one email. It had come in at 6:21 a.m., roughly the same time that I would have been dreaming. It was from Luzma, saying she thought I should come visit her teacher Tony in February. This was the first time that I'd ever heard from her. If I'd been waiting for a sign for the right person to take ayahuasca with, this was a billboard of neon lights. I marked my calendar and started making plans for a trip south.

That, in short, is how I ended up at the Trocha Amazonica, finally face to face with Luzma—the dark-haired woman of my subconscious. She skips over to me and gives me a hug.

"I'm es-sorry if I'm es-melling. I'm working with a new plant, and Tony won't let me use soap while on *dieta,*" she says, continuing her smirk and casting a lighthearted scowl back over her shoulder to, presumably, the place where her teacher holds court.

In the context of these ceremonies, dieta—Spanish for diet—is the tool that shamans and imbibers of traditional medicine use to heighten the effects of the ritual. Similar to the magic of the potato hack or flotation tanks, dietas involve cutting out stimuli from the outside world so that that the sensations that the medicine invokes in the body are more apparent. The more bland the dieta, the more powerful the experiences should be, and the easier to tune into subtle sensations. For people taking the ayahuasca brew, this means cutting out pork, salt, oils and other heavy foods and having a mostly bland diet of vegetables, fruits, fish and chicken.

For Luzma, working with other plants means even more restrictions. This month she's come to the Trocha Amazonica to learn about a secret plant—it's not ayahuasca, and she asked me not to name it—that will teach her a new way to heal people. Her dieta is even more restrictive; she tells me that she's only taking one meal a day, has cut out all chemicals that might touch her skin, and will bathe only by using mud from a swimming hole near the shacks where we are staying.

I think of this dream as Jake and I sling our bags over our shoulders and follow Luzma up a small hill to a cluster of tin-roofed shacks. She points to one with a handful of stray cats and chickens wandering in front of it. "That's where Tony lives. It's also the kitchen," she says. I notice that there aren't any lights on anywhere. No radio. My cell phone fruitlessly pings the ether for service.

"We really don't have nothing," she chirps happily when she sees me finger my phone. For the next week, I'll be here, and only here—blessedly extracted from the 24-hour news cycle, work emails, contact with agents, editors and incessant social-media interruptions that fracture my attention at home. The only thing that I'll miss is being able to talk to Laura. Before I left, she asked me if she thought taking the drug would make me suddenly want to divorce her. It was a scary thought. I'd wanted to reassure her. But what could I say when the point of coming here in the first place was change? I power down my phone and take a breath of clean and unencumbered jungle air. I'm excited and scared at the same time, anxious that this could turn out wrong, yet hopeful that I'll learn something new about myself. This week could change my life.

In my mind, I review the week ahead. I'll sit for three ayahuasca ceremonies. The first one happens tonight, just a few hours after my arrival, while I'm still dizzy with jetlag. If I'm being honest, I don't feel too great about jumping right in. I sort of want a little time to adjust to the new environment. But the three of us aren't the only ones at the Trocha, and the ceremonies happen on a schedule that I don't have any control over. As we make our way up the hill, we pass a cabin, where I spy a few people lazing in hammocks and around a rustic wooden table. They cast dour expressions at us as we approach. While Jake and I are effectively ayahuasca tourists—interested in using traditional medicine to explore our bodies and minds—most of the people who come to take ayahuasca with Tony are here for much more urgent reasons. In the hut are twelve Eastern Europeans—mostly from the Czech Republic and Slovakia—who greet us with only the faintest smiles and lazy waves. They're uniformly thin, with visible ribs and sunken stomachs, all suffering from one life-threatening illness or another.

We do a few very brief introductions. Zuzana Tesarova has the pale, haunting beauty of a consumptive. I find out later that she's been suffering from a rare form of Lyme disease for more than a decade and a half that makes her ultra-sensitive to light and almost unable to walk. Her skin is so light that it's almost translucent. She tells me that she spent a year in a dark room because it was the only way to make the pain go away. Andrej Turba flashes me the charismatic smile of an event promoter. He was born with three kidneys, all of which started to fail at the same time a few years ago. He tells me that although he's a candidate for an organ transplant, he's opted instead for three sessions of weekly dialysis and a Hail Mary pass that maybe ayahuasca will reverse his organs' degeneration. I see Martina Lupacova Svarcova reclining in a hammock. She's an artist and spiritual traveler who is recovering from heart and ovarian surgery that sapped her strength. And then Lubomir Jankovych extends a hand. He's a white-haired retiree suffering from prostate cancer, who later will tell me, "At home, ordinary doctors believe that there's no cure for our illnesses, but there's hope here that you won't find anywhere else." Together, all of their doctors predict steep declines, and in what is either a herculean effort of faith and bravery or a tacit embrace of their own mortality, they've come here as a last stop on a road to recovery or, maybe, death.

My compatriots all look like they're in varying levels of pain. I sense that they don't really want to talk. So we head to another hut to stash our bags. The hut—or, more accurately, the *maloka*—sits on five-foot stilts to keep it up and away from the bugs and flooded ground, and has an expansively high roof so that the heat floats upward, away from the beds. Smashed corpses of three-inch long cockroaches dot the rough-hewn floorboards, and our toilet is a porcelain pot that can only flush with a bucket of water.

Luzma smiles cheerily at the accommodations. "I can't wait for you to meet Tony. He changed my life," she says.

Luzma doesn't seem to have much to do. Life at the Trocha passes by at an almost painfully slow pace. Long stretches of napping and idle soft conversations make up most of the days, with only infrequent frenetic healing ceremonies to punctuate the calm.

The first of those happens tonight in a maloka deep in the jungle. The ceremony will go from dusk to dawn, and Luzma advises me to be clear about the intentions that I take to the ceremony. She also says that once the invocations start, I should be ready to abandon my preconceptions. "Just see where the spirit takes you," she says.

That seems easier said than done. If anything, all I have right now are the sketchy pre-conceptions based on books and friends' stories. It's hard to know what emotions lurk in my subconscious mind. I'm reminded of how a bad mindset after a fight with my wife turned a sensory-deprivation float into an excruciating experience.

I remind myself that I'm not only here for personal transformation. I'm here for the Wedge. The stakes seem bigger than ever. During my previous Wedge explorations, I maintained some control. I could exit the float tank. During the MDMA trip, I was safe at home with my wife. Now I feel a little out of control. I'm thousands of miles from home in a dense, remote jungle in a foreign country. I'll be under the influence of a drug I've never tried before. I'm the type of person who needs to feel some control. I don't do well with total chaos. *The Wedge. The Wedge.* I repeat those words to remind myself why I'm here—and to try to insert a sense of safety. I know it's futile. I remind myself that at the deepest level, I'm on this journey to try to understand what I felt on Mount Kilimanjaro with Wim Hof almost three years ago. I want to feel connected to the environment. I want to feel the world outside my skin and connect it to a gut feeling. I want to be all the Russian dolls at once. When I began this journey a year ago, I had a way to understand these things intellectually. But now I want to feel them from outside my own perspective. I want the ayahuasca to make it effortless.

The Wedge allows a certain sort of communication between the outside world and the automatic parts of the body's programming. Sensations link external stress to the mind itself. I know that if I choose to orient toward those sensations, it will alter how my autonomic nervous system responds and reacts to environmental stimuli. I can choose not to feel panic in the face of a threat, and my endocrine system won't produce the adrenaline that it normally would. Whatever mental attitude I can muster intervenes in what should be an automatic process. I know that I have a measure of control over my internal programming. And I know that the insight doesn't only have to look inward: I also explore the larger context, in which our bodies are simply facets of something incomprehensibly more vast than our own egos. On Kilimanjaro, I had a peek into another frame, one where I wasn't investigative journalist Scott Carney, but a product of the environment—an integral piece of life itself. I want to feel all the levels of the Wedge together. I want to be the superorganism and integrate body, mind and spirit.

Maybe those are more goals than intentions. I'm also a little scared of going crazy, and maybe coming to a destructive realization that impels me to wreck the things I value about my life.

Luzma and I chat as the sun dips low and the evening mosquitoes make themselves known. She tells me that she knows everything is interconnected. Plants, she says, have spirits and can talk to us if we know how to listen. She says that the things you feel on a plant medicine aren't just your body metabolizing a chemical, but actual messages between the plant world and the human one.

"In my opinion, the world belongs to plants, not people," she continues. "The world has far more plants than animals, and for millions of years they have used animals to do their bidding—giving them fruit in exchange for dispersing seeds, oxygen for CO_2, and medicines to keep the humans at work. Plants have their own agendas that they work without us even knowing."

Her description isn't as far out as you might think. Some researchers have made surprisingly similar claims about plant consciousness. Ecologist Suzanne Simard showed symbiotic relationships between plants that exchange energy and information through networks of fungus in soil. Simard's research catalogues how they respond to insect attacks and warn neighboring plants to ramp up their own defenses, and even expend vast amounts of resources to keep the root networks of trees that have lost their trunks alive, simply because they are related.[11]

But it became clear to me that Luzma had a very different way of viewing plants and healing than even the most flexible scientist. She believes that trees, grasses, flowers and fruits are actually *talking* to us all the time. The messages that I'm going to get from ayahuasca tonight aren't just a chemical reaction in my brain, she notes; they're the spirits of the plants made understandable. In a way, they're from the spirit of life itself.

That's a big thought—and one that I'm not entirely ready for. So I ask her what I should expect from tonight.

She paraphrases a medicine man, or *curandero*, whom she once asked the same question. "In the regular world, we live in a dark room, shining a flashlight on the parts of reality that our ego is most interested in. On ayahuasca, it's like someone flipped the light on in that room, and suddenly all perspectives are visible. You don't just see things from your own point of view, but you can access everyone's

---

[11]   See the work of Suzanne Simard at the University of British Columbia that shows how trees share and disperse carbon through their root systems. She has a very accessible TED talk on the topic. Also, see the book *The Hidden Life of Trees,* by Peter Wohlleben, for a more accessible description of plant relationships.

point of view all at once," she explains. I'm not sure I know exactly what she means, but the thought is appealing.

Perhaps one way to make sense of it is to go back to a 1992 book by botanist and psychedelic explorer Terence McKenna called *Food of the Gods.* McKenna is a sort of bridge between the West's desire for a scientific understanding of the world and more esoteric spirituality. In his book, he explores archaeological evidence that seems to indicate how human evolution and spirituality are intertwined with hallucinogenic plants.

McKenna spent years traveling around India and the Amazon cataloguing and sampling various plants and shamanic medicines, and reasoned that the very first religious experiences that mankind had must have started by ingesting psychedelic substances—most likely psilocybin mushrooms. Early man, he argues, lived in climates where such mushrooms would have grown freely in cow and ungulate poop. Over hundreds of thousands of years, people must have come across psychedelic plants, eaten them, and had predictably otherworldly experiences. Though no written records go back more than 5,000 years, McKenna finds evidence for his theory in how shamanic traditions around the globe use psychoactive plants in their ceremonies, along with drumming, fire or total darkness to accentuate the effects of the drugs. His book contains pictures of early cave paintings that depict mushroom-headed men and horses with mushrooms for manes. From those images, he posits that there's a tangible link between psychedelic mushrooms and early religious experiences.

McKenna sees psychedelics at the root of all the spiritual and religious institutions that eventually came to dominate humanity, and then he pushes his theory a step further. He argues that psychedelics could have actually helped change the way our brain structures function and may have spurred *Homo erectus* to communicate with language. Essentially, his argument is that psychedelics are what made us human in the first place.

This so-called Stoned Ape Theory of evolution (admittedly a terrible name) relies on the sort of logic that is impossible to prove through archaeological evidence. Many of today's anthropologists deride it. But it makes sense to me that humans would have always had interactions with the plants and animals around them, and that the intense hallucinations we feel when we imbibe them today would be similar to the experience of our ancestors when they took them half a million years ago.

While no one has run any experiments showing that hallucinogens can create hereditary changes in brain structures, perhaps early humans found the insights they got on psychedelic trips useful, or holy, and just maybe some of their visions helped spark what we now know as civilization. After all, the effects of psychedelic plants would be noteworthy to any human that used them. It's not crazy to think those experiences helped shape our early culture. McKenna believed that over the millennia, social and religious institutions started to downplay and even forbid self-exploration with hallucinogens that exist in many shamanic traditions in favor of the control and power afforded by more complex societies.

With all this in mind, I start to think that maybe the experience tonight will give me insight into the sorts of experiences my ancestors might once have had.

Just as I'm getting ready to duck back inside my hut and retreat beneath a mosquito net until the ceremony, Tony comes down the hill to sit with us. He's dressed in a red Lycra Adidas soccer shirt, baggy jeans and hiking boots. At full height, he comes only to my shoulders, and his belly comfortably precedes him everywhere he goes. He's an ordinary man who wouldn't draw a second glance on any third-world street. But there's something about his eyes and cherubic grin that convey a sense of contentment.

Unlike every other person that I contacted in my search for ayahuasca, Tony was the only one hesitant to bring me out. He prefers a low profile, and, since he knows I'm going to write about my time here, asks me to use only his first name, lest other people find out what happens at the Trocha.

A stump of a tree serves as his stool as he reiterates Luzma's question and asks me about my intentions for tonight. Luzma translates my vague ideas about connection and consciousness to him.

He nods. Then he raises his hand in the air and makes what little eye contact is possible in the now near-total darkness. "You must know that what happens tonight is not theater. This is serious business. Though I look like an ordinary man—and not someone who wears feathers and fake headdresses—I am a shaman. Tonight I will work in the world of spirit," he says, still trying to gauge why I would want to cross the globe to see him for something that wasn't a life-threatening illness.

For now, I'm going to be open to whatever happens in the ceremony. I will suspend my disbelief and give the experience the full force of my mind. Maybe plants *can* talk. Maybe the world *does* belong to plants instead of humans. Maybe this is a gateway into a surreal world. Luzma suggests a mantra for me: "Whatever happens, say to yourself, *'I'm willing.'*"

I have the power to choose my own orientation, to willingly accept the sensations and mental changes of the ceremony for my own betterment. "I'm willing" is my wedge.

...

A few hours later, I start walking down a deep jungle path. It's a new moon, but the Milky Way lights a bright swath across the sky. The jungle is alive with chirping birds, insects, frogs, creaking trees, vines, monkeys and god only knows what else. It sounds as if every creature in creation is deep in conversation. One animal calls out and a million buzzes and burps return in answer. I wonder what they are saying. Our headlamps bounce off a muddy path for about fifteen minutes until I spy another maloka. I can't say if I'm ready or not, but I feel that I'm on a path now that I absolutely won't veer from until I know where it leads. I creak open the door and see about ten people lying down on cheap foam mats circling the edge of the structure. A single candle in the center of the room provides some flickering light that casts deep shadows up on the roof and along the floor. Jake and I find places in the corner and put a couple buckets within easy reach. The buckets are for our vomit, an unfortunate inevitability for most people who take ayahuasca; we want to have them easily at hand if they're ever required.

Tony arrives about half an hour later.

He's holding a two-liter plastic water bottle that's about half full of a viscous black syrup. He finds a seat on a cube of wood on the west side of the room and fiddles with a bottle of scented water known as *agua de Florida* and a clutch of unfiltered cigarettes that were on the floor.

The room hums with silence and anticipation.

Time passes slowly until Tony lights one of the cigarettes, gets up onto his feet and blows giant puffs of tobacco smoke in the four cardinal directions. The smoke is the signal of the ceremony's beginning and is a ritual for purification. Luzma whispers to me that the tobacco cleanses the room's energy and invites spirits in. When he sits back down, he whispers a few words into the open plastic bottle and blows more smoke into its aperture. There's no other fanfare. We've begun. And I have no idea what's going on.

Tony taps his feet gently on the floor in a rhythm that starts as a distant rumble and then grows with the subtle intensity of a heartbeat. He purses his lips and whistles equally as softly. It's a simple tune that I almost remember from my childhood, but not one I've ever learned. The whistles turn into a chant that might be Spanish or the indigenous language of Quechua—or maybe they're just sounds that come to him out of the ether with no meaning in particular.

It goes on for a while, and when he's sung enough, he motions to a rail-thin man to his left and indicates that it's time to drink the potion. The man gets up and kneels in front of Tony. He's holding out his hands in a clasped gesture of prayer. Tony grasps the man's bony fingers and they whisper to one another. Tony is asking some sort of question. Once he's satisfied with the answer, he pours a flimsy plastic cup full of the black liquid and holds it up to the light of the candle. Judging that the dose is insufficient, he pours a few drops more. The man drinks, scowls at the taste, and makes his way back to the mat.

The process continues for every person in the room.

I watch as Luzma takes a cup in her hand, looks at the amount, squints her face into a screw and shakes her head no. Tony pours some back into the bottle and offers her what's left. She downs it in a quick movement like she's taking a shot. Within seconds of getting back to her seat, I see her rinse the taste from her mouth with water from her bottle.

About fifteen minutes later, it's my turn. I make my way over to Tony, and he asks me if I've done psychedelic drugs before. I tell him that I took psilocybin mushrooms a few times in college, and that the first time I tried mushrooms, I ended up in the hospital. In my psychedelic daze, I told a friend that I thought I was going to die, and he dutifully called an ambulance. They pumped my stomach. Cops got involved. I was wary of hallucinogens after that, but a few years later I tried them again. On *that* trip, I felt that I'd met something far greater than myself.

Tony nods, probably unsure what to make of my gushing. Then he pours a nearly full cup. He asks me to repeat my name and then whispers words into the brew. When he hands it to me, I look into the syrupy brownness and try not to smell it. I seal the back of my palate so I don't take in any fumes, then down the contents of the cup like a shot and hand it back. I go back to the mat and watch Jake take his turn in front of Tony.

The brew has the consistency of used motor oil and a taste somewhere between rotting fruit and coffee grounds. The fluid coats the inside of my mouth and slicks down my throat. The taste won't go away no matter how many times I swallow. Once the last of the lineup slurps down the noxious brew, someone gets up and blows out the candle in the center of the room. We plunge into inky blackness.

I know that ayahuasca is supposed to take about a half-hour before the effects kick in, but something is different almost immediately. Maybe it's because I'm just so tired from the flight that any change to my body is noticeable. At first it's like someone oiled the darkness of my closed eyes with a palette knife, moving swaths of paint over the flecks of blues, reds and greens that naturally populate my visual field. The darkness's texture isn't the same. The effect doesn't distract me; rather, it pulls my mind inward.

Going into this experience, my biggest fear was that ayahuasca would change my relationship with Laura. Maybe the psychedelic would un-moor one of the most solid parts of my life, create a massive personality change and instigate a divorce. As the effects start to sink in, her face appears in my mind's eye—not a visual hallucination, but more like turning my thoughts in her direction—and I'm overwhelmed by a feeling of pure gratitude.

I see the small actions she takes every day that I've grown accustomed to. Where I'm disorganized, she has the patience for details. She cooks (and, more important, plans out) meals a week in advance, where I would fall into routines of ramen or potatoes without her. I feel her generosity with time and willingness to accompany me on my rather ludicrous adventures. None of this is new to me, exactly. But the ayahuasca reveals her contributions from a different perspective. It's almost as if I'm inside her mind seeing the world through her experience. I feel loved. And I also see the hundreds of ways that I help and support her: with her own writing and creative projects, encouragement in dark times and in good ones. She trusts me to have her back when she takes a risk.

Those initial fears of radical change are almost laughable now. Ayahuasca doesn't open up an entire new reality; rather, it sends me into a place where I can see people, relationships and tendencies from multiple perspectives at once. It's not ego-death, where my own identity disappears. Instead it feels like I have the ability to peek into places from outside my own boundaries. And the information comes fast. Sometimes an insight flashes by so quickly that I can't examine and hold on to it. All I can do when this happens is rock back and forth on my foam mattress as my eyes flit left and right like I'm speed-reading a book.

About 45 minutes after gulping down the tea, something starts happening in my stomach that I can already tell I won't have a lot of control over. One reason that ayahuasca will never make it onto the party circuit is that, in addition to its psychedelic effects, it's also a purgative. That's a polite way of saying that almost everyone who drinks it either vomits or has a bowel movement once it starts working its way through their system. The human body simply does not want the toxic-tasting mixture of plant sap inside, and it will do anything it can to expel the brew. I'm very thankful that the bucket is by my side.

My stomach churns the sickly sweet syrup, and soon I can taste it again in my throat. I grab the bucket in the dark and bend over its opening. Unholy moments follow. The taste of tannin, rotten fruit and burnt coffee erupt into my mouth, but this time add to it the mixture of bile and stomach acids. It's horrible. Meaty. Fortunately, the horking is over as soon as it begins. I wash out my mouth with water. For maximum potency, drinkers try to hold back from the explosion as long as possible to allow the body to absorb a higher dose, but it's clear that my time had come. Once my insides quiet down, my mind goes back into contemplation. Now, instead of examining the world around me, I start to look at my own personality and habits.

Ayahuasca first tells me my strengths. While I'm rarely the best at anything I take on, I have a sort of determination and faith that I can finish anything I start. This skill—maybe "mindset" is a better word—has served me well in the uncertain waters of a writing career. I weather the risks of my projects and think strategically about books and assignments that can take years to complete. Somehow I've managed to stay afloat in the uncertainty of my career, even thrive. But ayahuasca also tells me that my greatest strength is also a weakness. And then it takes me back to my childhood.

When I was a kid, I was always fond of games, especially ones that focused on strategy or storytelling. More than any other, I loved Dungeons & Dragons, a role-playing game that involves creating open-ended stories about elves, wizards and medieval fantasy adventures. I distracted myself from school by memorizing the rule books (there were a lot of them) and planning out games with my friends. The beauty of D&D was that there was no way to win a game; there was only the adventure of playing. Over time those interests morphed into playing video games in worlds made by designers whose goal was to keep players at their computers. While imagination in D&D is essentially free, the industry that develops video games promotes its titles by their potential for addiction. They even employ teams of neuroscientists to create rewards that keep people locked into their computers. In many ways, the fun part of being an investigative journalist is sort of like D&D: I get to do my research in far-flung parts of the world, uncover people's secrets, and peer into subcultures that I ordinarily would never have access to. My journalist badge opens doors.

The less romantic part of the job is that there are interminably long stretches of time when simply nothing happens. I wait for assignments to mature, sources to get back to me and plans to align. My life can be 90 percent downtime interspersed with times of high-intensity, unadulterated excitement. Over the years, video games have filled in part of that downtime void, and I've found a few favorites—from strategic titles in the *Civilization* franchise to indie survival thrillers like *RimWorld* and, most recently, one called *Dota 2*, an hour-long team game that requires thinking ahead and mastering hundreds of characters, and only seems to gain in complexity the more I play.

I've dumped thousands of hours of my life into the digital medium of video games. It's something that embarrasses me. The time isn't productive—it's someone else's fantasy—but the games speak to a primal part of my psychology that needs stimulation. Games appeal to me because they keep a certain strategic part of my brain sharp, but the physiology of sitting in front of a computer contradicts what I know to be healthy. I rarely talk about my addiction, even though I can lose entire days to it.

In the darkness, Tony's drumming grows more intense as the floorboards creak under the force of his rhythmic blows. I come back to the sound of his voice to anchor me. The place that games occupy in my life comes into view almost as a singular object: something that is more than a habit. It's as if it fills a physical space inside of my body.

I can see that my best qualities (a steady, strategic mind motivated by excitement) intertwine perfectly with my worst ones (a predilection to waste time on tasks that don't actually nourish my life in any tangible way). This realization may only apply to me. Certainly not everyone who turns on a video console has the same tendencies or relationships. But I know now that even though I've deleted games from my computer several times, the habit never went away, because I never found anything else that could fill the space they take up.

I gaze out into the pitch-black room, and I'm aware of a pillar of white light. It reaches down from the middle of the ceiling and comes to rest in the center of the room where the candle was flickering earlier. The swath of pastel blackness engulfs the space around me so that the longer I look at the column, the brighter it seems. And yet the column is strange: It doesn't illuminate anything around it. I watch in timelessness until it fades away.

Tony chants for three or four hours. All the while, my mind races through fractal-like facets of relationships, long-ingrained habits, family histories and my desire to connect with the people around me. Tony's voice crescendos and then peters out, only to regain its strength. He shouts in tongues with the voice of an old man, then parrots back a response in the cadence of a woman. I have my doubts that it's a language at all. Eventually his strength ebbs into total silence. Only the sounds of the jungle keep us company.

Then he takes a deep breath and announces that the spirits have left.

The ceremony is over.

Jake and I drift off to sleep on our mats on the maloka floor. Eventually, blue morning light fills the cabin and I can see we are the only ones left in the room. Everyone else snuck out in the night. We clear the sleep from our eyes, and I ask him how the experience was for him. He describes personal things, then says that when the ceremony was about half over, he watched pillar of white light, about five feet long, in the middle of the room.

We'd seen the same light.

Yet both of us are fairly certain that it wasn't really there; it was a vision that came from inside of us.

We walk back down the jungle path in silence, find our beds and collapse. When I open my eyes, it feels like days have passed. The sun hangs high in the Peruvian sky. My mind whirls from the aftermath of the night before. I feel compelled to write it down before it goes away, so I scribble my thoughts into my black notebook. I feel that if I can just capture the feelings and insights from that night, then there's a chance that I can make changes. Jake is taking notes from his journey as well. We fill pages with ideas on how to implement what we learned from our experience. The inspiration comes almost automatically; we feel compelled to record. This is a common experience. Many people report that the most productive part of an ayahuasca trip isn't the ceremony, when images and ideas move so quickly that it's almost impossible to get ahold of them, but what happens over the next few days as your brain has a chance to process what it learned.

A few days later, I meet Peter Gorman, an investigative journalist and author of several books on Amazonian psychedelics. He sometimes holds court in the bars of Iquitos. He tells me, "For the next month, you'll keep downloading new information from the experience. You'll see, smell or hear something that you learned on your trip that simply passed by your consciousness too fast to recognize, and then *pop*, you'll realize something you already knew."

...

It's time for a rhetorical question. What do you call something that makes people change for the better and heals illness? For much of my life, I didn't understand the way that Native Americans used the word "medicine." I'd heard of medicine men, medicine talismans and bags, but the notion that these things were somehow the same as what a doctor prescribed for me in a clinic jarred my understanding of medicine as something in the domain of hospitals and pills. In the Amazon and among shamanic traditions around the world, anything that alters your body or mind is a type of medicine. In this sense, the Wedge is medicine, too. Sensations and feelings direct the immune and nervous systems to respond and adapt to the environment. Most traditional medicines guide and create sensations and feelings that make a person stronger and healthier. And this is what the Wedge is all about: We manipulate the stresses we encounter, the way we feel the world, and the way we relate to those experiences in order to give our bodies direction in how best to adapt to the challenges we face. We can control our automatic biology by altering the things that influence that biology to react in the first place.

As mentioned in the chapters on heat, placebos and MDMA, Western psychiatric medicine is often hard to distinguish from pharmacology. Most antidepressants aim to suppress moods—to bring them into a narrow range of experience, removing both the highs and lows. We reduce symptoms of an affliction to make it invisible.

Indigenous medicine takes a different tack. Experience takes precedence. Instead of reducing symptoms, medicines like ayahuasca accentuate them. Psychotherapy in the Amazon involves facing, not suffocating your demons. It can be unpleasant and uncover ugly things that you'd rather not look at, but if you weather the experience, you have access to the root of the issue. To put it another way, if we bury our symptoms in the West, then in the Amazonian tradition, we expose the symptoms to sunlight in the hope of burning them away altogether.

Still, that doesn't mean we can't also try to understand the chemistry of ayahuasca through a Western lens. The ayahuasca vine (*banisteriopsis caapi*) itself contains two primary psychoactive chemicals: harmine and harmaline, both Monoamine oxidase inhibitors (MAOIs), which are chemically similar to some of the first antidepressants approved by the FDA back in the 1950s. MAOIs prevent the brain from cleaning out serotonin, dopamine and adrenaline from its neural pathways. And they worked reasonably well to level out moods until they fell out of fashion in favor of SSRIs a few decades ago.

In Quechua, *ayahuasca* means "vine of death" because of the visions of mortality that many people experience during their intoxication. And yet drinking ayahuasca on thier own doesn't produce any noteworthy effects in most people. However, the brew we drank last night—the tea known around the world as "ayahuasca"—also contains leaves from the chakruna plant (*psychotria viridis*), which is where it finds its chemical fireworks. The chakruna plant has trace amounts of N,N-Dimethyltryptamine, better known as DMT, stored in diamond-shaped nodules at the place where the veins of the leaves meet the stem. You may remember that I mentioned DMT in the chapter on breathwork as a molecule the body produces as it's dying. Recreational DMT users typically smoke the chemical if they want to feel its effects. Taken in this way, DMT gives intense but brief trips, rarely lasting more than five minutes. On its own, DMT's chemical half-life is so short that it's hard for a person to take enough orally to have any effect. Indeed, a tea made only from the chakruna leaf doesn't do anything at all.

However, that changes in the traditional brew, where the MAOI in the ayahuasca vine stops the brain's ability to reabsorb and break down DMT, so that the psychedelic effects can last for hours. Without the chemical profile of those two plants working together, the neurochemistry would never produce any effects of note. And this leads to one of the most enduring mysteries about the brew: How did indigenous shamans thousands of years ago discover the properties of the two plants together?

The Amazon basin is one of the most biodiverse places on earth, with a bounty of more than 80,000 different plant species. An almost infinite number of vines, trees, fungus, flowers and fruits grow around the Trocha. A billion bugs flit unseen through its dense thickets. Amid all of this, chakruna and ayahuasca don't look like anything special: just a green leafy plant and a vine that looks pretty much like any other vine. They're plant extras in the *Where's Waldo?* picture of a jungle. On their own, neither plant has any interesting effect—certainly nothing like the near-magical properties of when they come together.

Generations of anthropologists and ethnobotanists have wondered how indigenous people in the Amazon discovered the preparation in the first place. Was it random chance? Did a shaman or cook happen to boil the two plants together and feel a mystical effect? Maybe. But with all of the Amazon's poisonous creatures and plants, simple trial and error would be an unavoidably fatal process. What we do know is that archaeological evidence suggests that the ayahuasca preparation we use today goes back to at least 500 B.C. Chemical analysis of Andean mummies discovered the presence of harmine in the preserved hair follicles, leading researchers to assume the mummies had imbibed some version of the ayahuasca brew in their lifetimes. There's no written record of how the two plants came together, no hard evidence that will make every expert agree. But Tony has a theory. He doesn't think ayahuasca got discovered at all. Instead, he says, "the plants found us."

A few days after the first ceremony, Tony says he wants to show me how he prepares the brew. It's a long process, but he hopes it will give me insight into his traditions. Jake and I accompany him into the jungle to a spot of muddy ground about halfway between our maloka and the ceremonial hut deeper in the jungle. Here, a giant cauldron on an iron grate hovers over the burnt leftovers of a hundred campfires. We haul a few fifty-pound bags of dried ayahuasca vines from his stash spot in the forest. He tells me to cut them up into small pieces and then break them apart with a mallet. It's hard work, and it isn't long until blood blisters form on my palms from the impact.

After an hour of pounding, Luzma makes her way to the fire and we take shifts reducing the vines to mulch. When the ground is thick with vine bits, we pour buckets of water into the cauldron and bring the mulch to boil over the fire until brown foam bubbles up from all sides. Luzma sings a song over the brew and shakes a shaman's rattle in the pillar of steam. She calls to the spirit of the vine for a potent concoction.

Once it's boiled for a few hours, Tony says it's time to gather the chakruna leaves. He grabs a machete and leads me into the jungle. It's impossible to move more than a few feet in any direction without breaking down a vine, plant or small tree trunk with a slash of the short sword. The jungle burbles with thick and thorny plants that make ribbons out of the legs of my pants.

A vulture circles overhead, perhaps hoping that we leave will leave a meaty snack in our wake. It takes a while, and we zigzag around the jungle looking for a plant that seems to be in hiding. Tony stops next to a tree that soars four stories above us and points to three interlaced vines that, to my eye, look like every other vine that we've hacked through to get here. "This is ayahuasca," he says turning it over to show how the plant's strands form a double helix, reminiscent of the DNA stored in every human cell. It's an interesting coincidence shared by many vines all over the world. However, we have enough ayahuasca already, so we move on. He hacks his way forward and points out plants by naming what sort of effect they have on human biology. One broad leafy shrub is good for the prostate and doubles as an aphrodisiac. A few feet away he finds a small tree and scrapes off an inch or two of bark, revealing the yellow sap inside. He hands the branch to me and tells me to rub it on the blisters on my hand. In a few minutes, the pain is gone. The next day, I'll notice that the blister has vanished altogether. Jake has similar wounds on his hands, but he doesn't use the herb. His won't go away for weeks.

Tony tells me that he never formally studied the plants of the jungle from other *curanderos*, but learned the pharmacology by listening. Every plant, he says, has a spirit, and if you can get quiet enough, you can hear them speak.

"Like in English?" I ask.

"They speak to me in Spanish, but to you, maybe yes, to you in English," he replies, adding, "They mostly speak in dreams."

My eyebrow can't help taking an incredulous posture. *So plants are multilingual*, I think.

Tony tries to give an example. Suppose, he says, he has been on his dieta for a little while and decides to take a walk into the woods. Every plant in the jungle has a message, and the forest is a symphony. In order to listen to any particular note, he says, all he has to do is touch a plant that he's curious about, and in minutes, or perhaps in a dream that night, the plant will tell him its secrets. It will tell him how best to use it. If for some reason a plant just doesn't want to open up, then he blows tobacco on it to loosen its tongue. However, if the plant is extremely stubborn, he might choose to sleep next to it for a night or two and ask it for help. "Eventually, they all speak."

Okay. So it isn't the scientific method. Maybe it's the intuition of a wizard. Or, less charitably, the ravings of a madman.

A few swings of the machete later and he smiles in triumph.

"Chakruna," he says, pointing to thin spindly twig of a tree that I couldn't tell apart from any other plant that we've hacked our way through today.

He swipes it down in a single hit and gives me a branch of leaves to pluck. Tony points to a small pouch at the base of where the stem connects to the ribs. "That's where the DMT is," he says. We fill a bucket full of greenery in a few minutes. Then we walk briskly back to the camp. He dumps the leaves into the boiling water and mashes them below the surface of the brown foam with the end of a broken stick.

Now all we have to do is wait until the watery brown mixture reduces into a sticky syrup.

So we wait.

And wait.

Four hours later, we're still waiting for the brew to concentrate.

Another hour and we're all a little grouchy.

It's taking longer than any of us wanted it to.

Our eyes are drab with boredom. Luzma has long since tired of singing to the medicine. And then seemingly out of nowhere, Tony breaks the monotony of watching water boil by grabbing a dry palm frond and thrusting it into the heart of the fire. When the papery leaves ignite, he holds it above his head like a torch. He walks away from the pit and then back down the path back toward the huts.

We call out to him, asking what he's doing, and he shouts back, "We need rain!"

Thirty feet later he comes to a dying palm tree whose once-lush foliage now hangs dry and dead by its sides. He touches his torch to the tree and flames arc up the trunk and into the canopy.

Luzma, Jake and I are still a good distance away, but the temperature in the grove rockets upward, taking the already oppressive tropical heat into another register. Barely taking time to observe his work, he walks toward two other dried-out palm trees by a reservoir on his land and ignites another conflagration.

"But...why?" I stammer as burning embers cascade down around us.

Tony returns my stare with an equally mystified expression as if to question my sanity. *Isn't it obvious?* it seems to say. When it's clear that I really don't understand, he points to the two small reservoirs and asks me to notice how low they are.

They're low. It's true.

"Without rain, we'll run out of water in a few days," pausing for me to fill in the rest of the sentence myself. He sighs when I don't.

"We sacrifice the trees to call the rain."

He says a few words in Spanish that Luzma catches, something about how burning the trees will eat up oxygen in the area and form new clouds, but it doesn't make sense to me.

I look up into the perfectly blue sky and wonder if I'm going mad.

In a matter of a few minutes, the trees' foliage burns to embers. Their charred trunks stand alone against the sky. Tony goes back to tending the fire as if nothing happened.

Night eventually falls on the Trocha, and the brew still isn't concentrated enough. There will be another ceremony tomorrow night, but we decide to let the fire go out and start up again in the morning. I look up into the sky to see billowing cumulus clouds. They don't look dark enough to me to hold much rain.

I make my way to the hut and close my eyes to drift off to sleep. That's when I hear the first drops of water on the thatched roof. The drips quicken into a patter, and then a full-scale deluge. It comes down so fiercely that the water falls through gaps in the thatch above me. Drips make their way through my mosquito net and onto my face. The storm keeps up all the way until morning, and when I come outside, I see that the reservoirs are filled to the brim. The most obvious explanation is, of course, that we are in the *rain*forest—and there's no reason to seek out any more complex reason than that for the storm. But when I see Tony later that day, he simply smiles and touches his finger to his forehead in the international sign for "I told you so."

I don't quite know what to think about Tony. Is he a prophet or a charlatan? A madman or a messenger? Perhaps that is the wrong question. With my second ceremony looming, I hope to have a more powerful set of visions than I did on my first night. I still want to understand something more about my own consciousness. For better or worse, Tony's my guide.

The next day passes slowly, and by night I make my spot in the opposite corner from where I was for the first ceremony. I sit next to Luzma. She says that even though she has drunk ayahuasca a hundred times before, she's always nervous before a ceremony: "Every time is different. And Tony says he is going to give me a 'bomb' tonight. I don't feel like I need a bomb."

A bomb: a giant dose.

Hell, I wonder if *I* want a bomb. I mean, it would be interesting, right? The chance to go as deeply as possible all at once? The thought makes me scared and excited at the same time. My stomach clenches tightly, like I'm about to drop from the top of a roller coaster.

The night has a familiar rhythm. Tony arrives last, sits for a while and then begins by blowing tobacco smoke into the air. He starts chanting, and I rock in my seat along with the rhythmic drumming of his feet on the floor. He starts offering up the medicine by candlelight, and I'm the first one in the lineup. I sit down in front of him while he whistles a prayer into the plastic bottle. He tells me that the brew tonight is much stronger than the one we had before. He hopes that tonight will be powerful.

I take the cup from his hand and down it as quickly as possible, trying not to taste it on the way down. I didn't think it was possible, but this tastes worse than before. My face puckers into a screw while I make my way back to the mattress. I'm holding back from gagging.

When everyone is full of the concoction, someone blows out the light and we plunge into darkness for a second time. Tony stops chanting for a moment and seems to scan the room. It's so dark that I can only see the ember of the rolled cigarette get faintly brighter when he pulls in smoke. He releases the breath with a soft *shoo*.

As the ember descends, I sense his breath transform in the air. I write "sense" because it's not quite sight. It feels more like the memory of a sight. This invisible cloud of smoke transforms in my mind into a ghostly figure of a Native American man in a full feather headdress. The vision whooshes through the circle, anointing everyone with sacred smoke, then evaporates in a cloud. The image passes so quickly that I don't realize I've seen it until it's already gone. There's no point in trying to make sense of it.

This must be the beginning of something profound, I think, eager for more.

But nothing comes.

For the next thirty or forty minutes, I just sit in the dark, waiting for something, anything, to happen. But there are no visions. No geometric patterns. No spirits communicating from beyond. I don't even have any interesting insights about my family or friends. All I feel is the rumbling in my stomach and the taste of the concentrated vine syrup creeping up my throat. My body wants to expel the ayahuasca, but I hold it in, hoping that I just need to absorb a little more of the chemical.

But there's nothing I can do. My hand reaches for the bucket almost of its own accord, and when it's in front of me, my stomach turns upside down and brown sludge erupts out of my mouth. It's made all the more noxious with the taste of my own bile. The taste makes me want to vomit again, and the purging alternates between cycles of relief and then the foul taste, which makes me want to purge again. It's painful. Physical.

And then it's something else altogether. As I hunch over the plastic bucket, I realize that I'm not exactly expelling poison from my stomach.

I'm vomiting up video games.

The puke splashing into the bottom of the bucket isn't bile; it's three decades of electronic addiction. Whatever I realized in the ceremony a few days ago congealed inside of me. And now it's all coming up in a watery sludge. I puke out the cycle of winning one game and my immediate desire to start another. I hork out the accomplishment they make me feel. I purge decades of subtle neurological training that the industry has spent billions wiring into my head. I barf it all out until my ribs hurt from the hollowness. It concentrated in my stomach, and now I'm kicking it all out of my body like it was poison.

A viscous string of spit dangles from my lip and I look back up into the blackness and feel a sense of relief. I wonder if it's the start of a long-term change. When it's all out of my body, I bring myself back to the constant thrum of Tony's chants. I somehow know that ayahuasca doesn't have any more messages for me tonight. The message, if there is any, is purely physical; I won't be traveling into the depths of my subconscious or revisiting my childhood. So I fall back to my pillow and just listen to the chants and stomps until Tony tires just before dawn.

My experience purging up an addiction is relatively common among people who take ayahuasca or other similar psychedelics. Indeed, researchers first began studying the anti-addictive effects of LSD from the 1950s to 1970s, until the War on Drugs put an end to promising clinical research in the United States. In the past several years, however, the Food and Drug Administration has shown a renewed interest in psychedelics. While double blind and randomized control trials on their effectiveness are still in short supply, upstart clinics in South America as well as underground clinics in North America report an endless stream of cases where ayahuasca and another psychedelic plant called ibogaine completely remove their patients' addictive tendencies.

Andrew Huberman once defined addiction to me as "the progressive narrowing of the things that give you pleasure." And while I do not think that the neurological bumps of video games have blinded me to all other pleasures in my life, more serious addictions to drugs and alcohol can absolutely do that.

According to a 2014 review article on the state of psychedelic research on addiction by medical anthropologist Michael Winkelman, the early research on LSD and alcoholism was similar to what I just experienced in Tony's maloka. "LSD sessions could produce a vivid awareness of one's personal problems, presenting graphic images of the immediate and long-term deleterious effects of the alcohol. The recovering alcoholics often credited these realizations as providing the motivation to change their behavior." He goes on to write that in ayahuasca ceremonies, "vomiting is seen as provoking an emotional release or unloading of psychological burdens, as well as provoking diverse emotional dynamics." Various theories abound about what happens at a chemical level to stop addiction, and they unsurprisingly revolve around how psychedelics rebalance dopamine and serotonin levels.

While I'm profoundly moved by how the two ceremonies seem to have given me a new lens to understand my own tendencies, that morning I also walk back to my hut without the answers I'd hoped to find. I didn't fly halfway across the globe into the Peruvian jungle to wrestle with my own demons. I wanted to understand consciousness. I wanted the sensation that I had at the top of Kilimanjaro, where the distinction between my body and the frigid air around me disappeared. I want to taste the continuum of all existence, not to turn inward.

Later that morning, I find Luzma lazing back in a hammock. Last night, in the total darkness, she says she saw a world of visions that came on so quickly, she doesn't think she could ever articulate them in words. But there was a consciousness there. She felt the universe. She spoke with an alien intelligence.

"For me, it is always like this," she says, explaining matter-of-factly, "I am sensitive."

I'm a little jealous. All I did was vomit. She reads disappointment on my face.

"You know, I once held a ceremony with a man a few years ago who said he wanted to connect with the universe. Nothing happened when he drank. So I asked him about his relationship with his parents, and he just waved his hands in the air and told me that he didn't care about that. His mother was a terrible person and he had already written her out of his life. Then I asked him how he thought he could connect with the universe if he couldn't connect to his own family," she says.

The parable hits home. If we *are* the environment, then all of the things that shape our experience of the world are part of the picture as well. I'm going to have to wrestle with myself if I want to understand anything bigger than me. I chew on the thought and Luzma laughs.

"Besides, it's the medicine that chooses what we see. Not you. Or me. Or Tony."

A little later, I walk to the kitchen, where Tony's sister is preparing the day's dieta of tasteless lentils, rice and some unseasoned chicken. I'm hoping that there's a boiled egg somewhere on offer. It's been about five days since I showed up, and just like with the potato hack, I'm not really hungry at Trocha. Bland food makes me just want to eat to survive, not to eat just for the sake of it.

There's a bowl with a lone hard-boiled egg in it, and I start peeling back the shell. Tony is at the table, and he asks me how the night's ceremony went.

I say I wish I had felt more.

He nods and says that he thinks the brew wasn't very good last night. Perhaps too much ash blew into the mix when we cooked it over the fire. It could have interfered with medicine. He knows that I only have a few days left before I head back to America, and he says that he'll give me a private ceremony, just me and the medicine.

"I want you to find what you came for."

It's an encouraging offer, and I eagerly accept it.

When my egg is gone, I meander back to my hut, still exhausted from the night's purging. I'm low on energy and content to rest and reflect on the experiences from the ceremonies and have slow conversations with Luzma and Jake over the next few days. The tempo gives me space to reflect, write and imagine how I might bring what I'm learning back home. Meanwhile, Tony travels to the city of Iquitos to procure a different brew of tea.

Two days later, I walk to the maloka alone. The jungle feels sinister tonight. Every branch creak, bird call and rustling leaf conjures unseen dangers. After all, I have to remind myself that this is the home of the jaguar: a fearsome predator so powerful that it can fish an adult caiman out of a river and devour it. It's also my last ceremony. My last chance for something big.

The floorboards groan when I step inside. I walk across the empty room and set up a place on yet another soiled mattress. The red light from my headlamp bathes the space in an eerie bloody darkness. I'm alone as a four-inch roach skitters across the ground in front of me. I check the bathroom and see that no one has cleaned it since the last ceremony. Feces and puke run up the sides of the toilet and the stink is almost unbearable. Worse still: There's no water in the plastic barrel reservoir. So I take the barrel out to a nearby creek and walk it back half full.

I wait in darkness until I hear rustling outside the door. Tony's flashlight seeps through the cracks of the entrance and then momentarily blinds me as he looks in my direction. He apologizes softly, and then his attendant lights a candle. Although I'm the only one taking the tincture tonight, he starts just as he did for the other ceremonies: humming to himself and whistling with his eyes closed. He blows smoke in the four directions and then asks me to take a seat in front of him.

"This is good medicine; I got it special for you," he says, and pours out a full cup of the viscous liquid. I say a quick prayer, asking the gods of the cocktail for an eye-opening experience. Then I prepare to taste its foulness. The minute it touches my tongue, I know this brew is different; it's lighter than the ones from previous nights and goes down smoother. I scoot back against the wall and sit back and wait for the visions to kick in.

And just like the night before, they don't.

Tony chants his familiar simple sounds for a half-hour, but nothing changes. So I ask him for another cup. It's one thing to take ayahuasca once in a night, but the second cup is worse. My body screams that I'm not supposed to do this twice. I gag. The bile churns in my throat, and it looks like I'm going to barf at Tony's feet.

Suddenly aware of his peril, Tony acts fast. He grabs a bottle of orange-scented *agua de Florida* and holds it under my nose. Rich floral notes rise with the alcohol vapor. It distracts me long enough to control my reflex. To our mutual relief, I hold it down and then move against the wall.

Ten minutes pass before Tony pauses his chant and asks if I feel anything yet. It's looking like another bust. Maybe the brew is broken. Maybe I'm just not the type of person to have visions.

So I try something new. I start doing the Wim Hof breathing—super-ventilation followed by full-lung breath holds. I quicken the pace of the air coming in and out of my lungs until I can feel tingling in my fingers and toes. If ayahuasca is not going to give up its secrets quietly, I am going to force the issue. Breath is the most fundamental wedge, and I'm going to draw on what I've learned over the past decade to make this experience as intense as possible. It's the same breathing pattern I used in the yoga studio with Elee so many months ago, the one where I turned purple and caused so much alarm that she worried I might pop. But I reason that if this is the so-called "DMT breathing," and DMT is the active chemical in ayahuasca, then maybe it will get things moving. So I take thirty deep breaths and hold with full lungs. I focus my mind on the black ether behind my eyelids. Then I contract the muscles in my feet, my legs, butt and diaphragm to push the breath upward past my shoulders and into my skull.

When the pressure reaches a spot in the center of my forehead, I see an explosion of color. Something has come unstuck. The vision starts out as a shimmering pattern of red and blue light and transforms into geodesic fractals, as if the rods and cones in my eyes have just crystalized. The shapes lock together—first around the periphery of my field of vision, and then they take it over altogether. As the hallucination grows stronger, my mind turns inward.

I start thinking about my mother.

First she appears in front of me like I'm watching a movie of her as an adolescent with a beaming smile on her face. The image, no doubt pulled from an archive of photos I've seen over the years, gets sharper and shaper until I feel myself transform. Now I'm not looking at her from the outside, but part of me *is* her looking at the world from her eyes. I'm feel myself as her, full of energy and looking forward to all the possibilities of life. A flash to a decade or so in the future, and I'm my mother falling in love with my father. There's excitement and possibility in the air. Then it's years later in a house full of young children. A beat and I'm growing claustrophobic, and my husband (my father) spends most of his time working at the hospital where he's a surgeon. When I think about him, I flash into his perspective. Now I'm him, and I feel alienated from my family and proud of my career. I can see myself as him trying to connect with his children but realizing it's a lost battle. My wife (my mother) has more time with the children and will always be closer. There's a hint of jealousy because of it. Fast-forward a few more years and I'm my mother again, this time going through a divorce and feeling an almost endless expanse of freedom in front of me. I traverse decades of life experiences in a matter of minutes. I exist in multiple perspectives like a great living fractal.

The visions are difficult to communicate in language because they exist in a space beyond the ability to convey meaning. They come fast like snapshots that I have no time to process or dwell on. By the time I realize what I'm seeing, I've already moved on to another thought, in another place in the timeline. The brew has buried the lessons in my memory for me to process later. I'm both the observer and the subject of the visions. I'm me and someone else at the same time.

Just as I start to feel I understand something about my mother, I speed across generation lines again. Now I'm my grandmother at a Christmas party meeting a five-year-old version of myself. The boy (me) says something flippant, and I (my grandmother) warns the lanky child not to think that he's too smart. A second later, I'm her lying on a deathbed in a hospital looking out at the world through a lens of dementia. The observer side of me apologizes for not seeing her in her last days. But there's no time to dwell on that vision, because I've already moved deeper into my maternal history. I'm now my great-grandmother Minna—a person whom I never met and know almost nothing about save for a picture on the wall. I have a sense of purely existing and being in the world. The observer in me wonders why so many of the women in my family are forgotten.

The winds of time and genealogy pull me back down the trunk of my family tree. There are individuals in my roots whom I'll never know but who all contributed to the person I am today. It's strange to say, but I feel that some part of my conscious stores the perspectives of every person that came before me and that I can *almost* access them. Maybe I need more ayahuasca to go deeper. Or maybe they're better left in my subconscious.

At one point over the last week, Luzma told me she believes that DNA stores the memories of our genealogical past, somehow twisted into the geometric forms of amino acids, nucleotides and chemical bonds. She says that the plant can be a sort of key that brings those memories into the front. Of course, no scientist I've ever met would agree that DNA can store memory—at least not the way I'm experiencing it now.

I opt not to explore the roots of my family tree much further than my great grandmother. Instead, I come back to Tony's steady drumbeat. His strange song centers the experience and pulls me back to the present. He hums a short, childlike tune and then falls into silence. After a full measure, he asks me to sit down in front of him. So I crawl from my spot and make my way through the total blackness by touch and sound alone. I sit facing him, and when he starts up again, the vibrations of his stamping the floorboards course through my bones and wash over my body. The vibrations connect my body to his song. Every stomp reverberates through the loose planks into my body. I look into the blackness where I know he is, but cannot see, and I perceive his face as if it were the head of a buffalo. The beast flares its nostrils and bounces out the notes of his chant through the void between us.

I breathe in his song, and it takes me back to my ten-year-old self. I'm in my childhood bedroom looking out the skylight that was my window. The knotted carpet squishes beneath my feet, and there's a pile of dirty clothes in the corner.

When was the last time I thought about this place? I ask myself.

The child me stands next to the bed and looks across the hall to my sister's room. It feels like I am actually in that space and time again, filling me with the sensations of what it was like to be a kid. I gaze at her door and feel sadness and frustration at how much my sister dislikes me. Like many an older sibling, she is jealous of losing our parents' attention. And even though she can be mean, I also feel how those emotions are part of a great life lesson where we were both teaching the other how to be human. It's a good childhood, I decide as the observer. The insight ends that vision.

And now I'm back in front of Tony, exhausted by the travels. So I lie down at his feet, and the song becomes a physical thing. It travels from his feet through the floor and along my spine, so that I don't know where the notes end and I begin.

I look up into the crystalized patterns that sprint across the blackness—the fractals of the ayahuasca hallucination—and feel an intense sense of gratitude for the experience. I may never know what to make of Tony or the world of spirits as it butts against my own rational mind, but I can choose to respect the process that brought me here.

Somehow the last few years of exploring my own mind and body have brought me to the feet of a shaman somewhere in the Amazonian darkness. It's one of the most remote corners of the world, and I hear him invoking spirits that I know nothing about. His vibrations course through the deepest part of me. It is a sacred moment. And I try to inhale as much of it as possible into my body.

Time passes—I don't know how much. Then Tony's foot makes a final stomp onto the floor. His humming trails off into silence, and there's a minute of eerie quiet. Even the jungle says nothing.

"The spirits say you are a good person," he says.

In any other context, this would be the sort of thing that I would try to deflect. In the rational world, I don't much like compliments and don't generally believe in otherworldly spirits. But in this moment it fills me with joy. I feel relief that the spirits he talks to see something worthy in me.

We wait there a little longer, and then Tony says that he thinks the ceremony is over.

We walk together back to the maloka in the pitch darkness as the world of geometric shapes crowds around the periphery of my vision. I don't fall asleep when I finally get back to my mattress. I stay up and think about what it all means, and I know that I'll never find an answer.

...

I barely speak to Tony after the ceremony, and I say my goodbyes the following morning, getting ready for my trip back to the Northern Hemisphere. He smiles warmly to me, and we converse in what little stable ground we can find between our broken Spanish and English. He asks if I found what I came for, and I tell him yes.

And yet how can I convey it? Writing about ayahuasca is difficult, because whatever answers do come often don't pair well with words. This is true of just about every aspect of the Wedge where the language doesn't necessarily jump up from the pages of a book, but arises instead out of the sensations that we feel. It's one thing to read about an ice bath, or to imagine what it might feel like to catch a kettlebell in midair as it transforms in your hands from a weapon into a dance. These are things you have to feel to understand.

What I can say is that, in the almost two years since I came back from the jungle to the time that I'm writing the words on this page, it continues to have a powerful impact on my life. I speak to Luzma every few weeks, mostly through messages on my phone. Sometimes I flash back to a moment of insight that I never had time to notice while I was bathing in blackness. Many changes are subtle; I didn't destroy my relationship or start a new career. I haven't filled my house with sage bushes, crystals and dense-smelling incense. Others are more obvious: I have almost no desire to play video games anymore. But that isn't to say that I don't know how easy it might be to get sucked in again; they're as available as a high-speed Internet connection. I spent one week in December immersed in electronic bliss before quickly seeing the unhealthy tendencies in myself. I deleted them and haven't gone back. I've instead filled that time with new hobbies—and even founded a tabletop D&D group with friends that meets once a week. The game from my childhood hits the same notes of high fantasy but has a social component that just couldn't exist online. In other words, I have the tools to occupy the space left after my purge.

Sometimes I find myself whistling phrases from Tony's childlike tunes in the middle of the day for no reason at all. I'm still breathing out parts of his song.

Let death be your greatest teacher.

—Buddha

CHAPTER 12

DEATH, RISK, AND THE MEANING OF LIFE

What lies beyond this life? Heaven? Hell? An endless cycle of re-birth? Simple nothingness? Opinions abound, but it's all speculation: No one knows. I've watched good people die, and I can attest that, more often than not, the final moment doesn't seem very pleasant. If life is a song, it ends in a minor key.

If we take it seriously—that is, if we don't avert our eyes from the truth that we have an expiration date similar to a carton of eggs—then death becomes the most powerful teacher that we can ever hope for. If we think of death in Wedge terms, our assured demise is the ultimate stressor, and thus our motivation to make choices that mean something. Death is the stake that all of us are born with. No matter our triumphs or failures, death will always be waiting. With the end inevitable, it's only our choices that matter.

In other words, life *is* the wedge between birth and death.

I sometimes think of life as being the captain of a small boat bobbing up and down on choppy seas. We steer our vessels into waves, or around them. Sometimes we navigate into placid lagoons, and other times we push our limits and challenge the high seas. And while we can never predict what the ocean will throw at us, every sailor knows that when you're caught in a storm and see a massive wave start to form, there's one option. You turn the bow directly into the threat and hold fast on the rudder until you make it over the top or let it take you down into the depths. Running from a rogue wave almost always invites disaster. But it takes courage to face doom head on. Only the bold can hope to make it through.

This is why the Wedge is so powerful. We always have one choice in the face of life's obstacles. We can follow reactions that are already hardwired into our body's physiological responses, or, for better or worse, resist those urges and will ourselves onto a different path. Either way, life's challenges—the crests and valleys of that turbulent ocean—are the stakes that define what we're made of. The decisions we make in the face of death are what make us real.

We may not always think about our death, but we sense death constantly on a cellular level. Evolution gave us this morbid gift. We are built to propagate the species. Every hormonal response, reflex, sensation and cognitive ability exists to serve this purpose. Every emotion, from fear, love and happiness to sadness, ambivalence and ennui, confers critical information that helps us stay alive.

Even so, our nervous systems can really only issue two commands: tension or release. This is the interplay between the sympathetic and parasympathetic wiring. In a moment of crisis, we can engage all of our physical and emotional powers to combat the situation we're in, or we can relax and let the chaotic forces do with us as they will. At some point our personal powers have limits. There's only so much that any of us can do. In the battle of man versus nature, nature always wins.

In the beginning of this book, I wrote that evolution seeks to preserve experiences. It's not a meaningless cycle of birth, reproduction and death. We struggle against challenges because they're worth struggling against. We feel happiness, sadness, anger, fear and lust because those are inherently meaningful.

The great spiritual adept Eckhart Tolle once wrote: "You are not *in* the universe, you *are* the universe, an intrinsic part of it. Ultimately you are not a person, but a focal point where the universe is becoming conscious of itself." The miracle of being alive is that you have a very specific perspective on things both larger and smaller than yourself. It might be just one of an infinite number of perspectives, but it's special because it's yours. You're responsible for how you want to live your life, and all the while, you know that every action you choose either moves you closer or further from the end.

This is why it's so important to take death seriously. It's why death is so beautiful. No decision you make will ever make it possible to avoid death. Which, in a strange way, means that the whole idea of risk is something of an illusion. If avoiding death was the goal, then we've already lost the game. But what if the point of being alive was instead to experience the entire bounty of human emotion, failure, triumphs, love and loss? To my mind, the goal of life isn't to live as long as possible, but rather to find our true selves as a reflection of the world that we inhabit. It's to test our mettle and resolve as we race to make the most of the time we do have.

Most of the experiences I've written about in this book are dangerous in one way or another. An errant kettlebell could land on a foot; a person could overheat in a sauna, fall into hypothermia in the ice or suffer hypoxia while holding their breath. Never mind the universe of unknown drug interactions with traditional medicines and illicit drugs. There's no doubt that at least something I've written in the last few hundred pages has made you pause and wonder if any of this is really a good idea. And, honestly, as a writer far removed from your own personal circumstances, I can't make that call for you. All I can say is that taking these risks have made me healthier, happier and stronger. I am more at peace with life because of the journey of reporting and writing this book. I've accepted that I don't have any control on how things end up. I just have control of how I get there.

A person can choose a life path of muted sensations, avoiding pain and living indoors protected by a cocoon of technological comfort. That person can work a 40-hour work week, fully fund a retirement plan, carry acceptable insurance, dutifully pay taxes, have a few children and ultimately die comfortably in bed. This is the default life plan that many Americans follow. But it's not as risk-free as it seems. On the one hand, we all risk the ordinary misfortunes of the modern world: cancer, car accidents, heartbreak, economic downturns and bankruptcy. On the other, by pathologically avoiding failure, we can miss out on the opportunity for unexpected rewards. The great paradox of life is that there's no obvious meaning to it. And so we need to supply our own meaning. If we don't, then life itself becomes unlivable. Purposeless.

Success doesn't happen if you only act when you are sure of a positive outcome. Real success means risking failure. We succeed only after we accept that we might fail and plan for the worst.

On a neurological level, the anticipation of failure is stress. When a person enters into an ice-cold bath, the first thing they feel is a desire to clench up and protect themselves. In a sauna, they want to escape the heat. Facing down a flying kettlebell, a person might cringe at the thought of it crashing onto their feet, and before an ayahuasca ceremony, it's entirely reasonable to fear going insane. These are all innate responses predicting some sort of bodily harm. They're sensations and emotions that we've trained into our neurology or inherited from a long line of evolutionary succession. However, when we tackle those sensations head on, when we insert a wedge into the space between stimulus and response, we don't just become better kettlebell throwers, sauna endurers and plant imbibers. Facing those challenges makes us more robust, healthier and more capable of just about anything.

Indeed, it's our anticipation of the worst possible outcomes that gets in the way more often than not. We envision negative consequences for our actions. And yet more often than not, a missed kettlebell lands safely on the grass, a sauna relaxes us, and an ice bath brings alertness. For me, the ayahuasca ceremony gave me a new perspective and answered questions that I didn't even know I had about the deep bonds I have in my marriage, my connection to a lineage of ancestors and my vulnerability to electronic addictions.

I began this journey by accepting the possibility of catastrophe. I knew my inquiry might lead nowhere. I also knew I might get injured or even die while seeking answers. But I kept going. I pushed through. Despite some doubts along the way, I believed I would come out the other side better, stronger and more resilient, that my life would be richer for it. When I think about my own death—no matter how I end up meeting it—I want to know that my choices made a difference. I do not want to have my final moments consumed by the notion that I was passive when I could have been active. Of course, I know that if I do this kind of work long enough, it's likely that I'll get hurt at some point. But that doesn't mean the journey won't be worth it.

This book and the wedges I've introduced are the tip of an iceberg. They're exercises, practices and ideas that speak especially strongly to me. They're examples of challenges that I needed to try, stressors that I needed to push up against in order to grow. Some of these wedges showed me powerful new ways to enter into a flow state. Others let me reprogram patterns in my nervous system. But it was my journey. Your life—the time between birth and death that the gods grant you—is your journey. It's your Wedge. What you do with this opportunity is up to you.

And just maybe, somewhere on your journey you will catch hold of that thread that connects the choices of every iteration of every Russian doll to a consciousness that none of the parts can comprehend on its own. In this way, we can all be individuals and the universe at the same time.

TECHNIQUES

How to Take a Cold Shower

Cold showers are an easy method to trigger a predictable stress response. Mastering your response to the cold will help you develop control over your body's autonomic reactions. Here are a few things to think about before you do the hardest thing any human has ever done and turn the knob to cold.

- Start with a hot shower.

- Take a deep breath.

- Turn the shower to cold and focus on the sensations.

- Exhale and relax as your body wants to tense up.

- Turn around in the shower, being sure to cover every part of your body—especially the places that you don't want to put in the water.

- Stay in the shower until the cold is just a sensation.

I often experience initial sensations of cold immersion as a sort of upward energy starting in my lower back or pelvis and then tensing up into my shoulders. If I mentally suppress these sensations before they start, I won't tense up, and the cold is much easier to tolerate.

Breathwork

If breathing is a remote control to the brain, then here are a few basic methods to start pushing the buttons. People with high blood pressure or a history of heart problems should be especially careful and consult with their doctor before attempting any techniques with a press or extended hold.

CO_2 Tolerance Test

The CO_2 tolerance test is a basic assessment of your innate ability to deal with stress and anxiety. Coupled with a personality assessment, this test can help personalize basic apnea breathing protocols that will help you build up passive CO_2 tolerance.

- Find a stopwatch.

- Take 3-5 normal breaths.

- Relax for 10 seconds on an exhale.

- Take one full inhale, and when you start to exhale, start the timer.

- Exhale as long and slowly as possible.

- Record your time. More than a minute-long exhale is good.

Apnea Breathing

The goal of apnea breathing is to raise your CO_2 tolerance. Apnea training should feel slightly uncomfortable, like you're trying to catch up to an oxygen deficit, but should not be painful or excruciating. Different apnea breathing protocol and timings will allow you to slow down before bedtime or prepare you for a workout. For more information, see Brian Mackenzie's website powerspeedendurance.com.

- Inhale for 6 seconds.

- Hold for 18 seconds.

- Exhale for 12 seconds.

- Repeat 3-5 cycles.

Wim Hof Basic Breathing

The Wim Hof Method also incorporates cold immersion and mental focus practices for the full effect. To learn more about the Wim Hof Method, see *What Doesn't Kill Us* or visit wimhofmethod.com.

- **Preparation:** Lie down comfortably on the floor, or in bed, preferably on an empty stomach before breakfast.

- **Power Breaths:** Take at least 30 full-lung breaths through your mouth: sequentially filling the belly, diaphragm and then lungs. Inhales are forceful and powerful, but exhales should be natural and without force. Keep the pace quick and steady with your eyes closed. You may feel lightheaded, see colors or feel a tingling sensation in your hands and feet.

- **Exhale and Hold:** After 30 power breaths, take one more full-lung breath and let it out completely, but without force. Hold your breath with your eyes closed until you feel the urge to gasp.

- **Recovery Breath:** Take a half-lung inhale and hold for about 10 seconds. These three steps constitute one round. Do a minimum of three rounds for full effect. Repeat for up to an hour as desired.

- **Power Push-ups:** After at least three rounds of breath holds, finish the practice with 30 power breaths. Exhale and hold your breath. Immediately turn over and start doing push-ups while holding your breath. You should notice an improvement in performance.

Note: It's common to experience cramping in your hands during power breathing. This is known as *hypocapnia*, which comes from having low CO_2 levels. It's not dangerous in short doses, but you can relieve the symptoms by breathing normally.

Head Clearing

This is a truncated version of Wim's basic breathing that I've adapted for a quick energy boost and to clear my head if I'm feeling foggy in the morning or I have a headache. It should make you more alert in the course of just a minute or two. This is a "push" technique and can potentially make you pass out. Select your environment appropriately.

- Start out lying down comfortably on the ground.

- Take 10 "power breaths."

- Breathe in and hold, with your lungs full of air.

- Sequentially tense your feet, glutes, stomach and chest as you envision that you're moving oxygen into your head. Push all of this gently upward to the place in your brain that is feeling cloudy.

- Keep pushing for 2-5 seconds.

- Exhale and hold your breath until you feel the urge to breathe.

"DMT" Breathing

DMT Breathing is *not* considered part of the official Wim Hof Method, but is something occasionally practiced by people in Wim Hof groups. It is unclear exactly what physiological processes occur during DMT breathing, or if there are any physiological benefits at all. Instead this practice is a shortcut to "going deep" into breathing meditation and often results in visual, physical and auditory hallucinations. People frequently report seeing faces or feeling the presence of other people in their vicinity whom outside observers cannot see. The method noted is the safest DMT breathing protocol that I'm aware of; however, Wim Hof has taught several other versions over time—all of which are variations on the theme of hyperventilation and altering blood flow to the brain with a "push."

WARNING: This protocol could be dangerous for people with high blood pressure or heart trouble. Consult your doctor before trying this technique. Never try this underwater, while operating heavy machinery, or even standing up.

- Perform the basic Wim Hof breathing protocol for a minimum of three rounds.

- Take a full breath for retention and hold it.

- Start squeezing muscles from the bottom of your body up to your head like you are rolling out pizza dough. Constrict your feet, calves, thighs, butt, stomach diaphragm, chest and neck. Squeeze your hands, forearms, biceps and shoulders. Focus all that pressure and energy to a point in the very center of your brain or at the very top of your head (the area where baby skulls are soft at birth).

- Hold the push until you feel the need to breathe.

- Relax and allow blood flow to return to normal.

- Repeat as necessary.

How to Throw a Kettlebell

Should you be brave enough to try throwing kettlebells yourself, the first step is to look for videos of Michael Castrogiovanni on the Internet to see how it's done. It's also smart to at least know the basics of lifting kettlebells on your own—preferably the Russian-style swing—before your start hurling one at your partner. There's a variety of weights available online at all price points, and most big-box stores have at least a small selection of kettlebells in stock at reasonable prices. Twenty-five pounds is a good weight to begin with, but feel free to use a smaller or larger one depending on your level of fitness.

ANATOMY OF A PARTNER PASS

- Location: Find some soft ground that won't be the worse for wear with a few kettlebell divots. Sand and grass are great.

- Stance: Stand about four or five feet from your partner. Square off your shoulders and legs. Place the bell on the ground. Partners take a wide stance so that a missed bell will fall between their legs.

- Connection: Partners lock eyes, and the person with the kettlebell asks if they are ready. The partner must say yes.

- The initiating partner picks up the kettlebell with two hands and a straight back and starts the count from one. They announce the number at the top of the swing while keeping eye contact with the receiver.

- On the one count, partners lock eyes with each other.

- On the two count, both partners move their eyes to the bell.

- On the three count, the initiating partner lets the bell go, letting it flip backward in the air for a half turn. The receiving partner keeps their hands stretched outward to catch the bell by the handle, or push it out of the way if it is off course.

- The receiving partner catches the bell and lets it follow its own momentum until it stops behind their butt. The less force the better.

- The receiving partner immediately returns the bell by using their hips and wrists so that it follows the same arc to the new receiver.

- Repeat back and forth for any desired number of reps.

- When finished, give your partner a high-five for a job well done.

- Heavier bells tend to rotate more slowly and can be easier to master than smaller bells that rotate quickly.

With practice and trust, partners can learn to improvise different types of kettlebell throws and start to freestyle their own routines.

Juggling

It's not always easy to find a partner to throw kettlebells with, so when I'm in a pinch, sometimes I'll juggle a single bell on my own. You can find Castrogiovanni's KPP solo and juggling programs online. These are a few of my favorite juggling moves—and they're good training for when you start to throw with a partner.

ONE-HANDED BACKWARD FLIP

- Start with the bell in a neutral position in one hand between your legs with the handle perpendicular to your stance, like you're holding a suitcase.

- Swing the bell one-handed between your legs to build up momentum.

- Hinge at the hips and feel your abs engage as you dip low. Bring the bell high and engage your glutes. This is a full-body workout.

- Pass the bell from hand to hand at the top of the move-ment when it is about chest height.

- Now add the flip. Let go during the up swing so the bell flips backward for a complete rotation.

- Catch with your alternate hand and repeat.

- You can catch on either side of your body, or along the centerline between your legs.

- Be mindful of your feet and knees, as well as nearby pets and children, who might be in the way if you drop the bell.

- Learn to do 100 of these in a row without dropping the bell before adding more weight or another move.

THE DROP STEP JUGGLE

- Start with a normal backward flip alternating from left to right hand.

- When you're ready, throw the bell to the alternate hand and come down into a single-legged lunge with your catching leg behind.

- Let the bell swing back in a straight line, then return to a standing position as you return the throw to the opposite hand.

- Be careful not to rotate the knee you are using to support yourself.

- Repeat.

THE U-TURN

- Start with a normal backward flip.

- Catch with your alternate hand and continue the momentum around your side and then behind your back.

- Gently throw the bell from one hand to the other behind your back. (Handing it off is generally too slow to do effectively, so think of the pass as another mini-throw.)

- Throw a forward flip in front of you, but catch with the same hand you just threw with.

- Return it behind your back.

- The bell takes a U-shaped path behind you.

Floating

Here's what you should keep in mind before you take the plunge:

- Intentions matter. If you go in with a good mindset, you're likely to come out in a better place than when you started. Don't do a float if you're in a bad place.

- Meditate in the tank. The environment of flotation lets you completely relax and will set you up to fall into an almost automatic meditation. However, if you bring a practice with you, you will be able to intensify the experience.

- Try the basic Wim Hof breathing or other meditation technique.

- Be mindful of the saltwater getting into your eyes, as well as cuts on your body that could end up stinging.

- Wear earplugs to keep the water out of your ear canals.

- Relax and enjoy it, but try not to fall asleep. The best experience happens in between the sleep and wakefulness of the float.

The Potato Hack

These basic rules for the Potato Hack come from Tim Steele's book *The Potato Hack.*

- Plan to eat only potatoes for 3 to 5 days.

- Eat 2-5 pounds of potatoes each day.

- No other foods allowed (this includes butter, sour cream, cheese, bacon and vodka).

- Salt and spices allowed but not encouraged.

- Drink when thirsty: coffee, tea, and water only.

- Heavy exercise is discouraged, but light exercise and walking are okay.

- Take your normal medications, but no dietary supplements.

- Break your fast with light, healthy foods.

Potato Recipes:

THE BOILED POTATO

- Place your potatoes in a pot of water and bring to a boil.

- Add ½-tsp of salt to the water once it's boiling.

- Reduce heat to low and cover.

- Boil for 15-20 minutes.

- They're done when you can pierce the potato with a fork and remove it without the fork sticking. It's good to have a little uncooked (resistant starch) in the middle.

Eat them like an apple, or mash them with a dash of salt or your choice of herbs and spices. Garnish with dill, oregano, paprika or flavored salt.

HASH BROWNS

- Grate 3-5 potatoes in a food processor.

- Fill frying pan to ½-1 inch deep with potato hash.

- Add light salt and pepper and cover.

- Flip when browned and repeat on other side.

- Serve

Surprisingly, hash browns aren't too bad without oil. You might even consider adding this one to your ordinary breakfast menu.

THE WEDGE ™

- Preheat oven to 425 degrees.

- Cut potato into 1-inch bite-sized wedges.

- Place on baking pan and garnish with salt and pepper.

- Bake for 20-30 minutes, moving wedges around occasionally.

When it's not possible to change the taste of your meal, at least you can change its shape. Wedges seem like an appropriate polygon for the intrepid potato body hacker.

How to Take a Sauna

Traditional Latvian saunas are all but non-existent in North America, so getting the full *pirts* experience will require a trip to the Baltics. That said, the concepts of misdirection and contrast are things that anyone with access to a sauna, hot tub or cold water can develop. Here are some things to consider:

- Lie down when possible. This will help even out your blood pressure and heat the body evenly.

- Don't base your experience in the heat on a timer. Pay attention to your sensations. If you start feeling claustrophobic or experience tunnel vision, get out and cool down.

- Drink lots of fluids.

- Pay attention to your feet. In a sauna, *pirtnieks* constantly check the temperature of their patients' feet, since these are the most difficult places to heat up. If your feet are cold, you haven't equalized the heat in your body.

- Try to use contrasting sensations at least three times in a sauna. Try immersing yourself in cold water after heating up, or roll in the snow, or fill a bucket with ice and put your feet in it while heating up.

- Incorporate scents into the sauna. This can be done easily in traditional hot-stone saunas by putting peppermint or other essential oils into a bucket of water and dripping the concoction on the rocks.

- Explore indigenous traditions, but do your research. Not everyone who runs a sweat lodge knows what they are doing. Keep your wits about you and trust your sensations.

ACKNOWLEDGEMENTS

No book is ever really the creation of one author in isolation. The ideas that I've put forward have emerged out of a lifetime of conversations with brilliant people as well as musings from every book I've ever picked up, radio programs my ears have digested and even half-remembered dreams. Saying that I've come up with something new would do a disservice to generations of seekers, biohackers, mystics and scientists who contributed something of their essence to my words. If anything, I'm merely a curator of thoughts, and my work perhaps lends a bit of idiosyncratic organization to a sprawling subject. That said, there are some specific people to whom I owe an immense debt of gratitude for helping see this through to completion.

Without a doubt, the person who invested the most in this book with her enthusiasm and gameness is my wife, Laura Krantz, who took time from her own journalism projects (including a must-listen-to-podcast called *Wild Thing*, about her year-long search for all things Bigfoot) to travel the world with me, float in tanks, sweat in saunas and try psychedelic substances against her better judgment. I love her so much.

And, of course, Wim Hof, the madman and mystic who, if I had never met him in a training camp in Poland, I would have never found my way down this path. I first saw the Wedge through his techniques, and he still has more to teach me.

More pragmatically, many people helped usher this manuscript from its most nascent stages into the version you hold in your hands today. My agent at Aevitas, Laura Nolan, has been with me for the majority of my career and has helped me manage New York's bewildering market for words. She sold *The Wedge* to Mark Weinstein of

Rodale, my editor for *What Doesn't Kill Us*. Then, when Harmony acquired Rodale, the book came under Diana Baroni's care. At some point, it was clear that I needed fresh eyes, and I was incredibly lucky to find Brad Wetzler, who edited the manuscript and brought it home.

As part of the journey to get this into print (and perhaps at considerable financial risk), I decided to leave the mainstream publishing world behind and bring the book out under my own small imprint, Foxtopus Ink.

Along the way I've been blessed to work with true publishing professionals. Robin Vuchnich designed the book cover. Sarah Pinneo reworked my website and marketing campaign. And Santosh MP produced an amazing book trailer.

Jake Holschuh took the vast majority of the photos in this book—following me down to Peru for an ayahuasca ceremony, throwing kettlebells in parks and mountain peaks around Colorado and diving into flotation tanks in downtown Denver. I'm looking forward to working with him more in the future.

Every chapter in this book relies on other people's expertise. In no particular order, my thanks go out to everyone who shared their time, knowledge and passion with me as this all came together. Andrew Huberman let me peek into his mind at his VR lab at Stanford, and we very nearly went on a real-life dive with great white sharks together in Mexico. I'm still miffed that those plans got squandered by a hurricane over our dive site. Vaibhav Diwadkar and Otto Muzik, both professors at Wayne State University, helped hone my understanding of neural symbols and helped steer my ideas from an early stage. Brian Mackenzie took me through his new breathing protocols at his house in the Bay Area. Daniel Schmachtenberger met with me early on as the themes of *The Wedge* were starting to coalesce; we spent several late nights talking about many ideas that are now in this book, even though the chapter about his own work on nutropics did not make it in. Elizabeth "Elee" Lee, a Wim Hof

Method instructor in Denver, watched over me as I turned purple in her class.

Kasper van der Meulen has been a friend and confidant since we met several years ago in Holland. I wish I had been able to include the chapter on chanting and sound that came together out of our discussions. Tone Floreal shocked my brain with electrodes while I considered writing about therapeutic electricity, and then introduced me to Michael Castrogiovanni, the creator of Kettlebell Partner Passing. Justin Feinstein at the Laureate Institute for Brain Research helped me understand interoception, and Sahib Khalsa, also at Laureate, walked me through his own innovative research. Paul Clift of the Samana Float Center in Denver gave me almost unlimited access to his tanks so that I could deepen my practice in the salty water.

Maris Zunda brought me to Latvia once my attempt to write about the Lakota sweat lodges hit a roadblock. He arranged the sauna with Ivita Picukane and Vilnis Lejnieks in the remote woods outside of Riga. I very much want to go back. Tim Steele was generous on Skype, taking me through the potato hack. Two anonymous therapists, who may or may not be in the Denver area, watched over Laura and me while we were on MDMA.

One of the most powerful experiences from this past year occurred in the depths of the Amazon jungle. I am grateful to have first dreamed of, and then met, Luz Maria Ampuero, also known as Luzma, who introduced me to her teacher, Tony. They have pure spirits. I highly recommend anyone who wants to explore their own shamanic journeys to look into Luzma's organization, Nuna Ayni (found on the web at nunaayni.org.pe). I'm saddened to report that one of our guides into the jungle—the indomitable spirit named Celso, who kept the jungle from overtaking Trocha Amazonica—passed on a year after he showed me medicinal plants whose names I will never accurately remember.

Once I had a complete manuscript, my work was still far from done. I've been helped along the way by numerous readers, including Jason Lilly, Matthew Markert, Daniel Wright and Chris Walker, who all weighed in on how to make my prose better.

And also. . . Jeff Vahrenwald. Just because.

GLOSSARY

Affective Nervous System - Part of the limbic system that connects raw sensation to your emotions.

Anxiety Sensitivity - The fear of behaviors or sensations associated with the experience of anxiety. Bodily sensations related to anxiety are mistaken as harmful, causing more intense anxiety or fear.

Allostasis - The process of achieving stability, or a new range of homeostasis, through physiological or behavioral change.

Entheogen - A chemical substance, typically of plant origin, that is ingested to produce a non-ordinary state of consciousness for religious or spiritual purposes.

Empathogen - A class of psychoactive drugs that facilitate emotional communion, oneness, relatedness and emotional openness—that is, empathy or sympathy.

Homeostasis - The state of steady internal conditions maintained by living things. This dynamic state of equilibrium is the condition of optimal functioning for the organism.

Hygiene Hypothesis - This hypothesis states that a lack of early childhood exposure to infectious agents, symbiotic microorganisms and parasites increases susceptibility to allergic diseases by suppressing the natural development of the immune system

Interoception - Sensory awareness of your internal bodily processes.

Limbic System - A complex system of nerves and networks in the brain involving several areas near the edge of the cortex concerned with instinct and mood. It controls basic emotions (fear, pleasure, anger) and drives (hunger, sex, dominance, care of offspring).

Neural Symbol - The combination of emotional and sensory experience that is stored in the limbic system.

Paralimbic Cortex - The part of the limbic system that specifically deals with emotions.

Parasympathetic - The part of the nervous system associated with "rest and digest" that counterbalances the sympathetic nervous system.

Placebo Effect - A beneficial effect produced by a chemically inactive drug or treatment that cannot be attributed to the properties of the placebo itself and must therefore be due to the patient's belief in that treatment and the spontaneous healing properties of the body.

Psychonaut - A person who induces altered states of consciousness for spiritual purposes, or for the exploration of the human condition.

Sensory Deprivation - Environmental interventions that minimize stimuli from the outside world in order to accentuate interoception.

Shaman- A person regarded as having access to, and influence in, the world of spirits, who typically enters into a trance state during a ritual and practices divination or healing.

Sympathetic Nervous System - A part of the nervous system that serves to accelerate the heart rate, constrict blood vessels and raise blood pressure associated with the fight-or-flight response.

WORKS REFERENCED

Araujo, Draulio, et al. "Seeing with eyes shut: neural basis of enhanced imagery following ayahuasca ingestion." *Human Brain Mapping.* Wiley-Liss, Inc. (May 2011)

Bobel, Till, et al. "Less immune activation following social stress in rural vs urban participants raised with regular or no animal contact, respectively." *Proceedings of the National Academy of Sciences.* (2017)

Bucko, Raymond. *The Lakota Ritual of the Sweat Lodge.* University of Nebraska Press: Lincoln (1998)

Carhart-Harris, Robin, et al. "Neural correlates of the LSD experience revealed by multimodal neuroimaging." *Proceedings of the National Academy of Sciences.* 113 (17). (April 26, 2016)

Carney, Scott. *The Enlightenment Trap.* Foxtopus Ink: Denver (2017)

Carney, Scott. *The Red Market.* William Morrow: New York (2011)

Carney, Scott. *What Doesn't Kill Us.* Rodale: New York (2015)

Catlin, George. *Shut Your Mouth and Save Your Life.* Trieste (2017)

Chuong, Edward, et al. "Regulatory evolution of innate immunity through co-option of endogenous retroviruses." *Science.* Vol 351, Issue 6277. (2016)

Craig, A.D. "How do you feel? Interoception: The sense of the physiological condition of the body." *Nature Reviews.* Vol 3. (Aug 2002)

Dauch, Carly. "The influence of the number of toys in the environment on toddlers' play." *Infant Behavior and Development.* (2018) pp. 78-87

Dennett, Daniel. *From Bacteria to Bach and Back.* W.W.Norton & Company: New York (2017)

Doidge, Norman. *The Brain's Way of Healing.* Penguin: New York (2015)

Escoll, P. "From amoeba to macrophages: exploring the molecular mechanisms of Legionella pneumophila infection in both hosts." *Current Topics in Microbiology and Immunology.* (2013) pp. 1-34

Fadiman, James. *The Psychedelic Explorer's Guide.* Park Street Press: Rochester (2011)

Feinstein, Justin, et al. "The elicitation of relaxation and interoceptive awareness using flotation therapy in individuals with high anxiety sensitivity." *Biological Psychiatry: CNNI.* Vol 3. Issue 6. (Feb 2018) pp. 555-562

Feinstein, Justin, et al. "Examining the short-term anxiolytic and antidepressant effect of Flotation-REST." *PLOS | one.* (Feb 2, 2018)

Feinstein, Justin, et al. "Fear and panic in humans with bilateral amygdala damage." *Nature Neuroscience* 16(3). (March 2013)

Feinstein, Justin, et al. "Sustained experience of emotion after loss of memory in patients with amnesia." *Proceedings of the National Academy of Science.* 107(17). (April 2010)

Fitch, W. Tecumseh. "Monkey vocal tracts are speech-ready." *Science Advances.* (2). (December 9, 2016)

Fox, Kieran, et al. "Functional Neuroimaging of Psychedelic Experience: An Overview of Psychological and Neural Effects and Their Relevance to Research on Creativity, Daydreaming, and Dreaming." *The Cambridge Handbook of the Neuroscience of Creativity.* (R.E. Jung & O. Vartanian, Editors). Cambridge University Press. (2016)

Grosset, Katherine & Macphee, G., et al. "Problematic gambling on dopamine agonists: Not such a rarity." *Movement Disorders : Official Journal of the Movement Disorder Society.* Vol 21. (2006). pp. 2206-8

Hanusch, Kay-u., et al. "Whole-body hyperthermia for the treatment of major depression: associations with thermoregulatory cooling." *American Journal of Psychiatry.* 170(7): (July 2013) pp. 802-804

Janssen, Clemens, et al. "Whole-body hyperthermia for the treatment of major depressive disorder: a randomized clinical trial." *JAMA Psychiatry.* 73(8):(2016) pp. 789-795

Kastrup, Bernardo. "The idealist view of consciousness after death." *Journal of Consciousness Exploration & Research.* 7(11): (2016) pp. 900-909

Kastrup, Bernardo. "Self-transcendence correlates with brain function impairment." *Journal of Cognition and Neuroethics* 4(3): (2007) pp. 33-42

Kastrup, Bernardo. "What neuroimaging of the psychedelic state tells us about the mind-body problem." *Journal of Cognition and Neuroethics.* 4(2): (2016) pp. 1-9

Khalsa, Sahib. "Interoception and mental health: a roadmap." *Biological Psychiatry: CNNI.* (2018)

Klein, Donald. "False suffocation alarms, spontaneous panics and related conditions." *Arch Gen Psychiatry.* Vol 50, (April 1993)

Kotler, Steven & Wheal, Jamie. *Stealing Fire.* Dey Street: New York (2017)

Labate, Beatriz Cauiby & Clancy Cavnar eds. *Ayahuasca Shamanism in the Amazon and Beyond.* Oxford University Press: New York (2014)

Langer, Ellen. *Counter Clockwise.* New York: Ballantine Books. (2009)

Laukkanen, Tanjaniina, et al. "Association between sauna bathing and fatal cardiovascular and all-cause mortality events." *JAMA Internal Med.* 175(4): (2015) pp. 542-548.

Lee, Calvin, et al. "Multigenerational memory and adaptive adhesion in early bacterial biofilm communities." *Proceedings of the National Academy of Sciences.* (2017)

Lowry, Chris. "Identification of an immune-responsive mesolimbocortical serotonergic system: potential role in regulation of emotional behavior." *Neuroscience* 146 (2007) pp. 756-772.

Lilly, John and Jay Shurley. "Experiments in solitude in maximum achievable physical isolation with water suspension of intact healthy persons." *Psychophysiological Aspects of Space Flight.* New York: Columbia University Press. (1961) pp. 238-247.

Matloff, Gregory. "Can panpsychism become an observational science?" *Journal of Conscious Exploration & Research.* 7(7): (August 2016) pp. 524-543.

McAuliffe, Kathleen. *This Is Your Brain on Parasites.* Houghton Mifflin Harcourt: New York (2016)

McKeown, Patrick. *The Oxygen Advantage.* William Morrow: New York (2015)

Meuret, Alicia, et al. "Feedback of end-tidal pCO_2 as a therapeutic approach for panic disorder." *Journal of Psychiatric Research.* 42: (2008) pp. 560-568.

Miller, Andrew, et al. "Inflammation and its discontents: the role of cytokines in the pathophysiology of major depression." *Society of Biological Psychiatry.* 65: (2009) pp. 732-741.

Molmeret, Maelle. "Amoebae as Training Grounds for Intracellular Bacterial Pathogens." *Applied and Environmental Microbiology.* 71.1 (Jan 2005) pp. 20-28.

Muzik, Otto, et al. "Brain over body—a study on the willful regulation of autonomic function during cold exposure." *Neuroimage* 172 (2018) pp. 623-641.

Mukherjee, Siddartha. "Cancer's Invasion Equation." *New Yorker.* (September 11, 2017)

Murphy, T.J., & Brian Mackenzie. *Unbreakable Runner.* Velo Press: Boulder (2014)

Ogalde, Juan, "Identification of psychoactive alkaloids in ancient Andean human hair by gas chromatography/mass spectrometry." *Journal of Archaeological Science.* 36 (2009) pp. 467-472.

Palhano-Fontes, Fernanda, et al. "Rapid antidepressant effects of the psychedelic ayahuasca in treatment-resistant depression: a randomized placebo-controlled trial." *Psychological Medicine.* (Feb 13, 2018).

Papa, Ilenia, et al. "TFH-derived dopamine accelerates productive synapses in germinal centres." *Nature,* Vol 547, (20 July 2017) 318–323.

Perel, Esther. "The Double Flame," from *Treating Sexual Desire Disorders*. (Guilford Press 2010) 23-43.

Raison, Charles, et al. "Somatic influences on subjective well-being and affective disorders: the convergence of thermosensory and central serotonergic systems." *Frontiers in Psychology*. 5(1580): (January 2015)

Rausch, JL et al. "Depressed patients have higher body temperature: 5-HT transporter long promoter region effects." *Neuropsychobiology*. 47(3): (2003) 120-127

Reber, Stefan, et al. "Immunization with a heat-killed preparation of the environmental bacterium *Mycobacterium vaccae* promotes stress resilience in mice." *Proceedings of the National Academy of Science*. (May 16, 2016)

Reeves, Roy, et al. "Nocebo effects with antidepressant clinical drug trial placebos." *General Hospital Psychiatry*. 29: (2007) pp. 275-277

Regueiro, Javier. *Ayahuasca: Soul Medicine of the Amazon Jungle*. Lifestyle Entrepreneurs Press. (2016)

Reimann, Michael. "Cliques of neurons bound into cavities provide a missing link between structure and function." *Frontiers in Computational Neuroscience*.11(48): (June 12 2017)

Schachter, Stanley, & Singer, Jerome. "Cognitive, social and physiological determinants of emotional state." *Psychological Review*. 69(5): (1962)

Shew, Joel. "Potato Diet," *Water Cure Journal & Herald of Reforms*. New York (1849) pp. 114-116.

Shurley, Jay. "Profound Experiential Sensory Isolation." *116th Annual Meeting of the American Psychiatric Association*. Atlantic City, New Jersey: (May 9 1960)

Siddiqui, Ruqaiyyah et al. "Acanthamoeba is an evolutionary ancestor of macrophages: A myth or reality." *Experimental Parasitology.* 130 95.95 (2012)

Siebler, Philip, et al. "Acute Administration of the Nonpathogenic, Saprophytic Bacterium, Mycobacterium vaccae, Induces Activation of Serotonergic Neurons in the Dorsal Raphe Nucleus and Antidepressant-like Behavior in Association with Mild Hypothermia." *Cel Mol Neurobiol* Vol 38 (2018) pp. 289-304.

Sood, Amit, et al "One Mind Wandering, Attention, Brain Networks and Meditation." *Explore.* Vol 9, No 3. (May/June 2013)

Steele, Tim. *The Potato Hack: Weight Loss Simplified.* Archangel Ink. (2016)

Uexküll, Jakob von. "A Stroll Through Worlds of Animals and Men. *(1934)" Semiotica* 89-4 (1992) 319-391

Wohlleben, Peter. *The Hidden Life of Trees.* Greystone Books: New York (2015)

Wolpe, Joseph. "Carbon Dioxide Inhalation Treatments of Neurotic Anxiety." *Journal of Nervous and Mental Disease.* Williams and Wilkins Co. (1987)

Winkelman, Michael."Psychedelics as Medicines for Substance Abuse Rehabilitation." *Current Drug Abuse Reviews.* Vol 7 No 2. (2014) pp. 101-116.

ABOUT THE AUTHOR

Scott Carney is an award-winning investigative journalist and anthropologist whose stories blend narrative non-fiction with ethnography. His reporting has taken him to some of the most dangerous and unlikely corners of the world. He is the author of three other books, including *The Red Market*, *The Enlightenment Trap* and *New York Times* bestseller *What Doesn't Kill Us*. He was a contributing editor at *Wired*, and other works of his have appeared in *Outside, Mother Jones, NPR, Playboy, Foreign Policy, Details Discover, Men's Journal, Men's Fitness* and *Fast Company*. His books are available throughout the world in at least 20 languages. He lives in Denver with his wife, Laura, and a couple of cats. Together they run a tiny media company called Foxtopus Ink.

You can find more of his writing at scottcarney.com.

INDEX

CONTINUE YOUR JOURNEY ONLINE AND IN PERSON

Learn breathing techniques, focus and environmental exposure that will help you unlock your innermost biology. For discounts on new training programs, equipment, the Wim Hof Method, XPT and more, go to:

scottcarney.com/courses

Connect with Scott Carney at: **scottcarney.com**

Twitter: @sgcarney

Instagram: @sgcarney

Facebook: scottcarneyauthor